VOICES FOR DEMOCRACY:
STRUGGLES AND CELEBRATIONS
OF TRANSFORMATIONAL LEADERS

The *Yearbook of the National Society for the Study of Education* (ISSN 0077-5762, online ISSN 1744-7984) is published in April and September by Blackwell Publishing with offices at 350 Main St, Malden, MA 02148 USA; 9600, Garsington Rd, Oxford, OX4 2DQ, UK; and 550 Swanston Street, Carlton South, 3053 Victoria, Australia.

Society and Membership Office:
The *Yearbook* is published on behalf of the National Society for the Study of Education, with offices at: University of Illinois at Chicago, College of Education (M/C 147) 1040 W. Harrison Street Chicago, IL 60607-7133. For membership information, please visit www.nsse-chicago.org.

Subscription Rates for Volume 105, 2006

	The Americas[†]	Rest of World[‡]
Institutional Standard Rate*	$136	£84
Institutional Premium Rate	$150	£92

*Includes print plus online access to the current and previous Volume. [†]Customers in Canada should add 7% GST or provide evidence of entitlement to exemption.
[‡]Customers in the UK should add VAT at 5%; customers in the EU should also add VAT at 5%, or provide a VAT registration number or evidence of entitlement to exemption.
For more information about Blackwell Publishing journals, including online access information, terms and conditions, and other pricing options, please visit www.blackwellpublishing.com.
All orders must be paid by check, money order, or credit card. Checks should be made payable to Blackwell. Checks in US dollars must be drawn on a US bank. Checks in Sterling must be drawn on a UK bank.

Volume 105 is available from the publisher for $40 a copy. For earlier Volumes please contact Periodical Service Company, L. P., 11 Main Street, Germantown, NY 12526-5635 USA Tel: (+518) 537-4700, Fax: (+518) 537-5899, Email: Psc@backsets.com or http://www.backsets.com

For new orders, renewals, sample copy requests, claims, changes of address and all other subscription correspondences please contact the Journals Department at your nearest Blackwell office (address details listed above). US office phone 800-835-6770 or 781-388-8206, Fax 781-388-8232, Email customerservices@blackwellpublishing.com; UK office phone +44 (0) 1865-778315, Fax +44 (0) 1865-471775, Email customerservices@blackwellpublishing.com; Asia office phone +65 6511 8000, Fax +44 (0) 1865 471775, Email customerservices@blackwellpublishing.com.

The *Yearbook* is mailed Standard Rate. Mailing to rest of world by DHL Smart & Global Mail. Canadian mail is sent by Canadian publications mail agreement number 40573520.

Postmaster: Send all address changes to *Yearbook of the National Society for the Study of Education*, Blackwell Publishing Inc., Journals Subscription Department, 350 Main St., Malden, MA 02148-5020.

Blackwell Synergy Sign up to receive Blackwell *Synergy* free e-mail alerts with complete *Yearbook* tables of contents and quick links to article abstracts from the most current issue. Simply go to www.blackwell-synergy.com, select the journal from the list of journals, and click on "Sign-up" for FREE email table of contents alerts.

Copyright 2006 National Society for the Study of Education
All rights reserved. With the exception of fair dealing for the purposes of research or private study or criticism no part of this publication may be reproduced, stored, or transmitted in any form or by any means without the prior permission in writing from the copyright holder. Authorization to photocopy items for internal and personal use is granted by the copyright holder for libraries and other users of the Copyright Clearance Center (CCC), 222 Rosewood Drive, Danvers, MA 01923, USA (www.copyright.com), provided the appropriate fee is paid directly to the CCC. This consent does not extend to other kinds of copying, such as copying for general distribution for advertising or promotional purposes, for creating new collective works, or for resale. Institutions with a paid subscription to this journal may make photocopies for teaching purposes free of charge provided such copies are not resold. For all other permissions inquiries, including requests to republish material in another work, please contact the Journals Rights & Permissions Coordinator, Blackwell Publishing, 9600 Garsington Road, Oxford, OX4 2DQ, UK. E-mail: JournalsRights@oxon.blackwellpublishing.com.

Disclaimer: The Publisher, the National Society for the Study of Education and Editor(s) cannot be held responsible for errors or any consequences arising from the use of information contained in this journal; the views and opinions expressed do not necessarily reflect those of the Publisher, Society or Editor(s).

VIOCES FOR DEMOCRACY: STRUGGLES AND
CELEBRATIONS OF TRANSFORMATIONAL LEADERS

105th Yearbook of the
National Society for the Study of Education

PART I

Edited by
PAUL KELLEHER
REBECCA VAN DER BOGERT

Distributed by BLACKWELL PUBLISHING MALDEN, MASSACHUSETTS

National Society for the Study of Education

The National Society for the Study of Education was founded in 1901 as successor to the National Herbart Society. It publishes an annual two-volume Yearbook, each volume dealing with a separate topic of concern to educators. The Society's yearbook series, now in its one hundred and fifth year, presents articles by scholars and practitioners who are noted for their significant work in critical areas of education.

The Society welcomes as members all individuals who wish to receive its publications and take part in Society activities. Current membership includes educators in the United States, Canada, and elsewhere throughout the world—professors and graduate students in colleges and universities; teachers, administrators, supervisors, and curriculum specialists in elementary and secondary schools; policymakers and researchers at all levels; and any others with an interest in teaching and learning.

Members of the Society elect a Board of Directors. The Board's responsibilities include reviewing proposals for Yearbooks and authorizing their preparation based on accepted proposals, along with guiding the other activities of the Society, including presentations and forums.

Current dues (for 2006) are a modest $40 ($35 for retired members and for students in their first year of membership; $45 for international membership). Members whose dues are paid for the current calendar year receive the Society's Yearbook and are eligible for election to the Board of Directors.

Each year the Society arranges for meetings to be held in conjunction with the annual conferences of one or more of the national educational organizations. All members are urged to attend these meetings, at which the current Yearbook is presented and critiqued. Members are encouraged to submit proposals for future Yearbooks.

Voices for Democracy: Struggles and Celebrations of Transformational Leaders is part I of the 105th Yearbooks. Part II will be *With More Deliberate Speed: Achieving Equity and Excellence in Education: Realizing the Full Potential of* Brown v. Board of Education.

For further information, write to the Secretary, NSSE, University of Illinois at Chicago, College of Education M/C 147, 1040 W. Harrison St., Chicago, Illinois 60607-7133 or see http://www.nsse-chicago.org

Board of Directors of the National Society for the Study of Education
(Term of office expires in the year indicated.)

ALLAN ALSON, Superintendent, District 202, Evanston Township, Illinois (2006)
ARNETHA F. BALL, Stanford University (2006)
GARY FENSTERMACHER, University of Michigan, Ann Arbor (2006)
MARY HATWOOD FUTRELL, George Washington University (2006)
DAVID HANSEN, Teachers College, Columbia University (2008)
DAVID IMIG, President Emeritus, AACTE; University of Maryland (2008)
PAUL KELLEHER, Trinity University (2006)
GLORIA LADSON-BILLINGS, University of Wisconsin, Madison (2008)
JUDITH SHULMAN, WestEd (2006)
JOHN R. WIENS, University of Manitoba (2006)

Contributors to the Yearbook

ALLAN ALSON, Evanston (IL) Township High School District 202
BEVERLY HALL, Atlanta Public Schools
LINDA HANSON, *School-Exec Connect*, Highland Park, IL
PAUL D. HOUSTON, American Association of School Superintendents
BECKY BAIR HURLEY, District 36 School Board, Winnetka, IL
BARRY JENTZ, Leadership and Learning Inc.
BENA KALLICK, Educational Consultant
PAUL KELLEHER, Trinity University, San Antonio, TX
LARRY LEVERETT, Greenwich, CT Public Schools
REBECCA VAN DER BOGERT, Winnetka, IL Public Schools
JOHN R. WIENS, University of Manitoba

Reviewers of the Yearbook

PAULA A. CORDEIRO, *University of San Diego*
JOSEPH CRONIN, *EDVISORS, Boston University*
GENE DAVIS, *Idaho State University*
THELBERT L. DRAKE, *Ball State University*
LANCE FUSARELLI, *North Carolina State University*
KRISTINA A. HESBOL, *DeKalb Community Unit School District 428*

GARY IVORY, *New Mexico State University*
LAWRENCE KEMPER, *University of La Verne*
JUDITH MELOY, *Castleton State College*
ROD MUTH, *University of Colorado at Denver*
FRANCES SEGAN, *New York City Department of Education*

Table of Contents

CHAPTER	PAGE
FOREWORD: THE SUPERINTENDENT: CHAMPIONING THE DEEPEST PURPOSES OF EDUCATION, *Paul D. Houston*	1
1. INTRODUCTION: THE LANDSCAPE OF THE SUPERINTENDENCY: FROM DESPAIR TO HOPE, *Paul Kelleher and Rebecca van der Bogert*	10
2. CONFRONTING THE UNIVERSAL DISBELIEF THAT POOR CHILDREN CAN ACHIEVE AT HIGH LEVELS, *Paul Kelleher* with *Beverly Hall*	29
3. ATTACKING THE ACHIEVEMENT GAP IN A DIVERSE URBAN-SUBURBAN COMMUNITY: A CURRICULAR CASE STUDY, *Allan Alson*	49
4. A TALE OF TWO CITIES, *Paul Kelleher with Larry Leverett*	78
5. A NEW SUPERINTENDENT EMBRACES THE ROLE OF TEACHER, *Linda Hanson*	105
6. THE IMPORTANCE OF A "GOOD FIT," *Paul Kelleher* with *Juan Martinez (pseudonym)*	125
7. DEMOCRACY DURING HARD TIMES, *Rebecca van der Bogert*	146
8. LEARNING ON THE JOB: THE EDUCATION OF A SCHOOL BOARD PRESIDENT IN SHARED LEADERSHIP, *Becky Bair Hurley*	170
9. EDUCATIONAL LEADERSHIP AS CIVIC HUMANISM, *John R. Wiens*	199

Commentaries

CONSTRUCTIVIST SUPERINTENDENTS, *Bena Kallick*	226
MAKING OUR OWN MINDS THE OBJECT OF OUR LEARNING: THREE REASONS TO SEEK SELF-KNOWLEDGE, *Barry Jentz*	230
PUBLICATIONS OF THE NATIONAL SOCIETY FOR THE STUDY OF EDUCATION	239
ABOUT THE CONTRIBUTORS	249

FOREWARD

The Superintendent: Championing the Deepest Purposes of Education

PAUL D. HOUSTON

As the executive director of the American Association of School Administrators, I have had the opportunity each year to meet the state finalists for Superintendent of the Year. For me, it has always been very uplifting to listen to these really very fine representatives of the profession who had come to Washington to talk about what they were doing to make their schools responsive to children and to the community's needs, and to help energize their communities around children and their needs. There were always these wonderful stories every year.

In the last few years, the stories have changed. They are now about what superintendents have done to respond to the state's standards or the state's testing system, or No Child Left Behind (NCLB) and what they have done to raise their test scores—a much more limited perspective. Superintendents seem to have been forced into being bureaucratic responders to other people's agendas, as opposed to creating their own agendas as leaders.

To be proactive and to broaden our leadership agenda, we must recognize that the first and foremost mission of the public schools is their civic mission. In these times of making education the foremost instrument of the global economy while making public schools the scapegoat for society's lack of will to tackle the messy issues of race and class, that mission has gotten lost. What would it take to recapture the deepest reasons we have public schools? What would it take to confront the issues of how we keep children whole and how we address the needs of the whole child in an era in which children are being sliced and diced into categories on standardized tests? What is the role of local districts, of local control, when state and federal bureaucracies are making the decisions and calling the dance? What are the implications of all this for education and for democracy?

The Journey

The history of the school superintendent has been a fitful journey from the role of manager to leader and now, to activist. The superintendency is a position of wide influence that is narrowly understood. Every community in America has a superintendent. In most communities, the public school system is one of the biggest operations in town and the superintendent has some of the greatest responsibilities in the community. Yet little is known about this position beyond what the educational community knows, and even then, the complexities, struggles, and demands of the work are often unacknowledged.

Education has historically been a state function; initially, state legislatures allocated money to local communities. As education systems became more complicated, legislatures created local committees to oversee the expenditure of funds. These local committees eventually led to the creation of state and local boards. A paid state officer was appointed to handle the accounting function for these committees. In essence, this was the beginning of the superintendent role. The very first superintendents, by and large, were bureaucrats carrying out state laws, collecting data, and accounting for expenditures.

For decades, superintendents were responsible for taking care of the business of the schools—overseeing the budget, buildings, and day-to-day operations. However, with the passage of time and the accompanying complexities and challenges, the centrality of the position increased. Despite the fact that this position was created by local boards and had no statutory authority or support, it emerged in the 20th century as a role of power and prestige. The golden era for the superintendency lasted from the beginning until the middle of the 20th century, with a generation of community leaders who were respected for their business acumen and their moral courage in taking care of the nation's future through its common schools. Superintendents were clearly the most powerful individuals in the organization, managing systems that hired hundreds or thousands of employees and spending millions of taxpayer dollars. School boards, as well as the states, ceded much of their authority to the superintendent. These leaders were respected in their communities and tended to have longevity in the position. Decades-long tenures were not uncommon.

The cultural upheavals of the 1960s and 1970s and the growing criticism of public education that began with Russia's successful launch of Sputnik in 1957 and that was accelerated by the civil rights, women's rights, and handicapped movements caused a serious deterioration in the status and role of superintendents. The rise of powerful teacher unions and special interest groups led to a change in how boards were constituted, and board members moved from civic leaders to grassroots advocates, often arguing for specialized concerns rather than the common concerns of public schooling. Relations between boards and superintendents reflected the resulting tensions.

While *accountability* remained, *authority* became dispersed. Superintendents moved from the role of benevolent father figure who looked out for children to the community scapegoat and lightning rod—taking the blame for the perceived shortcomings of the system and becoming the target for the dissatisfaction of the broader community for what was not working as it should be. The impatience of policymakers and business leaders, focused on outcomes, brought additional pressure to bear.

Throughout all these upheavals, the basic job description and expectation for the superintendency remained remarkably unchanged. They were to be managers of schools—the people who made sure that the buses ran, the lunchroom served warm meals, the books were delivered, the teachers were hired, and the buildings built and maintained—as well as leaders in the community.

The Picture Changes

The last third of the 20th century led to subtle but major shifts in expectations for schools and those who led them. Up to that point, public education was about access—American schools as mini melting pots where children from different backgrounds and with different values were educated together and were taught to see themselves as citizens of a common nation. It was to be the place where the *unum* emerged from the *pluribus*. Most of the major legal and policy decisions around schools during that time were efforts to ensure access to learning. *Brown v. Board of Education* (1954), the Elementary and Secondary Education Act of 1965, the Individuals with Disabilities Education Improvement Act of 1975, Title IX, and court decisions around the education of illegal immigrants all were meant to advance the goal of ensuring that any child who wanted an education had the opportunity.

As America approached the end of the 20th century, several major movements were gaining momentum and beginning to merge. For decades, America had paid lip service to the dual expectations of *equity* and *excellence*, while actually providing, for many students, mere accessibility. Anyone who wanted an education—regardless of disability, whether they spoke English or not, whether they belonged to the majority culture or not—had a place at the table. However, it began to become very clear that not everyone was getting the same meal. The promises of equity and excellence remained unfulfilled. Further, many meals lacked the nutrition that would allow a child to meet the increasingly complex standards of an information age. While schools continued to produce workers for an industrial economy, a new global economy was emerging that would require more sophisticated and much more highly skilled workers. Also, the emphasis on civic virtue began to get lost in an increasing focus on preparation for the workplace and, in particular, a growing concern about achievement outcomes.

At the same time, the gap between the haves and have-nots was increasing, and those at the bottom continue to this day to lose ground. The traditional family has been reshaped by social and economic demands. Support systems—neighbors, churches, clubs, extended family—often can no longer be counted upon to provide extra stability.

Throughout its history, America has placed its hopes and dreams in its public schools and the people who run them to address societal problems—a double-edged sword that frequently targets schools as both the source of and the solution to problems. As a result, wave after wave of reform policies were set in motion over the last few decades, often to little effect. Finally, in 2002, those who were dissatisfied with the progress schools had made on the equity front joined with those who were dissatisfied with the progress toward excellence. The result was NCLB, a landmark bipartisan piece of legislation, which completely reordered the relationship between the federal government and states and put extensive demands on local districts for accountability—chiefly through the provision of norm-referenced tests.

Over 1,100 pages long, NCLB set out all sorts of rules for schools— from setting the accountability system, to the requirement to hire only specifically defined *highly qualified teachers*, to the requirement that schools provide military recruiters with student information that had previously been considered highly confidential. Initially, there was an increase in federal financial support for education, but that contribution has never exceeded 8% of the total cost of education and has failed to cover even the cost of the increased accountability measures.

Educators have joked for years that there is a golden rule in education: that whoever has the gold makes the rules. With NCLB, the federal government dictates the rules, and states must ask for exemptions if they feel they cannot or should not meet a rule. In some cases, exemptions have been approved; in others, they have been denied. The loss of federal money has become the stick (unaccompanied by any carrot). Despite the fact that the federal contribution covers only a small portion of the total costs of education, it is difficult for a state to walk away from these funds given that they are targeted to the poorest children. As a result, local control, based on the notion that those closest to the work were best suited to make decisions about the work, has been severely compromised, and this has had a significant impact on the work of the superintendent.

The case for activism. With the formal powers of the position stripped away by bargaining agreements, court decisions, state and federal mandates, and local political infighting, 21st-century superintendents may be tempted to fall back into a management role that casts them as bureaucrats for state and federal officials and board supplicants. There is intense pressure from the policy community for superintendents to merely carry out mandates, and the business community wants superintendents to be more like them.

Ironically, never before in the history of public education has there been a greater need for leadership, advocacy, and activism from the superintendent. Because of the changing demands on the system to deliver a different and better outcome, because of the unfulfilled promise of equity that has, in fact, left many children behind, and because of the varied pressures from all those who have their own distinct and differing expectations and demands regarding the schools, school leaders today need to be nimble and need to remain focused on their larger mission.

Perhaps the greatest challenge facing school leaders is to lead the renewal of America's commitment to the concept of common schools and the renewal of the spirit of commonweal that has always been the central expectation of public education. A modern democracy cannot survive or thrive without a joint agreement by its citizens that they will put aside their differences and personal desires for the good of the whole. Public education has historically served as the cornerstone of our democracy. It is under assault from different directions and for different reasons, but it must survive to assure the survival of the democracy.

As a result, we must pay renewed attention to the needs of children, families, and communities—concerns that are often glibly known as social justice issues. The needs are broader than the political agenda that is being played out. The needs of children are much more extensive than what is generally understood.

The community context: nurturing democracy. When we look at events like Hurricane Katrina and the lack of understanding about the issues of poverty and race that became apparent in this disaster, and their impact in schools, we know that superintendents have a mission of transformation that is there before them. However, if they get caught in listening to those who are trying to call the dance, as opposed to understanding the music, then they have a real problem. They have got to go back and get in touch with the music—what the job is about, and what the real role of leadership is in this context. It is a difficult opportunity, but it is still an opportunity.

We must act on the understanding that so much of what happens in school and the school's ability to be successful is dependent upon what happens *outside* of school. Schools typically get children four or five years after they are born. Those are critical years in their development. So many of their cognitive tools are sharpened during that time. The research is clear—when factors such as social class, family strength, childhood health and nutrition, and even prenatal care are not supportive of the child, the child suffers and their later learning can be severely affected. Schools have children about 8% of their time from birth to 18, and if schools fail to be part of that other 92%, then we are missing a huge chance to help provide the learning and support that children need. Educational leaders must reach out to families and communities to rebuild the network around children that has been so frayed over the last few decades. We do not like to talk about these problems, but they are there. The toxic elements exposed by Katrina are still simmering in the pot, even if the politicians are trying to put the lid back on as soon as possible.

That is all part of this whole civic mission of education—not to let people get distracted from confronting those problems. And the other piece of it is that schools must be learning laboratories for democracy. The original mission of public education was a mission of *civitas*—the creation of a good and fair society by giving generations of children an understanding of their responsibilities in a democratic system. So one of the core obligations of leadership is getting children—all children—ready to participate in our democracy, and ready to understand their connections to each other.

The school context: nurturing engagement. Educational leaders must work to change schools from a one-size-fits-all model—a model that served when children were expected to fit the system, and the system was there to sort children for an industrial world. In the global information age, no child can be neglected or overlooked. All the skills must be nurtured and developed. To do that, school leaders must get the schools ready for children by making them places children *want to be* and where teachers *want to work*. Schools must become places that are charged with meaning for children and places that engage their imaginations, talents, and dreams.

This year I visited Olathe Northwest High School in Kansas. They were teaching an educational technology class. The kids were building robots. They were creating a *battlebot* that would go in and fight with other robots. In the process, they were developing an understanding of metallurgy, physics, engineering, higher mathematics, and other difficult concepts, now made concrete and understandable. They were so excited about what they were doing because it really connected to them as 17-year-olds. In addition, they could see how what they had learned in math and science classes actually was used. There was a connection between what was seemingly theoretical and what was useful to them. They were very excited by that.

What is missing in far too many schools is that connection. We give students one side of the equation, but we do not give them the other. Kids are thinking, "I will learn this because I have to pass a test. I may need it some day but I do not know how without seeing the connection." We understand enough about brain research to know that teenagers are not fully formed yet. That is why they are still teenagers. And we need to understand how to assist them in making these leaps, how to build these little bridges of learning and understanding that allow them to cross over to a higher level of thinking and learning. I believe you do that by saying, "Let us do projects that are really meaningful to you, that engage your imagination." What I saw happening in that Kansas classroom was very exciting. And this is in the midst of all the high school reform discussions about how we are not turning out enough engineers and how the United States is losing its competitive edge. I asked these kids, "How many of you are going to go to college?" Every one of them was going to go to college. I said, "How many of you want to be engineers?" And every one of them wanted to be an engineer. There is no shortage of potential in that classroom in Kansas because teachers had shown them what it would be like if they became engineers, and it was exciting for the kids.

Unfortunately, at the moment, the federal government is considering more testing in high schools as a significant part of their reform strategy. However, those who want to reform high schools should start in places like Olathe, where the district has figured out that the best way to get students to learn more is to give them work that engages their imaginations and creates meaning for them. If schools do not help kids see the meaning and relevance of learning, they do not make that leap into understanding why school is good for them—why learning is good for them. Instead, they only see school as a chore.

The Superintendent's Charge

If you look at the polling information, what parents and the public at large say they want from schools is happy children. They want children who can meet the demands of life in a very broad way. They do not want narrow responses. Leaders who can speak to and lead to those higher aspirations, even in the context of having to fight off some of the situations that they are dealing with, are actually empowered. There is a danger in taking on the powers that be, but doing nothing is even riskier, I think, because you know what the outcome is going to be.

I think the superintendents who are leading their communities to higher aspirations are the ones who are able to get their constituents to see that this accountability model is such a limited model and that there are many ways of being held accountable as a leader. We do not have to rely just on the test scores. We look at other indicators. When you can get the community convinced of that, you have a lot of elbowroom with them. You still have to deal with the state bureaucracies and mandates, but we know from polling after polling that people believe their eyes more than they believe somebody in a distant place. So they always look at their own schools in a different way than schools to which they have no connection. That has always been a useful strategy.

Over time the environment will start to shape behavior. It is like putting a leg in a cast. Eventually, the muscles whither away. So when you constrict people's leadership qualities, eventually they lose the ability to lead. What leadership means in the current context is a much more prescriptive definition than what it was a few years ago when people could create their own agenda and their own responses. The people have not changed so much as the conditions have.

Leadership at the highest level is about resisting this new prescriptive definition and creating conditions in schools so that teachers can examine what they are doing, with some of the deeper purposes of education in mind, and so that you, as a leader, can engage your community in discussions about what the deepest purposes of education happen to be. That is really what the role of a superintendent could be. We need to reinforce that and nurture that, or we lose sight of what really makes a difference in terms of our children.

REFERENCES

Brown v. Board of Education, 347 U.S. 483 (1954).
Elementary and Secondary Education Act (ESEA) (Public Law 89–10, 20 U.S.C. § 6301 et seq.) (1965).
Individuals with Disabilities Education Act (IDEA). 20 U.S.C. 1400 et seq., as amended by Public Law 108–446. (1975/2004).
No Child Left Behind Act of 2001, Pub. L. No. 107–110, 115 Stat. 1425 (2002).
Title IX, Education Amendments of 1972 (Title 20 U.S.C. Sections 1681–1688).

CHAPTER 1

The Landscape of the Superintendency: From Despair to Hope

PAUL KELLEHER AND REBECCA VAN DER BOGERT

Phil Townsend is 53 years old and has served as superintendent of schools in a small, blue-collar city in New York for the last 9 years. As he nears retirement, he finds himself counting the days until his contract ends and he is free of the overwhelming burdens of his job. He recalls the excitement he felt when the board chose him and his feeling that he could make a difference for the children of his community, and he ruminates on what has happened to change his attitude toward his job. His board, of course, has changed. Those that hired him and supported him in his early years completed their board service and were replaced by others who are more inclined to micromanage and with whom he has a more ambivalent relationship. He is not sure that they would extend his contract if he wanted to stay. His community certainly has changed. It has become poorer and more diverse. Fewer parents can see themselves and their life experience when they look at Phil. Fewer parents and community members are willing to grant him the assumption of good faith that he feels he deserves. They are quicker to distrust, quicker to make negative assumptions about his intentions. As the local economy has declined, budget resources have become scarcer, and the battles among interest groups for shares of the pie have intensified. Unions have become more adversarial and distrustful. The dream of interest-based, consensus-building collective bargaining with which Phil began his tenure is long dead.

Although Phil could not have anticipated all of these changes, he knows that when he chose to become a superintendent he had to expect adversity. And he has always been able to bounce back quickly. Lately, however, he has not felt as resilient. What have made his job feel impossible are the new demands, over and above the expected, predictable ones, that state and federal laws and policies have wrought. In the last decade, the New York State Department of Education has gone from developing broad policy to making detailed regulations regarding classroom and school activities, with a corresponding increase in student testing, compliance paperwork, and other monitoring for which Phil is responsible and cannot ignore. The advent of No Child Left Behind in 2002 added yet another layer of bureaucratic mandates to Phil's work life and intensified the public focus on aggregate, annual standardized testing as the primary measure of educational effectiveness. In his visits to classrooms, Phil sees how the fear of being publicly shamed by poor test scores leads his principals and teachers to narrow and constrict children's educational experience. Phil's vision of a rich, rigorous, developmentally appropriate curriculum now seems like a pipe dream. After repeated urgings from his elementary principals, for example, Phil reluctantly agreed this year to eliminate recess, a step that he thought he would never take. Phil feels exhausted and "burned out." He sees little hope for positive change and looks forward eagerly to an early retirement.

We, the editors of this volume, are both long-time superintendents of schools who have lived and enacted the role in recent years. Phil Townsend is a fictional character, but his story is typical of what we have heard from far too many of our colleagues across the country. We empathize with those like Phil and agree that what it means to be the leader of a local school system has changed dramatically and continues to change in response to the changing times and contexts.

We intend this volume to provide hope that despite the daunting challenges educational leaders like Phil face today, they have more to look forward to than retirement. Despite the external pressures that threaten to overwhelm them, they can still carve out areas of positive control where they can enact educational visions. They can still aspire to be transformational leaders. They do not have to settle for being transactional managers who maintain the status quo, meet state mandates, improve standardized test scores, and improve the efficiency of operations. They can, instead, attempt in significant ways to move their schools closer to the ideal of developing the human potentiality of every student and teacher. The stories here, told by and with practicing superintendents and board members, provide powerful examples of transformative leadership efforts in the face of the obstacles and challenges that all superintendents face today. We hope that these stories will also provide inspiration to a new generation of school district leaders who might otherwise see the problems of these jobs as too difficult and daunting to undertake.

In planning this volume, we read and talked with a number of experts on school district leadership.[1] From our research and reflection, we realized that we wanted to present the involved voices of practitioners rather that the distant discourse of observers. Our own experience as superintendents has taught us that work toward transformational success in school district leadership rarely follows a clear, straight, steady path of progress. Instead, its path is often murky, twisting, full of obstacles and wrong turns, and fraught with risks. The stories of superintendents and those that work with them, more than exposition, would foster intimate accounts of the struggle involved. Stories would go beyond logical presentations of successful outcomes. Although the stories might offer just one perspective or experience, they would lift the curtain on the struggles that even successful leaders undergo as they operate in the messy, complex, uncertain, conflicted reality of schools. With this purpose in mind, we chose authors who we felt would be willing to take the reader "behind the scenes" and reveal thinking about choices and consequences that would not otherwise be revealed. We asked that their stories involve a significant dilemma or issue that tested their ability to stay true to their beliefs in the face of adversity. We also asked that what was at stake be significant—that is, the long-term possibility of transforming the organization.

The superintendents and board members that we chose are diverse in terms of race, ethnicity, geography, age, and gender. They lead large and small, as well as urban and suburban, districts. Five authors chose to write their own stories; Paul Kelleher interviewed three others and wrote chapters with their collaboration. With one exception, all were willing for their identities to be public. One superintendent whom Paul interviewed felt, after his story was written, that he preferred confidentiality. We have provided pseudonyms and changed some of the details of his story to protect his anonymity.

These superintendents and board members hold in common the aspiration to significantly improve the schools they lead or led and the desire to enact democratic ideals of fairness, equity, and inclusiveness in them. Linda Hanson, for example, tells the story of her struggle as a new superintendent to convince her board to repeal a graduation-testing requirement that would have punitive, inequitable consequences for students. Both Allan Alson and Larry Leverett describe efforts to mobilize their school communities to confront the achievement gap between white and minority students. Beverly Hall talks of the obstacles she faced in overcoming what she calls the universal disbelief that poor, minority children can learn at high levels. Becky van der Bogert tells of her struggle to maintain a democratic commitment to decision making through adversarial negotiations of a teacher contract. Becky Hurley, van der Bogert's board chair, narrates the story from her perspective as a new board member struggling to understand and embrace the democratic, cultural values she discovered in her new role. Juan Martinez (a pseudonym) relates his efforts to stand up for all the students and parents in his community and not just those represented by the dominant faction on a highly politicized school board. John Wiens describes his work to promote inquiry and democratic values among the broader educational community of students, teachers, parents, principals, superintendents, and his board.

Why Now?

The decision to develop a volume now about transformational district leadership grew out of our increasing concern that the prevailing storm winds in today's educational world push superintendents like Phil Townsend toward a narrow, confined definition of their role—as bureaucrats, managers, and accountants rather than transformational leaders. In towns and cities across the United States, the public dialogue about education, as presented by the media, focuses on test score accountability and the consequences of meeting (or not meeting) state and federal mandates. Public debate about other forms of education—moral, aesthetic, civic—and even about aspects of academic education beyond those affecting standardized test results—literature, history, science, the arts—have disappeared from the public radar screen before the overwhelming force of the accountability storm.[2]

A powerful example of this constriction of the leadership agenda comes from Paul Houston's introduction to this volume. He describes how, in the past, finalists for the American Association of School Administrators' (AASA) Superintendent of the Year Program would come to Washington and tell inspiring stories about what they were doing to make their schools responsive to children and to community needs. More recently, finalists locate their pride in their successful responses to state testing programs and other mandates. Houston finds it troubling that today's equally talented district leaders seem to have a much more limited perspective on the range of leadership possibilities than earlier representatives. They lack the elbowroom to create their initiatives; instead, they become bureaucratic responders to other people's agendas.

The lack of elbowroom to create a leadership agenda makes the challenge of becoming a transformational leader more daunting. A recent survey of superintendents from 100 of the nation's largest urban districts indicates that they feel the "conditions of the superintendency set them up for failure," making the job impossible (Fuller et al., 2003). Among the obstacles to success that the survey identified were politics, especially patronage politics; conflicts with the board of education; and difficulty in narrowing the achievement gap.

Leadership Challenges

The stories we present here describe brave leaders stepping up to the challenges of district leadership despite these obstacles. They persevere in trying to create elbowroom to enact their leadership agendas. Their stories illustrate a number of important issues that research has confirmed as critical to understanding successful school district leadership.

The Pervasive Impact of Poverty

The impact of poverty on children's readiness and ability to learn is a controversial issue. Some commentators and researchers—the Heritage Foundation and the Education Trust are two notable examples—cite evidence that schools can enable many children from poverty to achieve at high levels. Others like Gordon (2004), Orfield (2004),[3] and Rothstein (2004) talk pessimistically about the likelihood of schools, by themselves, overcoming for most children the enormous social and cultural disadvantages of poverty. Rothstein, for example, argues persuasively that society will have to invest heavily in health care and supplemental educational programs in order for large numbers of poor children to overcome the demographic odds against them. This controversy notwithstanding, the superintendents who tell their stories in this volume have faith in the efficacy of schools to enable children to rise out of poverty and achieve at high levels. Beverly Hall in Atlanta, Georgia, Allan Alson in Evanston, Illinois, Larry Leverett in Greenwich, Connecticut, and Juan Martinez, in a southern state, all talk optimistically about their efforts to close the achievement gap. As Beverly Hall says:

> People never looked at poverty as a reason for not educating them. They looked at poverty as a given and then how to mitigate against it so we can get on with teaching children to read and write.

This controversy among researchers and policymakers about the impact of poverty on learning is a critical one to resolve. If people like Rothstein are right, then valiant efforts by courageous and able school leaders are likely to fail without more investments in the lives of poor children than the schools can realistically provide. A worse consequence, if Rothstein and others are correct, is that when educators' efforts fail, schools will be blamed, will accept that blame and the recriminations, and then begin a new cycle of doomed school-only efforts to again try to mitigate the consequences of poverty.

The controversy, unfortunately, is likely to endure as our society struggles with its commitments to the poorest and most unfortunate among us. Superintendents must recognize both sides of the dilemma, understand them fully, come to terms with their own beliefs, and act accordingly.

The Importance of Context[4]

The stories here illustrate not only achievement gaps between groups of students in local communities but also contextual contrasts among communities in our society. Larry Leverett describes the affluence and social capital in Greenwich, Connecticut, where the bottom line is getting as many students as possible into the best colleges. Juan Martinez describes the poverty and corruption in Sunnyside, where the school district has more financial resources than any other local entity and the bottom line is school jobs and business for local residents and voters.

Despite these contextual dissimilarities, research confirms three critical dimensions—educational, managerial, and political leadership—of any superintendent's role (Cuban, 1988; Johnson, 1996). Johnson also suggests three "embedded contexts" in which all superintendents perform these roles—the contexts of the times, the locale, and the organization (p. 14). In recent studies (Blumberg, 1985; Owen, 1998; Peterson, 1998), a reciprocal relationship emerges between superintendent and context. The superintendent first must understand the context as fully and quickly as possible. Then, the superintendent acts to change the context. But then, to continue to be effective, the superintendent must also then change his or her responses. So, in effect, the superintendent is also changed by the context (Johnson, 1996, p. 118). The context then affects the emphasis a superintendent places on each of the three dimensions of the role, as he or she "changes hats" to address a particular problem more effectively.

In these stories, we see the interplay between school leaders and the contexts identified by Johnson, and we also see how the contexts influence the choices leaders make among the instructional, political, and managerial dimensions of their roles. For example, *the context of the times* clearly influences the instructional leadership choices that Beverly Hall makes. She fully realizes that the expectation that all poor and minority students will learn at high levels is more rhetoric than reality for many Atlanta (and U.S.) educators. The urgency of the need for improvement leads her to choose a scripted literacy curriculum that can quickly raise test scores for her elementary schools. Yet she also recognizes that, as the context changes, so should her response. She views a scripted curriculum as a short-term solution, not a long-term one. *The context of the locale* is clearly an important factor for Linda Hanson. She confronts support for the ill-advised graduation policy from local business people as well as her new board of education, which sees a graduation test as improving workforce skills for its blue-collar community. The situation first demands political leadership but then requires instruction as well, as she and her staff educate the board and the community. In his story, Allan Alson also recognizes that the achievement gap he confronts in Evanston Township High School reflects broader local patterns of social and economic inequity. In a final example, *the context of the organization* is a pivotal factor for both Becky van der Bogert and Becky Hurley. They each struggle to maintain and strengthen the culture of consensus building that has historically characterized the Winnetka schools. As adversarial collective bargaining impacts the context, their responses change as well.

The contexts described in these stories also shape sharply different responses from leaders in terms of what dimensions of their role they initially emphasize and how they choose to enact them. For example, Beverly Hall's high-profile entry into Atlanta in which she first builds a base of political support in the community contrasts with Becky van der Bogert's "leading from the back of the room" approach to her early effort to build an instructional vision in Winnetka. However, the impact of these leaders also affects the context, generating that interplay between person and setting. For example, John Wiens, superintendent in Manitoba, aspired to be a teacher–leader rather than a systems manager. He shares his struggle with making this role a reality, and working within the system he initially embraced and then grew to see as limited.

Authoritative but Collaborative Leadership

The almost mythical belief that a single, powerful, and effective leader can enter a school district context and magically overcome chronic, complex problems remains a sad illusion. The cycle of impossibly high expectations for new leaders followed quickly by predictable disillusion and disappointment is still all too familiar, especially in urban districts. Elmore (2000) argues that we need to "de-romanticize" leadership to make large-scale improvements in school organizations. Rather than the illusion of an all-powerful personality who can "embody all the traits and skills that remedy all the defects" (p. 14), he suggests a definition of leadership that focuses on improvement in instruction and the "distribution" of leadership throughout the organization. In fact, Elmore suggests, there is no other way to accomplish the complex work of large-scale instructional improvement (p. 15). Johnson (1996) also depicts a more collaborative style of effective superintendent leadership. "The emerging conception of leadership is one of reciprocal influence, through which individuals holding different roles collaborate to improve education" (p. 13).

Today's effective superintendent practices a style of collaborative leadership that is both top-down—articulating core values, establishing expectations for accountability methods—and bottom-up—including all constituents meaningfully, developing leadership in others. In this process, leadership is less hierarchical. The superintendent's role has shifted from the top of the organizational structure to the hub of a complex network of interpersonal relationships (Peterson & Short, 2001, p. 539). In their new role, school district leaders must motivate staff to improve the academic program, share authority and responsibility with them, and provide support and hold staff accountable for making those efforts. They must be authoritative rather than authoritarian, employing personal rather than positional authority, and they must be collaborative rather than unilateral, inviting commitment rather than compliance.

Effective community leadership also is more collaborative and less heroic. The Annenberg Institute studied communities that came together around shared goals to improve their schools. In describing several examples of successful public engagement, Kimpton and Considine (1999) state:

Leadership isn't about pulling people along anymore. It is much more about orchestrating ideas, people, visions, potential and diverse organizations into a cohesive program of education improvement. (p. 5)

In differing ways, the stories here demonstrate leaders who understand and attempt to exercise authoritative, collaborative leadership. For example, Beverly Hall brings political and corporate leaders together to ask for their support even before arriving in Atlanta. Becky Hurley sees her role as board chair as reaching out to newly elected members who represented the opposition and involving them meaningfully in board dialogue. Linda Hanson brings her reading teachers to the board to help her educate them. Despite the opposition of his board president, Juan Martinez establishes a parent advisory committee to implement a bond issue to ensure broader, fairer participation in decision making.

Vision Setting

One of the primary ways that superintendents exercise instructional leadership is through the formulation of a vision for the district. A school district vision involves the collaborative process of articulating beliefs about the education of children, defining goals for the school organization that enact those beliefs, and developing plans to reach the goals. As this definition suggests, the "how" of developing a vision seems to be at least as important as the "what." Johnson (1996) finds that developing an effective vision involves a "delicate balance of control and collaboration" (p. 82). Superintendents who develop their vision independently risk political criticism about being unilateral and ignoring the local context. However, a superintendent who develops a collaborative vision risks being viewed as weak and ineffective if the power of the vision becomes diluted by committees and compromises. The most effective superintendents in Johnson's study not only articulate their educational values with "clarity and conviction" (Johnson, p. 86) but also adapt them to the needs of the context. In collaboration with others, they are able to put their personal imprint on a vision that, at the same time, is addressing important local needs, and they enhance their credibility by not only stating their values but acting on them as well. In describing his experience in Plainfield, New Jersey, Larry Leverett provides a powerful example of a superintendent developing a vision that is clear, personal, powerful, and yet collaboratively held. John Wiens also has a profound vision, not only of how to become a better educational leader, but also of helping the world to become more democratic and human.

Skepticism About Educational Change

The measure of the effectiveness of the educational leadership of district leaders is the educational change produced. Bringing about change in a school system, however, is a formidable challenge. Johnson (1996) describes how teachers and administrators are inured to the potential for change a new superintendent brings because of decades of school reform activity characterized by finger pointing, failed promises, and lack of follow through. Typically, a large group of veteran teachers have set down roots and stayed in most communities for 25 or more years. Superintendent tenure is generally much shorter—perhaps 6 to 7 years at best (Natkin et al., 2002). Johnson says that superintendent turnover makes staff especially skeptical and mistrustful of yet another initiative. Staff cynics cite the metaphor of the "revolving door" of administrative change to justify their inaction (Johnson, 1996, pp. 92, 93).

One of the obstacles that most contributors faced was this skepticism. Beverly Hall, for example, was the fifth superintendent in 10 years when she took over in Atlanta in 1999. In her story, she describes staff waiting to see whether or not she could be effective in dealing with a highly politicized and contentious board of education. Even in the much more stable administrative environment of Evanston Township High School, Allan Alson describes the "faculty wariness" when he announced that improving minority achievement would be his top priority as a new superintendent. He notes, "[e]ducators know that there is often a huge gulf between the creation of a study and a change for the better in practice."

Authentic Personal Relationships

In today's world of collaborative leadership, superintendents who do win the respect and confidence of their constituents and achieve transformational leadership make effective use of personal authority: their interpersonal skills, social attractiveness, knowledge base, clarity of beliefs, and charisma. Positional authority, the power that comes with the role, may have been sufficient to bring about educational change in the days of scientific management when the hierarchy of the school organization functioned effectively. However, positional authority is no longer sufficient. Who the superintendent is as a person matters:

Superintendents' capacity to lead rests in part on their own moral purposes, their commitment to education, and their courage to stand up for what they believe. (Johnson, 1996, p. 281)

Superintendents must be seen as authentic human beings to be credible and to win support. Johnson (1996) observes, "[b]efore personally investing in a superintendent's initiatives, constituents wanted to know about the person behind the initiatives" (p. 283). Whether Larry Leverett's Greenwich constituents agree with him or not, they know who he is and what he stands for. In his story, Leverett relates examples that illustrate the bluntness and honesty of his leadership style, examples that establish his authenticity. People trust that he is not holding back.

Peterson (1998) also finds superintendents establish their authenticity through personal visibility. Through frequent school visits, superintendents, first, signal their instructional commitment. Visits also offer the opportunity, through observing teachers and reviewing student work, to demonstrate the value and importance of district instructional goals (p. 12). In his first 6 months in Sunnyside, Juan Martinez did what he calls the "Giuliani thing," becoming personally involved with teachers, staff, and students in a range of activities, from school emergencies to classroom visits. He received an outpouring of praise and acknowledgment from staff constituents as a result. Ironically, his board had a less positive view, expecting a less dynamic and perhaps a less popular and less politically threatening superintendent.

Becky Hurley's description of Becky van der Bogert's leadership style provides a powerful example of this personal relationship building. As a corporate lawyer, Hurley was surprised upon entering board service that van der Bogert spent "a lot less time than I expected reading memos, having meetings, or putting out 'fires in the inbox,' and a lot more time just being available to talk." She describes "Becky's couch" as where much of this talk occurred. However, van der Bogert also had a weekly schedule for school and classroom visits to which she invited board members. Becky Hurley concludes that these activities were "very productive" and that they "helped her to build community" (p. 184).

Hardwired Tensions With the Board

The political dimension of the superintendent's role, especially in relationship to the board of education, remains crucial. Consistent with the new emphasis on collaborative leadership, the dialogue today in the education media and elsewhere about board–superintendent relations emphasizes the importance of teamwork. As one superintendent told us recently, "I tell my board that we have to build a tent and bring as many as possible into it with us."[5] Arguing that authority for moving any school district forward has multiple sources in the system and the community, today's superintendents talk less about themselves as "superintendents"—individuals in whom authority to run the system is vested—and more about the "superintendency"—the network they have built of staff, board, and even community members who participate with them in system governance. Several of the stories in this volume—Hanson, Martinez, Leverett, and van der Bogert—describe superintendents' explicit efforts, some more successful than others, to build such a board–superintendent team.

Despite these optimistic efforts at collaboration with the board, superintendents generally express strong frustration with politics and red tape in their jobs. For example, 8 of 10 superintendents who responded to the 2001 Public Agenda survey, *Trying to Stay Ahead of the*

Game, felt that "politics and bureaucracy" were the key factors that influence the decisions of talented people to leave the field (Farkas, Johnson, Duffett, & Foleno, 2001, p. 8).

The realities of shared governance are considerably messier and more complex than slogans and generalizations about the value of shared leadership suggest. Boards and superintendents have different roles and responsibilities, specifically defined in state law and, generally, in district policy. Among the responsibilities that set superintendents apart from the board is managing the relationship between the board and the school organization, an area fraught with possibilities for conflict. Board members want access to teachers and administrators to fulfill their oversight responsibilities. Superintendents want to be sure that board access does not lead to micromanagement. Amidst these role conflicts, board–superintendent trust is always tenuous. In her story, Hurley describes how a seemingly innocuous board proposal for parents to communicate with teachers by e-mail threatened to create a rift with the superintendent who appeared to have an otherwise trusting and trusted board relationship.

Board–superintendent tension is hardwired into their relationship, and it is not a new phenomenon, although it may have been exacerbated by the social upheaval of the late 20th century. At its essence, the superintendent's role has evolved historically through political conflicts with the board of education over the power that superintendents would have to run schools (Blumberg, 1985). In describing the early predilection of school boards to make day-to-day educational decisions, Blumberg cites the "anti-executive" tradition in colonial history (p. 20), noting "[c]eding public powers to a single individual is simply against the American tradition" (p. 74). Much of the conflict centered on the struggle for power over educational decision making. Superintendents ultimately "won" because of the rise of scientific management and professionalism in the superintendency at the beginning of the 20th century and because of the growing complexity of school systems themselves. Elmore (2000) agrees about the cultural and historical roots of today's board–superintendent tension. Citing Madison's *Federalist Papers*, he reminds us that "institutions of government exist to play the interests of competing factions against each other, so as to prevent the tyranny of one faction over all others" (p. 18). Competing factions, jockeying for more power, are "hardwired into the culture and institutional structure" (p. 18).

Because politics is so embedded in the role, the conflicts that result are often a function of the position, not the person; "It comes with the territory" (Blumberg, 1985, p. 1). Superintendents today often describe themselves in "no-win positions," where any significant decision they make will alienate and upset someone or some group. Unlike other visible public leaders, like elected politicians, they do not have partisan coalitions on whom to rely for support in times of trouble. And, unlike politicians who cannot be easily removed from office until the next election, superintendents serve at the pleasure of the school board and can be removed at any time. Juan Martinez's story clearly illustrates such a "no-win" position, as he gets caught in the political crossfire between different board and community factions.

Other stories in this volume also reveal these hard-wired political tensions among superintendents, boards, and unions. Beverly Hall describes how a fractious board refused for months to approve her recommendations for a major facilities program. Linda Hanson's story demonstrates how even a new superintendent encounters tension in working with the largely supportive board that hired her. Becky Hurley's and Becky van der Bogert's stories reveal the pain of discovering the hidden but still hard-wired tension between the board, the superintendent, and the teachers' union over the terms of a new teacher contract. Van der Bogert tells of her surprise and sorrow in realizing that the values of interest-based bargaining that she thought were shared were not.

These stories also illustrate that, despite the yearning for a board–superintendent team, the superintendent at times is the "person in the middle" who must negotiate political relationships with the board and between the board and the organization. The superintendents in our stories, however, define this "person in the middle" role differently. In trying to persuade the board to change a flawed graduation policy, Hanson assumes the role of educator and successfully reframes a political issue as a learning issue by involving members of her staff. She also describes how in the process she had to confront the inappropriate and unproductive behavior of one key board member. Leverett, in contrast, aligns himself more closely with his board as he tries to change the culture of the organization. Martinez tries to act as an advocate for staff and community who do not have a voice amidst the acrimony of board politics. Hall, finally, identifies herself more with community political leaders in trying to change both the board and the organization.

Leading Through Managing

Of the three dimensions of the superintendent's role cited earlier—educational, political, and managerial—educational leadership seems most highly prized by commentators as well as incumbent and aspiring superintendents. Managerial leadership is often described as a separate and less valuable or less important function. This devaluing of management does not capture the more complex interrelationship that appears to exist between effective management and the other dimensions of leadership. Johnson (1996) argues that the separation of leadership and management is a social construct that is misleading and inaccurate. In her study, successful superintendents do both simultaneously: "In no district did we find evidence of effective leadership without effective management" (p. 239). In fact, superintendents manage in order to lead, or to put it another way, they lead through managing.

The stories in this volume provide ample evidence of superintendents performing both functions simultaneously. In each case, upon first arriving in the district the superintendent discovered and then solved a vital resource problem that enabled educational improvement and built credibility that would enhance subsequent educational leadership. Larry Leverett, Beverly Hall, and Juan Martinez were all surprised to discover management dysfunctions in their new organizations. Larry found budget and management problems that took him 18 months to correct. During that time, he felt that he was providing no instructional leadership. But, in fact, he was building relationships with parents and community as well as creating fiscal stability and credibility that would strengthen his ability to induce educational change in the organization. Beverly Hall found herself immersed in facilities work for over a year. Yet she was also able to initiate school reform programs that would bring urgently needed instructional change and would strengthen organizational accountability. Juan Martinez found both urgent facilities and budget problems that required his full attention. But, in the process, he established himself as a hands-on, involved, visible, and accessible leader.

Conclusion

Each story here concludes with "Lessons Learned" that we hope will be of use, especially to current and aspiring superintendents. There are also more general lessons that can be drawn from these stories that can be instructive to those who prepare school administrators, those who aspire for school leadership, and those who hire or elect school leaders.

The Importance of Good Entry Strategies

Our stories illustrate how different organizational cultures are from place to place. Although they all manifest surface similarities—the regularities of American schools—moving from one district to another is like traveling between foreign countries. In our stories, all of the superintendents entering new districts prepared for their entry; they were all aware of these cultural differences—nonetheless, the differences were often sufficiently vast enough that there were surprises. Hanson, Leverett, and Martinez, in particular, talk of surprises that they immediately met and their responses. Bena Kallick's commentary describes "entry surprises" she has helped her superintendent clients confront. She tells of one veteran superintendent who, based on past entry surprises, included a 6-month entry period in a new contract to get to know the district before embarking on initiatives. Whether a contract provision is feasible or not, new superintendents and other entering school leaders need careful, thoughtful, and thorough entry plans. Our other commentator, Barry Jentz, has written extensively about this issue and has published entry plan templates for superintendents and other administrators to follow (see Jentz & Wofford, 1982). Leadership training programs should address entry strategies. Aspiring school leaders should read the literature on this topic and begin to draft entry plans as part of their preparation. Finally, the board of education and others involved in hiring school leaders should encourage and, in fact, expect written entry plans.

The Complexity and Unpredictability of School Organizations

All of the stories here illustrate convincingly the reality of how unpredictable, uncontrollable, messy, complex, tenuous, and uncertain school district leadership is. Logical, rational plans, skillfully implemented, continually meet unexpected, uncontrollable, nonrational obstacles. Leverett discovered unpredictability when he chose a more qualified external rather than internal candidate for a principalship. Instead of passively accepting the decision, a faculty and community firestorm of loyalty and support for the insider broke out. Becky van der Bogert discovered the tenuous nature of mutual understandings and commitments with faculty about core beliefs, when they failed to hold during contract negotiations. Beverly Hall discovered the uncontrollable nature of board politics when her board failed to pass her first major initiative. Juan Martinez discovered unpredictability when, despite publicly acknowledged leadership success, his contract was not renewed. Allan Alson discovered complexity when he met opposition to efforts to acknowledge and respond to the achievement gap from an unexpected quarter—the black middle class in Evanston. Finally, Becky Hurley explicitly acknowledges the messiness she discovered when she became a board member. She says, "The simple answer is usually the wrong answer," and warns board members not to heed the "siren song of simplicity" (p. 171).

The Importance of Learning

The uncertainty and complexity of school district leaderships mean that superintendents must be continuous learners. Heifitz and Linsky (2002) and Schoen (1983) have argued against merely technical approaches to school leadership. There is no manual that contains the solutions to problems on the superintendent's shelf; they must construct new solutions that take into account idiosyncratic variables of context and people. Bena Kallick and Barry Jentz, the experts we invited to write commentaries, are both long-term organizational consultants who have worked with many superintendents and their school districts across the country. They agree that school leadership demands continuous, on-the-job learning and change. Kallick describes the "habits of mind" of the best superintendents she knows as including listening, flexibility, and openness to learning. Jentz talks of the need for leaders to accept and even "embrace the confusion" they will frequently feel when confronting organizational problems, and to employ this confusion as a resource for mobilizing the energy for self-inquiry.

The Importance of Self-Growth

Jentz argues that the learning and change necessary is not just about others and about the organization, but also about the self. In his experience working with countless principals, superintendents, and others in leadership roles, he has discovered that all of us manifest discrepancies between what we *think* we do and how we actually behave. Through reflection and deliberate practice at learning new leadership behaviors, we must confront these discrepancies if we are to communicate consistently to others, to inspire their trust, to build credibility, and to be effective.

We agree that this personal growth is essential for superintendents and other school leaders. Three of the stories here illustrate leaders confronting the need for growth and change in themselves as well as in their organization. Becky van der Bogert tells us how she denied the cues teachers were giving her about their attitude toward upcoming negotiations and assumed that the existing good will would prevail. She learned, or relearned, the importance of testing assumptions. She also learned the painful lesson that others' perceptions of a leader do not always match a leader's self-perception. Sometimes this lack of congruence results from the leader's behavioral discrepancies and sometimes it results from the beliefs and assumptions about authority that others bring to a school organization from a lifetime of experience.

Becky Hurley describes her growth as a new school board member and then board president. She struggles with understanding the meaning of the values of democracy and consensus in Winnetka, but finds herself undergoing what she terms "360-degree learning" through which board members, administrators, faculty, parents, and community members reflected and reinforced the same values in the same language. Through that process, these abstract values came to have contextual meaning.

John Wien's chapter details his ongoing personal and professional journey to develop a meaningful and productive philosophy of educational leadership. His story powerfully illustrates how career-long personal growth and development are crucial to effective leadership. Preparation programs should devote much more time and other resources to enabling aspiring leaders to develop the capacities to undertake this work.

Support for Extraordinary People

As superintendents ourselves, we confess a strong empathy for the people doing this work. Our experience in editing this volume confirms our belief that some extraordinary people have chosen careers as educational leaders. They enter with a kind of missionary spirit—a belief that they can make a difference, especially for those who have historically been poorly served by public schools. We are concerned that some of the best people in district leadership leave the profession and some of the best potential new leaders choose not to become superintendents because they become disenchanted by the overwhelming nature of the job or their perception that the pain and sacrifices they must experience far outweigh positive job benefits or outcomes. Our stories illustrate some of the struggles and some of the pain that all superintendents experience. Although each of our superintendents emerges undeterred from the difficulties each describes, others, like Phil Townsend, our composite superintendent, do not. They resign or retire.

Our stories also illustrate that superintendents can be successful. They can be transformational leaders, even in today's complex school environment. We would like to increase the odds of this kind of success and read more stories about it. One key to more district leadership success is, as we have been arguing, better preparation and training for school leaders in areas—entry strategies, personal growth—that can be directly helpful to them. Another key is, to borrow from Becky Hurley, "360-degree support." Those who prepare, hire, and supervise superintendents and other school leaders—as well as leaders themselves—need to fully embrace the responsibility of helping leaders be successful. Preparation programs should extend training to on-the-job mentoring. Boards should encourage and, indeed, support personal and professional superintendent growth plans that are revised and re-funded annually. The growth plan should draw on various resources—books, organizational consultants, conferences, and other experiences—that will enable a superintendent to continue to grow in his/her capacity for dealing with the challenges of leadership. Everyone should encourage and support superintendents in establishing and participating in peer support groups, where problems can be discussed without fear, advice and pain shared, solace provided, and connections and collegiality encouraged. It is simply too easy to feel alone in the job.

We hope, finally, that these stories and their lessons provide both evidence and hope: evidence that despite the daunting challenges of school district leadership, success is still possible; hope that talented, committed people will continue to see the value and the benefits of pursuing a career in public school leadership.

Notes

1. We are especially indebted to Barry Jentz, Susan Moore Johnson, and Bena Kallick for their advice.

2. We are grateful to Gary Fenstermacher for this observation. See also Von Zastrow (2004) for more on neglected aspects of the curriculum.

3. Gordon's and Orfield's remarks were made at the 63rd Annual Superintendents' Work Conference at Teachers College–Columbia University, July 11–14, 2004. Highlights of their presentations are available at http://conference.tc.columbia.edu/archives.asp#

4. The next several sections draw extensively from Sergiovanni, Kelleher, McCarthy, and Wirt (2004).

5. Dr. Samuel Stewart, former superintendent in Ridgewood and South Brunswick, New Jersey.

References

Blumberg, A. (1985). *The school superintendent: Living with conflict*. New York: Teachers College Press.

Cuban, L. (1988). *The management imperative and the practice of leadership in the schools*. Albany: State University of New York Press.

Elmore, R. (2000). *Building a new structure for school leadership*. Washington, DC: The Albert Shanker Institute.

Farkas, S., Johnson, J., Duffett, A., & Foleno, T. (with Foley, P.). (2001). *Trying to stay ahead of the game: Superintendents and principals talk about school leadership*. New York: Public Agenda.

Fuller, H.L., Campbell, C., Celio, M.B., Harvey, J., Immerwahr, J., & Winger, A. (2003). *An impossible job? The view from the urban superintendent's chair*. Report prepared for the Center on Reinventing Public Education.

Gordon, E. (2004). Presentation at the 63rd Annual Superintendents Work Conference, *Closing the Achievement Gap*, at Teachers College, Columbia University, July.

Heifitz, R., & Linsky, M. (2002). *Leadership on the line*. Boston: Harvard Business School Press.

Jentz, B., & Wofford, J. (1982). *Entry: The hiring, start-up, and supervision of administrators*. New York: McGraw-Hill.

Johnson, S. (1996). *Leading to change: The challenge of the new superintendency*. San Francisco, CA: Jossey-Bass.

Kimpton, J.S., & Considine, J.W. (1999, September). The tough sledding of district-led engagement. *The School Administrator Web Edition*. Retrieved October 1, 2005, from http://www.aasa.org.publications/sa1999_09/kimpton.htm

Natkin, G., Cooper, B., Fusarelli, L., Alborano, J., Padilla, A., & Ghosh, S. (2002). The myth of the revolving door superintendency. *The School Administrator, 5*, 28–31.

Orfield, G. (2004). Presentation at the 63rd Annual Superintendents Work Conference, *Closing the Achievement Gap*, at Teachers College, Columbia University, July.

Owen, J. (1998, April). *The roles of the superintendent in creating a community climate for educational improvement*. Paper presented at the annual conference of the American Educational Research Association, San Diego, CA.

Peterson, G. (1998, April). *Demonstrated actions of instructional leaders: A case study of five superintendents*. Paper presented at the annual conference of the American Educational Research Association, San Diego, CA.

Peterson, G., & Short, P. (2001). The school board president's perception of the district superintendent: Applying the lenses of social influence and social style. *Educational Administration Quarterly, 37*, 533–570.

Rothstein, R. (2004). *Class and schools: Using social, economic, and educational reform to close the black-white achievement gap*. New York: Teachers College Economic Policy Institute.

Schoen, D. (1983). *The reflective practitioner: How professionals think in action*. New York: Basic Books.

Sergiovanni, T., Kelleher, P., McCarthy, M., & Wirt, F. (2004). *The superintendency today*. Upper Saddle River, NJ: Pearson Education.

Von Zastrow, C. (2004). *Academic atrophy: The condition of the liberal arts in America's public schools*. Washington, DC: Council for Basic Education.

One of the findings that we found fascinating was the variety of sources of energy and the courage that kept our authors going when confronted with obstacles that might be insurmountable to many. As you read Beverly Hall's story, you will feel the passion that she brings to her superintendency, passion that is fueled by her beliefs—belief in poor children's ability to learn at high levels and belief in her staff that they can make it happen.

CHAPTER 2

Confronting the Universal Disbelief That Poor Children Can Achieve at High Levels

PAUL KELLEHER WITH BEVERLY HALL

In her first year as superintendent of the Atlanta Public Schools, Beverly Hall encountered what she describes as the nearly universal disbelief that poor children of color can achieve high levels of learning. This chapter recounts how she confronted this and other obstacles and challenges as the new leader of the Atlanta Public Schools.

The chapter resulted from collaboration between Paul Kelleher, volume coeditor, and Beverly Hall. Paul interviewed Beverly twice, and produced transcripts of those dialogues for joint review and revision. In writing the chapter, he consulted other sources, such as local newspaper reports and board of education minutes. He and Beverly then discussed and revised the chapter. As much as possible, the chapter presents Beverly's story directly. Her words are in italics throughout.

Atlanta History—Beverly's Perception

Unlike many urban school systems, the Atlanta Public Schools have a unique cultural history. As a hub of the Civil Rights Movement, Atlanta is renowned for being home to many of this nation's civil rights leaders. Indeed, Martin Luther King Jr. and other notable activists graduated from the Atlanta Public Schools. In addition, several of the historically black colleges like Spelman and Morehouse are in Atlanta and they provide educational resources and support to the community.

Despite these resources, like many urban systems, the Atlanta Public Schools have had a troubled recent history.

Here you have a system of predominately African-American children that always had low achievement scores. When the system was desegregated in the middle 1970s through the early 1980s . . . there was a tremendous amount of white flight . . . Even though there wasn't as much of an emphasis as there is now on achievement data, people always knew that the system was low performing compared to surrounding systems. Many families moved out of Atlanta to the suburbs or surrounding counties just for that reason. They felt the school system was not adequately preparing children for success after graduation.

If you look back to the era of greatest stability and examine the data, you'll see that the schools weren't showing great progress academically. Yet if you look at press articles and public perception, people thought it was a very good urban system.

That perception, and the stability it engendered, resulted from expectations for schools that did not include high achievement for all students. If urban schools were safe and nurturing, and if the system appeared to be managed well, then people were satisfied.

I saw on television just by accident a clip of a superintendent from that era testifying in Congress . . . At that time, he was considered a good urban superintendent. He was going on about all the good things that were going on in Atlanta. Then some senator or congressman cuts to the chase and says, "But if you look at the test scores, the kids in Atlanta are at the bottom." . . . The superintendent's whole demeanor changed. He was clearly blindsided because he had been told to go there . . . and promote the school system.

By 1999, when Beverly was appointed as superintendent, leadership stability in the Atlanta Public Schools was a distant memory. Beverly was the fifth superintendent in 10 years. Board conflict was the leading cause of instability.

It's legendary. If you go back into history and look at videotapes of board meetings . . . you will see board members fighting with each other and fighting with the superintendent. It was totally out of control.

Prior to the selection of her predecessor in 1994, community leaders had tried to restore order and integrity to the board of education. In 1993, the Metro Atlanta Chamber of Commerce created a political coalition called EduPAC that helped overturn the school board ("Atlanta School Board," 2000). They ran *a campaign called, "Erase the Board." And they had removed the majority of old board members. They brought in what appeared on the surface to be a much more sophisticated, well-educated board . . . That board's first task was to go out and find a world-class superintendent.*

With the support of the chamber and other community leaders, the new board recruited and selected a new superintendent, Dr. Benjamin Canada. After just four years, however, the new superintendent left for another job. The *Atlanta Journal-Constitution* later reported that

[h]is tenure in Atlanta was mixed. As an agent of change, Canada helped get higher academic standards set, elementary and middle school initiatives passes and 13 schools shut down. But scores dipped on the Iowa Test of Basic Skills, construction projects ran over budget and behind schedule and administrators left for better paying jobs. Parents didn't like the school closings, and employees complained about meager raises. ("Ex-superintendent," 2001)

Entry Into the System

With a renewed desire to put the Atlanta Public Schools on sounder footing, a powerful combination of political and corporate leaders became actively involved in the effort to find and recruit yet another superintendent.

They [the Chamber of Commerce] played a much more active role again. And this time, the governor, who had an aggressive education legislative agenda, also participated. He said, "As goes Atlanta, so goes Georgia." Since we have the largest number of minority students doing very, very poorly, he wanted a role in the selection of the next superintendent.

The broad-based committee that screened candidates included the governor's representative and corporate leaders. The governor had the Chancellor of the Georgia University System sit on the committee. In addition, Coca-Cola and UPS had two of their senior executives sit on the committee. They played a critical role. So, for my first two interviews, they were all there. It wasn't until the final interview that I sat with the board.

Through the search consultants it hired, this committee actively sought out, researched, recruited, and interviewed the best candidates it could find. The board, of course, also interviewed Beverly and other finalists before offering her the job. However, concerned about the history of instability, Beverly took the process a step farther.

Before I accepted the job, I asked to come back and meet with the board members, either individually or in pairs . . . I wanted them to know who I was. I wanted to know who they were. *I wanted to hear from them, their expectations . . . I told them this system had had five superintendents in 10 years. They couldn't all have been bad guys. Something structurally and fundamentally wasn't working here. I said, "I need to have a sense of what you are looking for and see if that coincides with what I have to offer." We had very good conversations resulting in a common understanding of where we were going to start and try to go.*

In the first days and weeks of her superintendency, Beverly moved to strengthen her political and corporate support even more. At her request, her initial contract linked her pay to student test score results.

This gave me a lot of support from business leaders in the community because they're very in tune with that kind of thinking.

She met tirelessly with local civic groups where she found people who wanted change in the school system:

The civic groups, too, were fed up and wanted change . . . I met with dozens of organizations, was open and honest, and strategically established relationships.

A meeting that she called in the last week of June 1999—before her actual starting date of July 1—was a critical event in cementing community support, especially for her first initiative, Project GRAD, a school reform program that began in Houston and that she had earlier implemented in Newark.

I asked leaders at Georgia Pacific to host a meeting and to invite my entire board and major funders in the system . . . The board could convene as a group because . . . it was not a meeting.

Convictions About Children

Beverly came to Atlanta as an experienced teacher and school and district leader with a core belief that large numbers of poor children can overcome the obstacles of poverty and achieve at high levels.

In the Teaching Commission Report, convened by former IBM Chairman Lou Gerstner, a key finding is that there is research to show that quality teaching can really offset the impact of economic deprivation . . . So, we have that from the research folks. We also have a lot of evidence when you look at what happened before desegregation and poor black children were going to one-room schoolhouses. There's evidence to document that these students learned and achieved at high levels.

No one ever attempted, whether white or black, to educate every child to high levels until very recently in America. But significantly large groups of poor kids from all groups have been educated. If you look at the immigrant waves in New York when the Europeans came in, those children often didn't know how to take care of their own hygiene. There are curriculum guides going back into the early part of the 20th century when teachers were teaching them how to clean their teeth, how to wash . . . and at the same time teaching them to read and write. A huge segment of that population went on in two generations to become highly successful, well educated, and wealthy . . . People never looked at poverty as a reason for not educating them. They looked at poverty as a given and then identified ways to mitigate it so we can get on with teaching children to read and write . . .

Then there is my own personal experience as a teacher in inner-city Brooklyn. We ran schools there where large numbers of poor children did very well.

Several years ago, I spoke with one of America's wealthiest citizens right here in my office. He told me that two generations ago his grandfather pushed a handcart in the garment district of New York . . . Examples such as these are fairly common—there is an entire generation of individuals who have done extremely well financially even though their parents came to this country with absolutely nothing.

It Is Like Walking on the Moon

The biggest obstacle that Beverly faced in Atlanta was that most people did not share her conviction.

The biggest challenge that I've faced—it was the same in New York as it is here in Atlanta—was convincing the very people that needed to work toward transforming the school system that it was doable. In spite of what people say, slogans that they put up, there is a fundamental disbelief in the educability of poor children—large masses of poor children. It's not just from any one segment of the population. It was easy for me to say early in my career that this or that group didn't believe in the kids. But I've come to the conclusion at this late stage of my life that there is almost universal disbelief in the possibilities of educating children. And it's not because people are mean. They haven't seen the evidence to say, "Yes, we can do it." It's like walking on the moon. It's much easier now for this generation to accept it than it was for my grandparents.

The expression of disbelief was a constant theme from a lot of constituency groups . . . "You don't understand where the children are coming from. You don't understand all the issues that we have to face in teaching the kids." This came from not necessarily evil people . . . I got the sense that many people almost felt sorry for me. "You're taking this on? You don't have a clue what you're up against." As opposed to people saying that it can be done, and we expect it to be done, and "Let's get on with it." When I decided to link my bonus to student performance, I probably was one of the

34   CONFRONTING A UNIVERSAL DISBELIEF

first superintendents in the country to do that . . . people thought I was absolutely insane. "You'll never earn it!" "What are you doing?"

We administered the High Places Survey, produced by a researcher at the University of Rhode Island, to faculty . . . Even the majority of kindergarten teachers in Atlanta said they did not believe the kids would finish high school. Kindergarten teachers are usually the most optimistic, the most hopeful. And here you have the kindergarten teachers saying . . . based on the data and what they saw around them, these kids aren't going to make it.

Another early example of the disbelief I encountered was a city council member who would be considered an advocate for the people. He attended a meeting in my conference room with a group of parents and teachers from a school where I was attempting to remove an unsatisfactory principal. He came to argue that I allow this principal to stay in spite of a track record of low student performance. His argument was based on the rationale that the children in the school now are not the same as the children that used to go to the school years ago when they had better results. These children, many with migrant parents, can't do it. He was arguing with me, "Dr. Hall, you've got to get real. Stop holding this man to such a high standard. Look at who the children are."

The disbelief came from all sides—except for some in leadership roles who really do believe like I do that if we establish the conditions and we focus on issues like good principal leadership and teacher quality we will be able to get it done. Those are a handful of people. The rest just believed that we were not going to get there. Or they didn't think they'd live to see it. It's going to take just too long.

Beverly thinks that people do not believe in student achievement possibilities primarily because they have never experienced large numbers of poor children of color succeeding academically. In Atlanta, at least, racism seems to be a minor factor.

If you've never seen it, it's hard to imagine it . . . So I think people just came to accept it that the children are poor. They're coming from very, very challenging environments, and they will not be able to do well in school. Of course, the students are African-Americans, so there is an element of racism there. But . . . we have a predominately African-American teaching staff. That's why it's not easy to call it all racism. It would be much simpler if the teaching staff was predominately white, but that is not the case. The leadership of the system . . . We've had African-American superintendents in here ever since the late 1970s. The board has been predominately African-American, and the teaching staff and the administrators have been predominately African-American.

One tacit way that people expressed their skepticism about the possibility of high-level achievement for all students was to focus their energies on other priorities.

People won't pay as close attention to the core business. They don't want to devote as much time to teaching and learning because that's not where they see the big win to be. They want to pay attention to a lot of what I call the glitzy stuff—technology, computers in classrooms, lots of computers in classroom, if you can get the buildings fixed. All of which have value, but they're not the main course. And they almost try to sabotage you getting on with the core business by putting out, "Fix the business operation ... Get going with that because that will give us a big win." But when you talk about really devoting a lot of resources, time, and attention to developing teacher skills so they can teach children, so children can learn, people almost don't want to hear it. It's too hard. It's never been done. It's not going to happen in my lifetime. So let's fix those other things so people will think things are happening.

To begin to combat this pervasive skepticism and to start the overhaul of the system, Beverly knew that she had to respond with confident words and competent actions.

In response to the disbelief that poor children could achieve at high levels, I told people that I had personally experienced just the opposite. And that I had looked at the research. For some people, that carries more weight than even your own personal experience. The research really does indicate that if children are taught by qualified people who know how to teach them, who have high expectations for them, they can succeed academically.... In the 1960s, Ron Edmonds of Harvard came out with the correlates of school effectiveness. He had done research to show that poor children could learn and did learn if certain things were in place. I kept responding with that.

I think that the challenge is that you have to say "Suspend your disbelief. Work with us." And then, as the results begin to come in, then you begin to make believers out of people who wanted to believe. So, once they begin to see some evidence, some data, some success—experience it—you find that you get a significant number then who will take this leap of faith and go along. And also, of course, I knew full well that I had to demonstrate it early on or else nobody would believe me after a little while.

Project GRAD: "Jump-Starting" the System

To convert a critical mass of nonbelievers to believers and to begin to transform the schools, Beverly felt that she had to "jump-start" the system immediately. In beginning to take action, however, she knew that she would encounter the ambivalence most people feel about leadership and change.

In spite of what they tell you coming in—"We want you to come in, fix the system, set some standards, and hold people accountable"—the minute you start doing it, you realize that they really don't even believe that, that you are going to get results if you do that.

When you begin to implement . . . "change everything but not what's important to me." Whenever they're hiring you, they want a change agent. They want a visionary, someone with high standards. When you come in, what they really want is someone who is just going to maintain the status quo, and let sleeping dogs lie.

Despite the resistance she knew she would meet, the urgency Beverly felt about getting early academic results led her to launch her first major initiative at the meeting she called with political and corporate leaders, along with her board, before she was even officially the superintendent.

Project GRAD was a program that began in Houston with the support of the CEO of Tenneco, Jim Kettleson, who was just really fed up with doing the usual Adopt-A-School, tutoring, mentoring at the high school level and not seeing any significant improvement in the drop-out rate, in the graduation rate, and in the student performance over time. He really went out and looked at research-based programs—how do you teach kids to read in the elementary level, to do math on grade level. And, of course, teachers told him that they couldn't manage a classroom. Were there any research-based programs around discipline that taught kids to discipline themselves and so forth so teachers could teach them? And he put together this whole reform model that was very comprehensive and piloted it in Houston. The achievement levels of the feeder patterns where he piloted it in . . . the improvement was just tremendous.

When I was in Newark, he came to see me along with Henry Schacht, who was the president of the Ford Foundation and also CEO of Lucent Technology. The two of them came to me and said, "Look, Ford has been providing money for this Project GRAD in Houston. The results in this one cluster of schools are just phenomenal. We'll bring it to a second cluster. And we think Newark ought to look at it." At first, I didn't believe it. I said, "There's no such thing as a silver bullet." But I went to Houston, visited the training sessions. The heart of Project GRAD is a lot of professional development for teachers around best practices. After I spent a lot of time watching that, I saw the schools, saw the transformation of the schools, heard it from teachers, from students, and from parents. I also looked at the research coming out of the University of Houston on the program. I said, "They've something special going on here." So I brought the program to Newark with the assistance of the Ford Foundation and Lucent Foundation. And I was beginning to already see the changes in the schools when I was recruited to come to Atlanta.

I decided to use Project GRAD as a vehicle to jump-start the lowest feeder cluster of schools here in the city and to spend the first year planning for that, involving all stakeholders and raising additional funding. We needed $20 million and I wanted to reach out to the community with a campaign to raise the money. At the end of the day, when the kids finish high school, maintain their average, finish in four years, take high-level courses and attend two summer institutes on a college campus, they will *receive a $4,000 scholarship. So we had to raise money for that in addition to raising money to provide all of the professional development for the teachers in the elementary, middle, and high schools. And we had to phase the components in over time. All of that was estimated to cost about $20 million to do the first couple of feeder clusters. We would start with one, and then we were going to pick up another one.*

I then announced that I would start it in our lowest performing cluster of schools, the Washington High School cluster. Several of my trusted corporate friends said to me, "Why, Beverly? If you want a win, go to not the lowest functioning but to the second or third lowest functioning." I knew that the lowest performing schools—when provided the resources, the attention, and quality teachers—show progress faster. Sure enough, the results were dramatic after the first year of implementation. And the teachers began to feel better about themselves. They knew what they were doing. Within two years, we brought on two more clusters. We brought them on together because people were saying, "It's having such a tremendous impact. Let's hurry and get the other schools on the way." So, that's how I jump-started the system.

Based on her previous experience in Newark, Beverly felt that there were two keys to making Project GRAD successful in Atlanta. The first was the need to hire skilled, district-level staff to lead the program. The second was the need to bring extra resources to the school in the form of social workers, tutors, and staff, as well as for professionals to train and develop staff capacity. Providing those elements depended in part on raising the $20 million.

We were trying to raise it over five years. And we raised it in two. I was also very fortunate by having a very respected community leader agree to chair the GRAD initiative . . . At that point, nobody would have given Atlanta Public Schools their money. It was like throwing it into a bottomless pit. But forming a 501c(3) and finding this really esteemed leader in the community to chair the effort helped to lend credibility in terms of the fund raising and helped to keep away any political factions that could have attacked GRAD. This kept opponents at bay and allowed Project GRAD to get some legs under it.

As the funding support materialized and as the early student achievement results showed impressive gains in the first cluster of schools, the support for the program also broadened and strengthened.

These schools began to win awards. They began to be mentioned everywhere, featured in publications . . . Nothing breeds success like success. That played a large part in it . . .

It's institutionalized, and we're funding most of it now from within. We've reallocated funds. We've gotten the schools to give up lots of things that weren't value-added and to replace them with the GRAD programs and strategies. Now, principals own GRAD.

It would be difficult, particularly in that first cluster, to abolish the program. The second and third feeder clusters are just beginning to get all the components in place. So, the buy-in probably isn't as strong yet. But that first cluster is very, very committed to Project GRAD.

You Could Cut the Tension With a Knife

Although Beverly's recapitulation of the Project GRAD story makes its success seem relatively straightforward, easy, and predictable, in fact, she confronted significant resistance from principals in the system as she implemented the program.

When I brought them together and told them they were going to be the first feeder cluster because they were the lowest performing schools academically in the district, serving some of our poorest children, they were not happy campers. As a matter of fact, one of them later told me she was so angry that day she felt as if she could hit me. She couldn't believe that she was being told that the school was so low functioning and that this had to happen. She later, of course, came to believe that this was the best thing that we could ever have done.

We had disaggregated the data. I didn't say you're bad people. I didn't attack them. I showed them the trend data for the five years preceding my tenure and how the kids were just failing wholesale in their schools. I explained that we had to do something different and we were going to do this program. I was honest that it was going to require a lot of intensive intervention with people coming into your schools to work with you and change what you're doing. But, in addition, we were giving the schools extra social workers and tutors. There were lots of components of the program that they would come to really like . . . to the point where some of my other schools often say, "Oh, the GRAD schools have everything."

Additional resources eventually helped to reduce resistance. But providing more staff and other program components took time to impact schools. In the meantime, Beverly dealt with the negative reaction.

At the end of each school year, I have a huge superintendent's leadership retreat. We were fortunate to get a grant from the Wallace Foundation to conduct leadership development. We were able to really carve out time—for the principals and myself and central office leadership—to go off site for a couple of days at the end of every school year. We usually have a national speaker who helps to tie things together. Then the heart of the conference has to do with how we performed this year as a district. We analyze the data. It's very public. We have lots of breakout groups.

But the resistance in the room . . . You could cut the tension with a knife during those first couple of years when I would get up to speak . . . They were polite. People respect the position. This is the South. Even if you hate the person, you smile and say, "How are you?" But it was evident that people were angry . . . Yet there was always a group that felt that this was long overdue.

Beverly's decision to devote a year to planning prior to implementation of Project GRAD helped to increase support for the program and to decrease the likelihood that principals would undermine the program.

Remember that we had a year of planning. Once I announced it and selected the feeder cluster, then we had . . . 7 months of planning. During that time, we also selected an executive director for Project GRAD and staff who were going to be just dedicated to this. They were very skilled in dealing with school-by-school, principal-by-principal issues. What could have been sabotage, I think we managed so that we were on top of it.

Improved test results also reduced resistance.

When the results started to come in, they began to say, "Now, wait a minute. You know these are better than we've had in the past." It was not every school . . . There were 16 schools in that feeder cluster. I would say there might have been four believers who said, "Look, I'm ready to try anything." And then there were another four who had the attitude of, "Oh, whatever." Then the rest were angry. So the ones who were okay and the ones who said "Whatever" weren't fighting as much but there was a group that just really didn't want it, didn't think it would work. They didn't want to hear from the developers of the program . . . When they saw the results, they began to say, "Now wait a minute . . . this is different. Things are improving here."

The turnover of principals, however, has had an impact on the reduction of tension.

We had some principals who did not seem to have a sense of urgency. So, each year . . . they have gotten fewer and fewer in numbers. Until now, at the last leadership retreat there is almost a feeling that principals really do like what's happening and are excited about it.

In reshaping her cadre of school leaders, Beverly relied more on changed work expectations to induce resignations and retirements rather than on more overt measures.

We knew the kind of work that would be required of the principals. We knew everything they were doing. We were doing the benchmark testing—looking at data, constantly talking to them about what's going on. And that was the beginning of the peeling off. So, some principals decided to retire. And the others who were determined to stay then began to buy in. Now, I think if I tried to remove GRAD, I'd probably have a worse fight than when I introduced it.

In addition to increased work demands, increased personal accountability for results also motivated principal turnover.

We looked at the data and saw where each school was in terms of the number of kids in the bottom quadrant. Then we set very specific targets school-by-school. So, there was heightened accountability, public accountability. We said to principals that a part of your evaluation will also be linked to the degree to which you attain these goals. A part of . . . additional compensation . . . was linked very specifically to schools attaining their targets . . . The percent of targets they hit . . . determined how much each person in that school personally received.

The high stakes accountability, the transparency of where each school was—and we weren't comparing schools on the North East to schools on the South West—we were comparing you to yourself and asking you to please make these targets. The further behind you were, the faster you had to run to catch up.

Sometimes Beverly's strategy required a more direct and confrontational approach. An example is the principal described earlier who had the councilman's as well as parental support to remain in his position.

Because I've been in situations like this before, I realized that the principal is usually the driver behind all of this. They can get the parents to say and do things . . . You're just amazed at parent support for them. So, I realized that he was as much a part of creating this groundswell of support, as he was the target of the support. I more or less confronted him on a one-to-one basis. When he realized that the game was up, he decided to just fold, retire, and go on about his business.

More Challenges in the First Year

Although Beverly wanted to concentrate her time, energy, and talent on the "core business"—improving teaching and learning through Project GRAD—as a first-year superintendent, she had other immense and time-consuming challenges to meet.

That first year was extremely difficult. Part of it was I did not have a team in place. I had brought the person who is now my deputy for instruction with me from Newark but I had only hired her, maybe a year, before I came here. And I had hired her as executive director for high schools and was not sure when I came to Atlanta that she would be ready to take on the deputyship . . . I had hired other members of my leadership team based on limited information because no one wanted to come to Atlanta given the history of superintendents leaving in short order. And it turns out that they were not the right people for the job. So, I was busy trying just to put bodies in place.

I knew early on . . . by winter vacation . . . that I had to make changes. It ended up taking me three years before I had a skeleton leadership team that worked. So the system was kind of running itself and I was trying to establish some kind of working relationship with the board.

"Build Smart" and the Board

Most new superintendents and boards go through a "shake-down" period as they work out their differing roles in system governance. In a system like Atlanta, which had experienced such rapid superintendent turnover prior to Beverly, working out the governance relationship can be especially difficult. In the absence of consistent and continuous superintendent leadership, board members may be naturally drawn into direct, day-to-day management of the system that must be reduced for the new superintendent to be effective.

Beverly and the board did experience some early success in clarifying governance. A crucial area of agreement involved termination and removal of principals.

When I came in, I was able to get from the board their commitment that they would not intervene in that process . . . I was very pleasantly surprised that they stuck to their word, and they really allowed me to go toward those people who were not performing.

In other areas, though, governance issues became more complicated. Prior to Beverly's arrival in Atlanta, the board had contracted with an outside consultant to develop a facilities master plan, called "Build Smart."

We spent the first six months of my tenure . . . creating a superb facilities master plan. There had been a referendum passed that had given over $500 million to the system for facilities. They had hired a reputable firm, Sizemore-Floyd, to do the planning . . . So, I inherited that process underway that was great.

We also knew that we were going out for a second referendum to give us an additional $400 million because the school system facilities were in really horrible shape. We needed to . . . get buy-in into the plan. I spent, I can't tell you how many nights and days poring over the plan, meeting with board members in small groups, having the consultants explain it to them, getting their endorsement, getting them to understand why we had to consolidate schools . . . We did a lot of what I call "spade work." Days and days in conference rooms with charts, consultants, and board members.

When she brought the Build Smart plan forward for board approval in April 2000, Beverly felt the stakes were high because not only were the facilities' needs urgent, but the recommendation for approval would be her first major proposal to the board.

It was my first big initiative. The whole system was watching. This was a system where there was no respect for the superintendency because . . . they knew superintendents didn't last. So, people are watching to see what's really going to happen to the lady from New York and this board. This was the first big item. We have all these routine items that come up month after month. But this was the first significant item.

Beverly was surprised and disappointed when, at the meeting, the board—in what the *Atlanta Journal-Constitution* ("Backward Step," 2000) called a "last minute modification" and a "sudden decision"—voted by a 5–4 margin to remove three schools from the list of those to be closed through Build Smart. After the meeting, the newspaper quotes Beverly as saying that the board's decision "compromised the integrity" of the plan. Because of the interrelationships among plan recommendations for school change, "To say you are going to remove three schools, the plan in my view ceases to exist." She concluded her comments to the paper, though, by saying that she was optimistic that board questions about the three school closings could be addressed.

Others at the meeting seemed less optimistic. A board member who supported passing Build Smart as recommended said he was "disappointed that politics continue to play a role in the decisions that affect children and that the board should accept the plan that has been presented by the professionals." Another board member expressed her concern that "the vote was an example of what the public will see as micromanaging" (Atlanta Public School [APS] minutes, April 17, 2000). The chair of a local think tank with a school task force said, "the move was yet another example of the a board trying to run a school system itself instead of trusting people they hired to operate it" ("Backward Step," 2000).

The public criticism of the board's Build Smart decision intensified over the remainder of Beverly's first year in Atlanta. In May, the paper described the criticism of the board's "micromanagement" and "putting politics above doing right." The Chamber of Commerce voted to reestablish EduPAC, and its chair told the paper that "EduPAC is looking for new candidates who will not micromanage the Atlanta Schools to run for the school board in 2001" ("Build Smart Program," 2000).

Despite the criticism, the board remained at a stalemate on the plan. In June, a new recommendation to close the three schools "died in committee . . . The nine member board maintained a 5–4 split . . . as Superintendent Beverly Hall and some members continued to press for the closings" ("Three Schools in Atlanta," 2000). In July, the paper again reported the board's split on closing schools but also reported on other issues dividing board members.

But Build Smart isn't the only issue dividing the board. It took two months for the board to approve next school year's calendar . . . And in June, after months of fighting the board finally agreed to have the Chief Financial Officer report to Hall—as in most systems—instead of to the board. ("Atlanta's Board Split," 2000)

The continuing disagreements impacted board relationships negatively.

The board members' inability to work together has erupted in outbursts during public meetings . . . the tension is so thick that board members have refused to meet to discuss issues. ("Atlanta's Board Split," 2000)

Although Beverly was upset by the Build Smart stalemate and by the ongoing conflicts, she remained publicly positive and professional.

She downplays the tension saying she must stay focused on improving the Atlanta schools . . . "I am committed to making every effort to work with the board," said Hall, who marked her one-year anniversary in Atlanta last week. The relationship, she said, "is a work in progress." ("Atlanta's Board Split," 2000)

Her supporters on the board and in the community, however, were concerned about the toll the conflict might be taking on her. The paper reported, "All the bickering and the board's inability to agree has made some wonder if the superintendent will stay." One of her board supporters told the paper, "Hall could easily land a new job elsewhere . . . This kind of behavior makes good people say 'you can't take it.' " And a chamber leader said, "We've got a good superintendent, and it's not easy to find great urban superintendents" ("Atlanta's Board Split," 2000).

Beverly, of course, did not choose to leave Atlanta at the end of her first year or anytime subsequently. In January 2001, with a new board president, the board voted unanimously to close the schools recommended in Build Smart and to enact the plan fully ("A Sharper Focus," 2001). Beverly makes sense of what happened with Build Smart in the context of the governance issues that existed between the board and her in her first year.

I was having more difficulty with the board at that time in establishing what was administration and what was governance. So, the Build Smart actually, when the vote came, was more the result of the tension between the board and myself at that time around that issue than it was of the actual Build Smart project itself.

Out of adversity can come opportunities for improvement. After the Chamber of Commerce and other civic leaders became mobilized around school issues again in the spring of 2000, these corporate and political leaders in the community decided that structural change needed to occur in school governance. With the support of local legislators, changes in the governance charter for the schools that clarified and strengthened the formal authority of the superintendent passed the state legislature in 2003.

Separating the Personal from the Professional

One characteristic that enabled Beverly to weather the board and other first-year conflicts is her ability to control her personal, emotional responses to what happened and to take broader and more dispassionate perspectives. In reflecting back on her response to the conflicts with principals, for example, she says

On a personal level, the good thing I think about me is that I'm able to separate that [their antagonism] *from a personal dislike . . . I am able to almost step out of myself and look at myself in a third-party kind of way, which I find a lot of people are not able to do. And so they get very, very emotionally distraught about this. But I was able to mingle with them* [the angry principals], *laugh with them—even though I knew they were probably calling me all kinds of names. You know . . . chitchat and attempt to reach out to them without feeling, well, I'm a horrible person. I think that was what helped me.*

I remember the first year we went on a boat ride . . . They were dancing, and I got up and started doing one of those line dances . . . And this was after a day where I knew they would have thrown me overboard if I weren't watching carefully . . . I mean you're human and you're sensitive . . . But I'm not personally upset by it. I would walk into the building, even the central office building, and people would barely speak. They would look away because we were at the same time cutting off a lot of practices that were inappropriate but that people were benefiting from. We had to establish a lot of things. But I was able always to come into my office, my area, laugh with the people who work in my office and just keep on going.

You want people to say, "You're really doing the right thing." But it's never going to happen . . . and I learned it early in my career . . . when you get there and you're making the changes, they want to burn you in effigy. When you announce you're leaving people are crying. They want to plant trees in your memory. These are the same people who for four years said "If she doesn't leave soon . . ."

It Nearly Killed Me

By most objective measures, Beverly had an enormously successful first year. She juggled competing priorities for her time and attention but kept a focus on the "core business" of teaching and learning. She linked her salary to student performance on standardized tests, and the test scores improved. She initiated a systemic program to improve teaching and learning, set in place a program to raise money to fund it, and confronted system resistance to it. After initial mistakes, she made considerable progress in finding the right people to work alongside her on her leadership team. Finally, after controversy and delay, she got Build Smart approved. In the process, she weathered a board crisis, clarified governance issues, and confirmed strong public support for her leadership.

Despite her experience—Atlanta is her third superintendency—and her personal and professional strengths, her first-year experience in Atlanta took its toll

The first year probably was the most difficult year I've had in my entire professional experience. And I've had a few . . . But it almost killed me. I mean the truth be told, people say, "You did a wonderful job." It literally almost killed me. I worked Saturdays. I was here all the time . . . And I said to myself, "Why would anyone want to do this again?"

Lessons Learned

Beverly is now in her seventh year in Atlanta. The length of her tenure is itself an indicator of her success. As she reflects back on her years there, she identifies some important lessons for other superintendents and boards in how to confront critical obstacles, like the disbelief that poor, minority children can learn at high levels.

Developing the Capacity of Teachers and Principals

For Beverly, transforming the Atlanta Public Schools is not just about improving test scores. It is also about increasing the knowledge and strengthening the skills of teachers and principals.

Project GRAD, for example, used Success for All as its literacy program. That's very scripted, as you know. The reason we did that was because when we did our first assessment of why teachers were leaving—we had a terrible turnover rate—the finding was that many of them came from area colleges and felt totally unprepared to teach in Atlanta Public Schools. They had not been taught what they needed to know to be able to teach children in an urban setting. With the Success for All that's so scripted, it almost says, first, "Do no harm." We knew that was not going to be the strategy for long-term success. At the same time, we brought in CORE—the Consortium On Reading Excellence . . . to do system-wide training on the teaching of literacy. The teachers to this day who had CORE still say it was perhaps the best professional development that they ever had . . . We have our own model teacher leaders now who can provide it. But for three years, we had to bring in CORE. We also brought in the folks from Modern Red School House to teach us how to teach to standards.

A key to success with teachers and principals is recognizing them as learners—phasing the introduction of new programs and aligning them so staff can make sense of them as well as absorb and apply new materials effectively.

We didn't want to overwhelm people. So, we had to stage it. Here you're being taught how to implement Success for All with a facilitator on site. You're going for quarterly training off site . . . on how to implement that. We also have CORE coming in. We don't want you to get confused. So it was aligning what was going on so people didn't wonder what they were doing and also phasing it in. In doing the Modern Red, how do we phase it in so we didn't have a feeling of, "Oh, I can't listen to one other thing or learn one other thing."

Overcoming the disbelief among teachers and principals that poor children can achieve at high levels—strengthening their sense of efficacy—is a critical indicator of success.

I have an outside consultant to annually come in and do focus groups with new teachers, veteran teachers, new principals, and veteran principals. I always read very carefully the findings of those reports because he goes in with them without any administrators or anyone. So they are very candid. You can see that they really have a sense of efficacy now around the teaching of literacy in the elementary schools. They know what they're doing.

If we gave that same survey now (the High Places Survey from the University of Rhode Island), which I think we're going to be doing again, there has been a sea change. Because when you walk into the schools, they really are talking about the kids in kindergarten outperforming their peers in the state. They've begun to see that we are narrowing the gap significantly with the state. And our first, second, and third graders are doing extremely well.

Staying the Course

Beverly believes that transforming any urban school system, including Atlanta, takes 12 to 15 years of enlightened, stable, continuous, and professional leadership. She views her mission in Atlanta as only partially accomplished.

We decided to take on literacy first. And then to begin to think about math. Right now, we're in the middle . . . I'm six years in and we're just beginning to crack the nut with math. We've got the literacy piece going really strong at the elementary level. We still have lots of work to do at the middle and high school. They don't teach reading . . . So we still have that nut to crack. At the elementary and also at the middle and high school, we are focusing intensely now on how to get teachers to teach the content, math and science, when they themselves may not know the subject area. People want all the scores to go up, but you can't overwhelm staff. It takes time.

Understanding That Self-interest Is a Powerful Motivator

Like many superintendents, Beverly is a realistic optimist. She continues to believe that people can rise above self-interest and act in the best interests of children, but she recognizes the reality that often they do not. However, she is not a pessimist; she has not become cynical about the possibilities for bringing out the best in people.

You overestimate your ability to get people to support you. You always think that if they seem sincere, and you're sincere, and the children are at the core of this thing, their well being, then we'll be able to cut through. I knew resistance was there. I'm not naïve. But we would be able to cut through it for the greater good.

That very few people really are able to rise above that to care for the greater good . . . is a scary thing to accept. But the reality is that's just what it is. And yet, I don't want to come over as jaded. It's an acceptance. That's the reality that you're up against.

Taking Pride in the Success of Others

Superintendents who commit, as Beverly does, to develop the capacity of others—in other words, to foster the growth of leadership throughout their organizations—must be able to locate their feelings of pride in the accomplishments of others, to feel personal satisfaction and fulfillment when others are recognized.

Margaret Spellings came recently. We visited Capitol View Elementary School, and then she had a little roundtable discussion involving two teachers, the principal, a PTA person, the local business council member, the business partner to the school, the instructional liaison specialist—that's the staff developer from the school—the executive director who oversees that cluster of schools, and I was at the table as well as the state superintendent and one of our U.S. senators.

It was amazing to me . . . to listen to the level of discourse as the teachers and the principal and the ILS talked about instruction in their schools. I mean they know it . . . I know I didn't do it myself. But I was a catalyst for making it happen. That they could have that kind of conversation with the secretary of education. I knew it blew her away. It blew me away.

References

A sharper focus: New president of Atlanta school board calls for "one system, one goal." (2001, February 1). *The Atlanta Journal-Constitution*, p. JD1.

Atlanta school board on chamber agenda. (2000, April 21). *The Atlanta Journal-Constitution*, p. D2.

Atlanta's board split on closing old schools. (2000, July 9). *The Atlanta Journal-Constitution*, p. C1.

Backward step will cost Atlanta schools. (2000, April 19). *The Atlanta Journal-Constitution*, p. A12.

Build smart program in trouble: Board defends keeping three schools open, cut critics say action shows micromanagement, politics and distrust of staff. (2000, May 4). *The Atlanta Journal-Constitution*, p. JD4.

Ex-superintendent of Atlanta schools resigns similar position in Portland. (2001, May 19). *The Atlanta Journal-Constitution*, p. E9.

Three schools in Atlanta get a reprieve. (2000, June 13). *The Atlanta Journal-Constitution*, p. C3.

In one of our conversations with Allan Alson, he shared his belief that superintendents need to be politicians before they can be educators. His story illustrates that political and educational leadership are inextricably linked, as he describes his 14-year focus on and commitment to narrowing the achievement gap while working tirelessly with his different constituents to bring them into the process.

CHAPTER 3

Attacking the Achievement Gap in a Diverse Urban-Suburban Community: A Curricular Case Study

ALLAN ALSON

The persistent and significant achievement gap between black and Latino students and their white and Asian counterparts at Evanston (Illinois) Township High School (ETHS) has existed for as long as anyone can remember. Stories real and apocryphal abound about the institutional barriers that have denied fairness and opportunity for minority students.

Despite a long history and the complexities involved in making substantive reform, real change has occurred during the 14 years of my superintendency. In 1992, the achievement gap was shockingly large in mathematics, as in other subjects. Only 6% of students in Calculus were black. Thirteen percent of all black students in math classes failed, and 40% received a grade of D or less. Just as distressing, neither staff nor community was in fact acknowledging or discussing the problems in any sort of public or productive way, although there were undercurrents of dissatisfaction and resentment. The school climate contributed to the finger-pointing and blaming that characterized math teachers' discussions; even decisions about textbook purchases became controversial.

In 2005, in contrast, the achievement gap was narrowing. American College Test (ACT) and Advanced Placement (AP) scores showed real growth. Twenty percent of students in Calculus are black. Black students are also receiving 10% fewer Ds and Fs in math classes. Awareness and acknowledgment of the achievement gap is widespread among staff in every department and among community members. More important, there is a growing sense of responsibility among math teachers for doing something about this as well. Within the Math Department, for example, the school climate now enables healthy dialogue among teachers, who invest their energy in promising new instructional approaches. And this change is evident in other departments as well.

What accounts for these changes is the subject of this story. It describes my personal struggles to understand and to define the issue, to develop by trial and error appropriate responses, to engage staff and community, including students, and to develop their capacity for addressing the problem. Most important, the story illustrates how we—board, staff, and community—have created the conditions over the past 13 years, through clarity and continuity of focus, for substantive and sustainable change to occur. I will focus in particular on our Math Department as a useful illustration of the effort taking place throughout our school to attack the achievement gap.

Evanston Background

Racial politics provide the difficult, complex, and inevitable context for discussions about the achievement gap. ETHS is a single school district set directly north of Chicago. Its enrollment boundaries include all of Evanston and a small portion of neighboring Skokie. As a stop on the Underground Railroad, Evanston became home to large numbers of African-Americans. Despite this apparent welcome to the community, there were virtually no aspects of social life that did not include segregation and disparity of resources. Separate schools, hospitals, social service agencies, and YMCA all defined Evanston's racial way of being. Interestingly, in 1883 and again in 1923, when the current building was constructed, the town leaders decided that there should be a single high school open to all students. Despite this, the racism that pervaded all the other social bureaucracies virtually guaranteed that the same expectations, curriculum, and quality of experience would not be available to all students.

Sadly, ETHS has had a history of explicit racism. This racism has purposely excluded students of color from the rich curriculum of the school and the postsecondary opportunities available to its high-achieving students. Most of this structural discrimination ended by the early 1970s. However, more subtle forms of bias have played out in the way individual adults and sometimes offices or departments have treated students of color and their parents. Over the years, there have been many stories about how, until the 1970s, counselors would steer students of color away from college preparatory courses, limiting their opportunities for postsecondary education.

Currently, ETHS houses nearly 3,200 students. For the 2005–06 school year, the racial composition is 46, 38, and 10% white, black, and Latino, respectively, and 3% each Asian and multiracial. Approximately one-third of the students qualify for free and reduced lunch. Of students who fall into this category, almost all are black or Latino. There are 35 different language groups represented at the high school. These demographic descriptors have remained constant with little variation during my 16-year tenure—the one exception being the Latino population, which has more than doubled in that time period. Variance between white and black student populations is virtually unchanged.

The Historical Context of the Achievement Gap

The achievement gap, with all its discordant strains, greeted me in 1990 in my role as assistant superintendent for curriculum and instruction, and defined the platform for my educational agenda when I became superintendent two years later. When I arrived in the summer of 1990, I spent an extensive amount of time getting to know administrators, teachers, parents, and community members. Various themes became evident regarding school structure, curriculum, race relations, and the academic performance of students of color. In terms of issues of race, there was a palpable lack of trust in the school administration. In fact, an array of comments made it clear that anger simmered just below the surface. At that time, not only did we not have the answers for how to close the gap; we did not, in fact, know what questions to ask. This was further complicated by a total lack of the data necessary to describe the scope of the problem, let alone the details essential for understanding the deeper intricacies of the gap.

In late January 1992, I heard that a teacher had made a terrible racial insult during a class. Spoken not to an individual student but about black students in general, the comment sparked controversy, deep anger, and widespread community tension. While much of the lingering effects of this tension was ascribed to the manner in which the previous superintendent handled the situation, the incident forced to the surface the wounds of injustice suffered by prior generations of students. Many people, both white and black, felt that the superintendent had not taken swift, decisive action and had, in fact, treated the matter like a bureaucratic blip. Specifically, he chose not to inform the staff or the community about the incident or the consequences; the teacher received a very mild two-day suspension and never apologized until ordered to do so.

The failure to notify staff and public backfired in dramatic fashion. I had urged the superintendent to send a letter to staff and parents describing the situation and detailing how the administration would respond to this racist incident. Black administrators, sensing the public outrage that would occur, urged me to convince him of this need. However, it was made very clear that he did not think this incident merited public alert, and I was told in no uncertain terms that he would no longer entertain my request for letters.

Word of mouth and, ultimately, a teacher letter in staff mailboxes made everyone intimately knowledgeable about the incident. Within 48 hours, the story made the front page of the Metro section of the *Chicago Tribune*. A student walkout, meetings with community leaders, and a series of town meetings that brought over 400 community members to each meeting followed. Despite the outrage, the superintendent continued to refuse to host a staff meeting to discuss the matter.

Finally, when the white-led teachers' union demanded a meeting, he relented. However, he told me that while he would factually recount the incident for the staff, he did not want to take questions. Much to my amazement, he gave that assignment to me. I actually said to myself, at that moment, that he was handing me the superintendency.

Observing this series of misplays, my own views regarding leadership during the racial strife were deeply etched. My instincts for full and immediate disclosure were reinforced. Sincere acknowledgment of the problem and its implications demanded explicit recognition. At the town meetings, I learned that the current racist behavior by adults fueled and exacerbated deep levels of mistrust of the school for its intentional, explicit, and even subtle acts of discrimination over the years. Black community members expected that any hope of long-term healing would include recognition of past behaviors as a precursor for going forward. Again the superintendent, this time publicly, said there was no reason to apologize for past behaviors from school officials. This, of course, fueled the discontent.

Confronting the Neglect

Attempting to champion social equity, let alone academic parity, requires navigating a tricky path with certainty of spirit and direction. Yet it also necessitates a process that is transparent, honest, participatory, and open to frequent midcourse correction as the unexpected happens.

When I became superintendent in August 1992, I vowed that our number one priority would be to improve minority student achievement. My opening day talk for the 1992–93 school year reinforced that, together, this would be our foremost goal and would remain so during my tenure. The term "achievement gap" was not yet part of the national lexicon, but there was no other way to describe the achievement of black students at ETHS without comparing them with their white counterparts. As part of this initiative, I announced that we would create a new academic direction through the work of two committees.

One, the Teaching and Learning Committee, would be the overarching group that would set the blueprint for future curricular and instructional endeavors. I explicitly charged this committee with promoting greater equity in terms of opportunity and results. The second, known as Career Pathways, was charged with totally revamping our vocational education program. While intended to be coordinated with the Teaching and Learning Committee, Career Pathway's explicit goal was to develop curricular sequences that would lead to workplace opportunities for our graduates. In addition, I indicated that we would issue the first of regular statistical reports on the academic and social status of minority students at ETHS.

I was certainly unprepared for one reaction to my speech. I expected that these words would be welcomed by some and would be greeted by apprehension and skepticism by others. All schools face faculty wariness when new initiatives are launched. Educators know that there is often a huge gulf between the creation of a committee or a study and a change for the better in practice. These views I anticipated. However, I did not expect a small but vocal set of white and black teachers to question why we had chosen the term "minority student achievement."

These teachers questioned whether it was not sufficient to simply refer to the education of *all* students and to avoid singling out any one group in conversation or in reporting. Through follow-up conversations with teachers and with administrators, I learned that this anxiety came from two different directions. One group, mostly white teachers, feared the inevitable tensions and anger associated with conversations about race and achievement. They were conflict averse, especially when it came to racial matters, and they were palpably worried that they would be labeled as racist. For concerned blacks, I believe their reaction was a combination of potential embarrassment and hopelessness. The constant focus on and analysis and public discussion of the academic plight of black students would cause the embarrassment. Their experience with previous initiatives that had, at best, resulted in a sense of empty promises provoked the hopelessness. During the Teaching and Learning Committee meetings, it also became evident that some white teachers and parents feared that the push toward higher achievement for minority students (defined as black and Latino, now generally referred to as students of color) would lower standards and academic rigor for *all* students. This played out in faculty and administrator discussions of academic placement in all curricular areas, especially math.

Moving Forward

As I considered these reactions to my newly proposed initiatives and thought about my options for moving forward, I believed that I was fortunate in having the kind of life experiences that would allow me to navigate these tensions. Beginning with my part-time job from age 10 in my father's North Philadelphia grocery store, which served a black clientele, to starting my career as a math teacher in all-black Sayre Junior High School in Philadelphia, to my desegregation work in Boston, and to my Teacher Corps leadership in multiethnic, multiracial Lowell, Massachusetts, I felt prepared to confront the politics and social dynamics of a highly defined racial achievement gap in Evanston, Illinois.

What I did not fully appreciate was the impact of economic diversity; in particular, when that diversity, as it does in Evanston, parallels racial achievement differences. These intertwined racial and economic complexities created an unusually charged political atmosphere. In practical terms, it meant that, in general, wealthier white families expected to fully take advantage of the school's academic and extracurricular resources. Honors and AP classes were enrolled with almost all white students. Poorer black and Latino students took vocational classes at a far greater proportion than their white counterparts. It seemed that in almost every aspect, two schools were simultaneously operating—one for whites and one for students of color.

Issues of racial equity permeated formal and informal conversations at school and in the community. Academic and operational policies were developed to account for race and disparities in income and achievement, often with unintended negative consequences for those meant to gain advantage from these policies. For example, in the mid-1980s, the school board created a policy that gave parents the final say in student course placement and level of courses. This was intended to ensure that counselors did not arbitrarily place black students in less challenging courses. In reality, it has been mostly white parents who have taken advantage of this policy. Despite such examples, the school had significantly struggled to develop a sustained will to make the structural changes necessary to ameliorate and, ultimately, to eliminate the academic disparities among racial groups. Hope for change was in short supply among black staff, parents, and community members.

The Political Context

It seemed, however, that a change in leadership bought a longer than expected period of goodwill toward me. Teachers, administrators, parents, and community members, mostly enthusiastically, agreed to serve on the Teaching and Learning and Career Pathways committees. The school board, made up of most of the people who had hired me, supported the proposed work of these committees. The belief was that proposals for systemic change would lead to improved achievement and a school more explicitly and implicitly responsive to students of color. Constituents were particularly interested to see the minority student achievement report in order to learn exactly what the gap looked like. When I gave that assignment to a relatively new black administrator whom I had recruited, I charged him with being scrupulously honest. However negative the results may be, I knew ethically and politically that we could not risk any perception that we had shielded or distorted data.

Because the school had suffered from the rancor of community meetings after the racist statement by the teacher, I knew it was essential to forge a unified administration that needed to be seen by staff, parents, and community as standing up for children and making fair decisions that were seen to be in the best interest of student concerns. This was far easier said than done, as many decisions are complex, and each one can have shifting support from adult constituencies. Although in my heart I knew it to be right, it was still emotionally difficult, for example, to come to the decision to terminate two administrators who were viewed by other administrators, and more importantly by the black community, as harsh in style and discriminatory in action.

Following rumors of my imminent appointment as superintendent, I had been lobbied by fellow administrators, people I deeply respected, to take this action. Negotiating the dismissal of these two administrators taught me a lot about board politics. The same board that had wondered out loud when they appointed me whether or not I would be "too nice" now were not sure it was fair to displace two people who had each worked for over five years at the school. After some healthy give and take, the board was unanimously supportive of this decision. I was reminded that in this relatively small environment, board decisions might frequently be shaped by personal concerns as much as educational views.

A second note relating to personnel politics was a curious one indeed, but a valuable lesson for the years that would follow. Some teachers who had come to me and privately urged the dismissal of the two administrators now came forward to voice their worry that, no matter how bad the fired administrators had been, they might now be unable to find new positions. This concern surprised me, because I had given them each over nine months notice. One teacher even asked if she had been personally responsible for the firings. Developing support for tough personnel decisions requires chess-like skills. Deciding that student and institutional interest outweigh job security is clearly a necessary judgment of the superintendent's work. My actions regarding these administrators made me realize that more tough personnel decisions would be required and that the politics of these decisions would be distracting. The stakes rise significantly when trying to create a successful political climate that will galvanize adult effort for important tasks such as closing the achievement gap.

The Report on Minority Student Achievement

The first in what is now an annual event, the minority student achievement report, released in May 1994, displayed great disparities in achievement on every imaginable measure—grades, class rank, ACT scores, percentage of students of color in honors and AP classes, college attendance rates, dropout rates, and graduation rates. White students, as we knew, were outperforming their black counterparts by wide margins. (It is important to point out that at the time, and still to a lesser degree, the sample size of Latino students was too small to be statistically significant.) The local and Chicago press carried all the painful details.

The report showed that the gap entering high school on the Stanford Reading Test was a shocking 37 points. White eighth graders were reading at the 84th percentile, while their black peers were reading at the 47th percentile. Black students who failed at least one course during high school total 36.8%, whereas white students in the same category total 6.3%. White students had a graduation rate of over 96%, almost 10 points higher than black students. ACT scores showed white students averaging almost a 27 score while black students averaged just under an 18. Interestingly, black scores on all standardized measures surpassed the average black scores in Illinois and nationally. Even so, with such high scores attained by white students, the gap at ETHS was larger than the national gap.

The report mainly drew praise, in particular from many black parents and community members, for its clarity and honesty. It provided the first comprehensive foundation of data from which to measure ourselves going forward. By far the harshest criticism, however, came from an unexpected source. The black middle class was angered, and as they said in calls and meetings, "Where were the success stories?"

I came to see that they were absolutely right, and I resonated with their concern. It immediately made sense to me that this work was more complex than simple numbers can reveal. In our haste to tell "the complete truth," we had neglected to offer positive examples, of which there were many. The result portrayed black students as monolithically poor achievers. We had insulted those whom we were trying to serve. The lesson? Never lose sight of complexity as you make information easy to digest. However, many black community members felt vindicated—their long-time allegations concerning the gap had been verified.

This would not be the last time we were surprised by Evanston's black middle class; I will offer another example later. In order to respond to the concerns about this first achievement report, we promised to do a study that we thought would paint a rosier picture. We compared the academic statistics of the top 20 white juniors with the top 20 black juniors. We learned that the black students were taking far fewer honors classes and a much less challenging curriculum overall, and had significantly lower grade point averages and lower standardized test scores. Despite this disparity, ultimately all 20 black students matriculated in very fine colleges and universities. This, of course, raised questions similar to those posed in *The Shape of the River* (1998). As William Bowen and Derrick Bok demonstrated in their book, despite differences at a younger age, the gap among high achievers tends to narrow over time. The disparity also forced us to think hard about the course of study that students pursued.

Staff and Community Response to the Report

As superintendent, it was my job, with the help of staff and community, to respond to the dismal results highlighted in the report. The prevailing view of my administrative team was that there was an enormous need for staff development. (The current preferred term of professional development—an interesting distinction in itself—did not come into favor until the late 1990s.) Black teachers asserted that their colleagues lacked an understanding of black culture and that racist views could be countered by raising awareness of history and heritage. There was a clear consensus among administrators and among the staff development committee that raising awareness would change attitudes, which in turn would lead to new instructional approaches and improved achievement. Whatever resistance was felt by the white staff remained unspoken. I think the difficulties surrounding the racial incident brought a certain level of compliance, even though it was no doubt accompanied by some degree of wariness.

So, the administration and the staff development committee jumped in with a vengeance to raise awareness and goodwill. Over the next few years, the ETHS faculty and staff would be exposed to some of the best contemporary minds on the issue of race and schooling. Our auditorium has been graced by James Anderson, James Banks, Gloria Ladson-Billings, Ron Ferguson, Kati Haycock, Jesse Jackson Jr., Carol Lee, Pedro Noguera, Clarence Page, Warren Simmons, Beverly Daniel-Tatum, and Uri Treisman. In addition, Charles Johnson, an ETHS graduate and author of the award-winning *Middle Passage* (1998), written about the slave trade, has visited us twice to reflect upon his own schooling and even to teach a class on writing.

Generally, our strategy was to have these noted authorities open the day with a speech. This would be followed by workshops for teachers, in varying size groups, that they would normally lead. Speakers would also visit classes and engage teachers in small group discussions. Occasionally, speakers would meet with parents and community members in the evening. It should be noted that we set aside a relatively modest budget for this endeavor and usually had only one or two speakers per year.

Speakers were not our only strategy to change adult views and behaviors. Our entire "required" staff development program was oriented around "multicultural awareness." The term multicultural seemed a safe umbrella under which we could tread lightly around the hot button topic of race. Of course, we were not alone. Multiculturalism was the "in vogue" word of the early and mid-1990s.

At the time, faculty raised few objections to this strategy of increasing awareness through information (didactically presented) and discussion. I distinctly remember feeling that this form of communal learning would bring about deeper understanding and therefore, commitment. In retrospect, I think three other factors were at work. First, Evanston as a school and community with liberal traditions welcomed this dialogue as a natural progression. Second, influential faculty explicitly supported this approach. And third, teachers who may have been in opposition probably felt it was not politically correct to state that opposition among their white liberal and black peers.

Our workshop topics (none explicitly connected to one another) included Multiculturalism in the Classroom; Addressing the Caribbean Student at ETHS; a speaker program on African-American, Hispanic, and Asian Perspectives; Gender-Ethnic Expectations and Student Achievement (a packaged program from the outside); a multicultural book club and film series; ethnic bus tours of Chicago; and even a theatre series in Chicago dealing with multicultural themes.

In the 1993–94 school year, we divided faculty and staff into two groups with each group receiving two different forms of training during the year. One program was "Black and White: Styles in Conflict," presented by the author Thomas Kochman and his staff from the University of Illinois at Chicago. This program dealt with cultural differences as well as perceptions and approaches that impeded communication between blacks and whites. The faculty and staff loved the program and believed it helped build better working relationships among the adults.

The other program did not fare as well. Jeff Howard's "Efficacy" program from Boston was brought in to challenge teachers' expectations of black student achievement. I had seen Howard present three times previously when I worked in Massachusetts. Tough, with a "take no prisoners" mentality, Howard believed *all* high school seniors could complete a quality 25-page research paper, 3 years of a world language, and a calculus course. The only real barrier for students, he asserted in his presentations, is low expectations held by educators. While I knew his style would create some ill feelings and a lot of cognitive dissonance, I thought the long-term results were worth the discomfort.

Unfortunately, Howard was not the presenter; instead, he assigned a professor from Galludet University in Washington, D.C., a very nice man who worked to introduce the Efficacy program without tension. However, my teachers found him condescending and believed he did not validate the knowledge they already held. After the third session, a group of black faculty requested that I cancel the remainder of the program. They were adamant. My perception of the way it was going led me to conclude the program was not salvageable. When I informed the professor of my decision, I could not help but wonder if, in addition to the presenter, the teachers also were unhappy with the level of challenge being cast their way. My own actions were an easy acquiescence based on the reality of presenter quality and on the fact that the protestors were black teachers who, I believed, were both sincere and good teachers themselves. In hindsight, it raises the clearly unresolved question as to whether I would have responded to white teachers in the same manner. Perhaps I failed to acknowledge the extent to which black teachers could also be made to feel discomfort when their expectations of student achievement were being challenged.

My decision to cancel the rest of the sessions is a reflection of the leadership style I have followed both consciously and intuitively. Upon hearing what I believed to be loud and widespread unhappiness with the program, I sought to verify the depth and breadth of that displeasure. My first awareness came from the leader of the multicultural staff development program, a black woman. She expressed her concern that negative feelings were widespread across an array of teachers. After I inquired about who exactly felt that way, I sought to confirm those views and to probe why those views were held. I concluded that there was a significant lack of openness among faculty that was not going to be altered by this presenter. There did not seem to be any teachers advocating for continuing the program at all. I am left to wonder what level of contrary views would have been sufficient to conclude the rest of the program.

In order to gain deeper insight into the racial achievement dynamics of ETHS, it is instructive to look at an individual academic department. Specifically, a more micro view of the school through the lens of the Math Department helps reveal authentic teacher conflict and value differences.

The Math Department: Curricular and Instructional Conflicts

ETHS has long been known as one of the premier high schools in the country for the preparation of its students in mathematics and the sciences. For example, the school provides a highly regarded 3-year integrated Chemistry–Physics (Chem–Phys) sequence, culminating in AP credit in both courses. The famed Westinghouse (now Intel) Science Awards for original research have been won by our students more frequently than all but two other high schools in the country. To be eligible for the Chem-Phys sequence, as it is known, students need to be on a track to complete Calculus by senior year. Yet in the early 1990s, it was highly unusual to see black students in Calculus or Chem–Phys, and there is no record of a black student ever submitting a project in the prestigious Westinghouse competition.

The Math Department, with 24 teachers, offered a curriculum that included courses such as Fundamental Mathematics, Freshman Mathematics, Elements of Algebra, Consumer Mathematics, and Statistical Projects. These were all intended to help poorly skilled, unmotivated students pass 2 years of math in order to graduate from high school. Content in these courses was weakly aligned, if at all. A quick visit to any of these classes immediately revealed a room full of utterly disengaged black students taught by poor, uninspiring teachers, both black and white. These students were destined never to see real Algebra or Geometry.

Contrast this set of circumstances with the other end of the curricular spectrum. There were almost no black students in the three levels of Calculus. In the 1991–92 school year, only 6% of the 124 Calculus students were black. In the same year, black student grades in mathematics were abysmal. Thirteen percent of them failed their courses, while 40% received a grade of D or less, and a whopping 60% of them received a C or below.

In my role as assistant superintendent for curriculum and instruction, I was able to make a number of firsthand observations about the Math Department. There was little, if any, formal discussion in the department about the performance of black students or about the content of what they studied. Students were simply assigned courses on the basis of the Stanford test taken in eighth grade and, subsequently, on their teacher's recommendations. No conversations were held about rigor or about the support students might need to become successful math students. As if this was not bad enough, the quality of teaching and content knowledge of teachers was quite disparate and was acknowledged only privately and through nasty insinuation. Not surprisingly, there was a wide divide in beliefs and approaches between black and white teachers. For obvious reasons, I found this quite disconcerting. I deeply believe (and hold this belief firmly today) that addressing the achievement gap depends on teachers building and sustaining their own learning communities to discuss and to analyze student work, and then to plot uniform approaches to address identified student deficiencies.

In the process of gaining familiarity with ETHS, I attended department meetings and over time held individual discussions with numerous teachers. Perhaps they perceived they could influence me with their views or maybe they just needed to vent, but at any rate, black and white teachers shared their long-held views of their colleagues. The teachers in the Math Department had deep and explicit racial differences that were known and discussed throughout the school. Overgeneralizing to explain this divide, I will characterize their differences in the following manner: black teachers believed that their white colleagues cared about content, not children. They felt that the white teachers, especially those who taught Trigonometry (Trig) and Calculus (only one black teacher taught Trig), had little, if any, interest in the struggling black students, and that even when they were assigned to teach those courses, their attitude was at best one of indifference. In essence, according to this line of thought, these white teachers were inflexible, unresponsive to students in "lower level classes," and affixed blame on only the students for their supposed failure to take responsibility for their own learning. It was also presumed that teaching high-achieving white students was a far easier task than working with disengaged students who were seriously behind in basic skills.

In contrast, white teachers felt that their black colleagues had little interest in the content of math. To the white teachers, this meant that black students were receiving lots of nurturing, but little in the way of challenging curriculum. White teachers were annoyed that black teachers lobbied to teach more honors and AP courses but from their point of view were ill prepared to do so. Even more worrisome to this set of white teachers was their view that the instructional repertoire of black teachers was extremely limited. Specifically, they allegedly used lots of drill and rote teaching techniques and rarely, if ever, employed problem solving and analysis.

In almost caricature form, the teachers had typecast one another in an unforgiving manner. They believed that they had fully explored with one another every conceivable possibility to change their ways. Their conversations were never this direct. They had reached the point where they believed no one had any new insights to offer. While I wanted to reopen dialogue even in small ways, I was acutely aware of how much anger lay just below the surface. It exploded in the spring of 1992 around the issue of textbook adoption.

Curricular Battles

The textbook committee was chaired by a black teacher who was one of a few who could gingerly navigate between the two factions. Interestingly, she was one of the two black teachers who were regularly "entrusted" to teach honors classes. Two of the white teachers had authored a math text that was one of the final two texts under consideration. District policy was clear that they could not receive royalties if the district purchased their text. The authors chose not to recuse themselves from the debate and the vote, which alienated their black counterparts, and finally the department administrator ruled as a compromise that they could participate in the debate but could not vote (it is worth noting that this administrator, since retired, is black and was universally respected.). Ultimately, the department voted by a narrow margin to adopt the other text, despite the fact that most area high schools had adopted the book written by the Evanston teachers. As a result of this angry textbook battle, opinions became even more polarized, and negative attitudes toward colleagues seemed as though they would be forever locked in place.

Unexpectedly, some issues emerged that began to ease the tensions between white and black teachers. Shortly after the textbook battle, the department learned that four of its teachers had been placed on probation. In a strange way, this brought the rest of the department closer together. Three of the probation teachers were white and one was black. Fortunately, the department supervisor and the department chair had done a great job of documenting the problems. With a cooperative yet very watchful teachers' union, two teachers were placed on "job improvement" (a less serious category) and two were placed on remediation (career threatening). As superintendent, I directed this process and participated in all critical decisions.

Needless to say, all department members and, indeed, the whole school, paid attention to what was happening to their fellow teachers. To my knowledge, no department members came to the defense of their colleagues. Within 2 years, two teachers resigned, one literally did not return to work one year, and the fourth improved significantly and remained until retirement. This strong and successful action on the part of the administration enabled us to signal and then to push for talks to honestly discuss curriculum, instruction, and most important, expectations for student learning.

Two other changes at that time began to unfreeze the balkanized department. The department chair, who was considered one of the elite white teachers and who was one of the coauthors of the textbook, resigned. He was largely regarded as well intended, but sarcastic and flippant in style. In truth, his black students fared rather well, compared with other black students, and spoke highly of him. But his style had clearly worn thin on the teachers. In response to his resignation, two teachers volunteered to cochair the department for a couple of years. These two white teachers, male and female, were deemed by consensus to be acceptable to the department. It felt like everyone had exhaled.

Also, the administration took a proactive stance regarding curriculum. I announced to our Curriculum Council (department chairs and administrators) that, as a school, we had to dispense with all courses that were not considered a contribution to the core curriculum. Essentially, all courses had to be "no escape" courses. For instance, students were not to be able to leave Algebra and to move to Fundamentals of Math. Elements of Algebra, Consumer Math, Fundamentals of Math, and Statistical Projects were all deleted from the available course offerings in math. This decision was essentially a directive from me. There are simply times when leaders must impose their will in order to foster change. This step was easier to take, knowing we were entering the arena of standards.

These course deletions forced all students to take a core curriculum within mathematics. It meant that all students would begin their high school math curriculum with a course no lower than Pre-Algebra, and this would ensure that all students would be able to complete math through Algebra II, assuming they made yearly progress. (It is important to note that approximately 30% of entering freshmen were beginning with Geometry and the vast majority of the remaining freshmen were starting high school with Algebra I.) The ability to complete math through Algebra II is extremely important, because Algebra II represents a key requirement for application to most four-year colleges and universities.

Some teachers, notably black ones, worried aloud that this change would present challenges that might be too difficult for a small number of incoming freshmen, but they made no effort to block the deletion of the courses. Their stated desire instead was to be sure that appropriate support would be in place for those students who needed it. While ETHS already had a math lab (a math tutoring center open throughout the day with a teacher's aide), we now assigned a teacher there every period, as their duty, to be available to assist students.

The Mission Statement: Including the Community

In the fall of 1995, I brought in a new assistant superintendent for curriculum and instruction, Dr. Laura Cooper. She had been a colleague in Massachusetts and was highly regarded for her intelligence, deep knowledge of curriculum, instruction, and assessment and her understanding of the social and political dynamics of schools. During Boston's desegregation, she held a parallel position to mine (working through a university to provide assistance to Boston Public

Schools) and had the opportunity to see race and achievement issues up close.

Shortly after she began, with my approval, she created (using our School Improvement Team) a series of community conversations to discuss the state of the high school, particularly the achievement of students of color. These meetings were very well structured and included small groups composed of students, teachers, staff, administrators, parents, and board members. The large group kickoff was facilitated by Warren Simmons from the Annenberg Institute at Brown University. These meetings were characterized by a high level of positive energy and goodwill. The purpose of these conversations was twofold: to build community and staff involvement and ownership, and to set a future direction and focus for closing the achievement gap between white students and their black and Latino counterparts.

The work of these community conversations and an impending accreditation review led to a process to revise the district's mission statement. The committee that set to work on this task included all appropriate constituencies. One key phrase was hotly debated for an extended period of time. I was insistent that the phrase remain in the final revision. The contested phrase was: "We will prepare all students to be able to apply to an Illinois college or university."

There was significant concern that this statement embraced the goal of college attendance for all students but diminished the value of the workplace. I felt that even though the statement articulated the same goal for all students, those who did not want to attend college or those who had not done well in high school would still have the choice to enter the workplace. There existed room in the ETHS curriculum for students to complete both a core curriculum and to finish a sequence of career preparation courses.

For me, the debate about including this phrase was really about making an explicit, permanent statement about equity. Retaining and highlighting the mission statement's phrase on college preparation ensures that all students will always be afforded the same opportunities. These opportunities are much less likely to be eroded by subjective and biased adult behavior, even over time.

Specifically, this meant that ETHS would expect all students to complete a core curriculum—4 years of English, 3 years of history, 2 years of a laboratory science, and 3 years of mathematics. Most colleges require math through Algebra II. The achievement gap in math completion at ETHS mirrored the achievement gap in college attendance rates between white students and students of color. Setting forth a concrete expectation that all students would achieve at this level and therefore would be capable of applying to college meant that we administrators and teachers were now obligated to create the curriculum, instructional strategies, and support that would ensure that all students would meet these expectations. This expectation and its related strategy was intended to close the achievement gap by pushing more students of color to apply to and enroll in four-year colleges. In fact, beginning in 1998 and continuing today, there has been more than a 10% jump in college attendance among Evanston's students of color.

The Minority Student Achievement Network (MSAN)

I began to have conversations with other educators beyond Evanston about the achievement gap. I was frustrated that people in Evanston—faculty, community members, and even board members—periodically referred to the achievement gap in Evanston as unique. It was quite evident from the popular press and media that many other urban-suburban districts were experiencing the same achievement gaps that we were. I was curious about what they were learning and how we might learn together.

My outreach to fellow superintendents across the country led in June 1999 to the formation of the Minority Student Achievement Network (MSAN) (http://www.msanetwork. org). We started with 15 districts and have grown to 25. Our decision as an organization has been to remain small despite a long waiting list from similar districts throughout the United States. This decision is predicated on the belief that by being small, we teachers, administrators, parents, board members, and students have a much greater opportunity to build working relationships.

The network hosts national student and teacher conferences and an annual conference for teams of educators and parents from member districts. MSAN also has a clearly defined research agenda. We have been fortunate to have our network guided by highly respected academics including Edmund Gordon, Ron Ferguson, Anthony Bryk, Wade Boykin, Uri Treisman, Gloria Ladson-Billings, Theresa Perry, and Pedro Noguera. Thankfully, Edmund Gordon of the University of Texas at Austin assumed the role of assembling most of these researchers and of bringing them into a series of meetings with the MSAN superintendents and practitioners. The three major components of our research agenda are literacy, math, and the connection between student–teacher relationships and academic work. Our survey of over

41,000 middle and high school students has yielded fascinating data regarding differences between students of color and white students, and how they approach and experience schooling.

The network has had two major research projects in math. We received a National Science Foundation (NSF) grant to study the barriers to high academic achievement in mathematics for students of color. Our study demonstrated that network districts and other school districts generally do a poor job helping students and parents understand the explicit pathway to upper-level mathematics. One lesson for superintendents and districts was the need, especially for first-generation college goers, to help parents know what the decision points are regarding acceleration into higher levels of math and when they are used by the district, along with information on how decisions are made and with what data. The second key learning from the NSF project was that, not surprisingly, teachers need well-sequenced professional development directed to the barrier concepts in algebra that cause the greatest number of students to stumble in math. In turn, professional development should be structured to enable teachers to work together to examine student work and, collaboratively, to examine instructional practices. This report is available through the NSF and is entitled *Overcoming Barriers to Higher Level Mathematics for African-American and Latino Students.*

The network's more recent study of math has been under the guidance of Uri Treisman from the Dana Center at the University of Texas. Treisman and his team have further refined the notion of barrier concepts in Algebra, and they have devised instructional strategies employing technology to help students overcome these barriers. Agile Mind, as it is known, is a professional development intervention that offers a lot of promise. Network districts, including ETHS math teachers, are currently using Agile Mind, as are other districts across the country. It has begun to elevate the confidence of our teachers as they work with students to master algebraic concepts. Information about Agile Mind can be obtained through the Dana Center.

Participation in the network has engaged numerous math teachers from ETHS. They now feel like they are connected to a much larger effort and are therefore not as alone in the struggle to close the achievement gap. Math teachers who have attended MSAN conferences have brought back concrete ideas to share with colleagues. These connections have helped develop a critical mass of teachers who feel better equipped, with a broader instructional repertoire and a deeper understanding of the impediments to learning experienced by students of color. They also feel that being a part of a community of adult learners fuels their own motivation to improve their practice. The network has successfully served as a forum for honest dialogue about race and achievement. Both black and white educators say they have gained understanding as well as classroom strategies through these dialogues. But the journey to this point has been demanding and full of complexity.

Closing the Gap for Low Achievers in Math

This section and the subsequent one are intended to demonstrate that achievement gaps exist in multiple places along the learning continuum and therefore require multiple and appropriate strategies to address them.

Low math achievers are those students who enter high school struggling conceptually with fractions, decimals and percentages, and perhaps even basic operations. Their success in Algebra and beyond requires a specific set of interventions and support. High achievers are students who enroll in Algebra I when they enter high school. They are students who typically might end their high school math career after Algebra II or Trig, but with appropriate opportunities and support, they may complete Calculus. The interventions we have attempted have met varying degrees of success. Some, such as dropping nonchallenging courses, have been easy to implement, gaining early and virtually complete support from all constituent groups. Others, such as the use of double periods, have been controversial and caused great strife on their road to implementation.

One important intervention was hiring Treisman, the math educator who is guiding our work on Agile Mind, as a consultant in the early 1990s. We asked him to look at our curriculum and some of our instructional practices, particularly in Algebra and Geometry. It was on his advice that I recommended dropping the nonchallenging math classes. He also believed quite strongly that time is a critical factor that can be used to help struggling kids. So, instead of using two years at a very slow pace for Algebra I, he recommended double periods. Treisman also thought that Calculus teachers should teach Algebra I in order to discuss with younger students exactly what it would take to get to Calculus.

Our teachers liked the idea of double periods so much that within two years, we moved Algebra I and II and Geometry to double periods for those students who needed the extra time. But initially, when we first implemented double-period Algebra I, there were two kinds of pushback from teachers. And although I intuitively thought each was a bad idea that would not stand the test of time (and might even ruin the concept), I relented on both in order to get a toehold for the double periods.

The first teacher worry was that, given the Evanston climate for choice rather than for direction, perhaps parents should be given a choice as to whether or not they wanted double-period math, especially because this would mean the loss of an elective. I wondered aloud to teachers, department chairs (some of whom had a vested interest in keeping student time free for their departmental electives), and the school board why math simply could not be deemed more important. Others won the battle, but student success after a couple of years had math teachers, and even the school board, advocating for direct assignment rather than choice.

The second concern was when to schedule the second period. Most of the teachers could not imagine being with the same struggling students for 90 consecutive minutes. They wanted a mix of students in the second period—their own plus a mix of other Algebra students. I chose to save the concept despite my perception of the logistical flaws. Five years later, after new, younger, vibrant teachers had joined the department, they came forward advocating for consecutive periods with the same students. These energetic teachers, confident in their capacity, had effectively lobbied their peers to change practice.

Earlier, I had discussed the painful divisions among the math teachers, often split along racial lines. One consequence of their disagreements was that they could no longer hear one another. They were so used to what they *thought* each other was about to say that they did not really listen. In the past 5 years, eight new teachers who have become close colleagues have joined the department. Three women in particular, two black and one white, have forged a strong professional bond and behave differently than their more seasoned peers.

They believe deeply in and represent a middle ground that argues for high expectations, rigorous content, and a nurturing support system. One request they made was for common planning time for each of the teams of teachers teaching double-period Algebra and Geometry. *All* teachers now crave the time together to discuss individual student work, to examine specific curricular units, and to share their instructional struggles and successes. The climate in the department has not been fully transformed, but lines have softened, opening the way for a more honest dialogue about what it takes to build student achievement, especially for students of color.

One battle that did split along racial lines had to do with the development of common assessments linked to the standards. The focus was on Geometry and took over 2 years to resolve. The arguments came out of a profound desire for fairness and consistency for students. A set of black teachers advocated for a separate common assessment in Geometry for honors versus nonhonors classes. They were worried. They did not put it in those terms, but that is how I heard it—that black students and other nonhonors Geometry students would not fare as well as their classmates. The counter view was simply that "common" meant that all students should be measured against the same standards and that those who had mastered more would demonstrate their greater proficiency.

There was a lot of sniping and attempts by each teacher group to influence various administrators. Intellectually, virtually all the administrators concurred that a single assessment should be used. Black administrators (about 50% of line administrators), however, were far quieter in their views, unwilling to publicly disagree with the black teachers. Eventually, the voice of persuasion was provided mostly by the newer black teachers siding with the need for a single assessment. However, an interesting added dynamic was the influence of the newer white teachers, who seemed to be trusted to a greater extent by the veteran black teachers. While not purposefully acting as a block, the newer teachers have found ways to build alliances that did not previously exist.

The most important math war, from my perspective, occurred in November 2001 when I proposed raising graduation requirements in math from 2 to 3 years. I clearly saw this (and stated so in many venues) as a structural lever to gain equity and to promote achievement. At the time of the proposal, 80% of black students as opposed to 97% of white students were completing 3 years of math. To realize the mission of all students being able to apply to an Illinois college or university, we would have to require that all students complete 3 years of math, specifically through Algebra II. While I understood, as did others who advocated for the 3-year requirement, that it would take a few years to get there, the goal of equity, higher achievement, and college access seemed worth the fight.

Three-and-a-half months elapsed from when I made my proposal known to when I brought it to the board for formal action. The proposal was made available to the general public and was specifically delivered to all parents of the feeder elementary district (the proposal was being made for the class of 2006), our staff, and students. Discussions were held with my administrative team, the Curriculum Council, the School Improvement Team, the Principals' Advisory Committee, students, the Math Department, the executive committee of the teachers' union, the entire staff, and the community in two meetings—one in the black community and the other in the Latino community.

I wrote to the board: "Embedded in this goal (of a three-year math graduation requirement) are two essential principles—equity and achievement. By enabling all students to meet this standard, the opportunity for higher education remains an open possibility for every student." My proposal acknowledged that to successfully implement the 3-year requirement, the "requisite curriculum, pedagogy, and supports" were necessary. I further attempted to make the case that core curriculum completion for all students was one key to closing the achievement gap. To sweeten the pot, I requested that a teacher be released one period per day to take the lead with faculty in designing appropriate curriculum and support.

All of the garnered feedback demonstrated almost unanimous support to raise the graduation requirement. However, yet again, I was surprised by the deep level of skepticism voiced by black staff, parents, and community members. What I find so interesting is that the black community members who voiced their concern were virtually all parents of recent graduates who had been quite successful in high school. They were worried that this requirement would raise the dropout rate. It was never clear to me if they did not believe some students were capable of completing 3 years of math, if they did not trust the school to provide adequate support and flexible instruction, or both, although I think it was both. Either way, it saddened me. The black community endorsed the proposal with a request for a one-year delay in implementation. I altered my proposal and accepted the delay. The board voted unanimously for the change. Three years later, the Illinois state legislature raised the state graduation requirement in math from 2 to 3 years.

The implementation of the new requirement included the teacher release time, a new tutoring arrangement for Algebra I double-period students designed and run by the Algebra I teacher team, semesterizing courses so no students would fall further behind (also providing opportunities for students to accelerate their coursework), and a new course known as Bridge Algebra. This course is designed to support and to prepare students who, after sophomore year, are not quite ready for Algebra II. At this time, fewer students are failing math. Black students are receiving 10% fewer Ds and Fs, and more students of color are successfully finishing 3 years of math, including Algebra II.

Closing the Gap for High Achievers in Math

The measure for closing the achievement gap for high-achieving math students is enrollment in one of three levels of Calculus. For the 2005–06 school year; Calculus enrollment has exceeded 340 students, 20% of whom are students of color. The initiatives subsequently described are responsible for this enrollment boost. Each one has a common theme, a component that makes it race-based in approach. Race-based programs clearly cause some discomfort in our diverse communities, and these initiatives have been no different.

QUEST (Questioning, Understanding, and Educating Students Together)

At around the same time MSAN was being formed, a group of almost 40 academically successful black students approached me with an idea. They wanted to mentor black eighth grade students and to teach them how to be successful in high school. Their intent was to mentor double their own number, meeting regularly with the mentees to plan for rigorous high school coursework, and help them learn self-advocacy skills and set a plan for college. The student founders insisted on choosing their own faculty advisors and have done so wisely; the original advisors have remained with the program since its inception. QUEST (Questioning, Understanding, and Educating Students Together), as the mentoring program is known, mentors approximately 70 students a year. It has been so successful that shortly after it began, a Latino version, Latino QUEST, was formed serving Latino students in a parallel fashion.

On more than one occasion, I have been asked by other students and parents about allowing white students to tutor and to mentor the QUEST mentees. It was and is my belief that this focused opportunity for black students to work with younger black students provided role models and a cultural affinity that white students could not provide. Making this change would have altered the fundamental precepts of the mentoring program. Despite an early failed civil rights challenge from a parent, the QUEST program continues to be an important tool in the effort to raise expectations and to build better student connections to school.

Clustering

QUEST has helped stimulate black student interest in honors and in AP classes. There is, however, still reluctance on the part of black students to enroll in classes where they see too few fellow black classmates. While our black enrollment in honors and in AP has risen, it still does not reflect the overall black population of the school. To counter this, we began to cluster students of color in all honors and AP classes in core subjects. The goal is to have as many of those classes as possible be half white and half students of color. We believe this has been an important factor in the increased enrollment by students of color in these classes, and more important, their grades and AP test results have also improved. When we implemented this strategy, there was some pushback from faculty, because it seemed to run counter to our stated goal of creating as much mix in classes as possible. The result of clustering, of course, left some classes with only white students. Thankfully, discussions on this topic were never rancorous; generally, faculty understood that a greater good was being served by clustering.

Summer Bridge Classes

Obviously, mentoring and clustering of students is not sufficient to change achievement patterns. It is critical to get at the heart of the matter—curriculum and instruction. Two veteran teachers, one white and one black, came forward to propose adding a new summer course in Pre-Calculus. They recognized that too many students of color were stopping math after Trig. The design they proposed would bring energy and would create support and a spirit that did not previously exist. Their idea was that the summer teachers (themselves, of course) would start with the same students in the fall and would be available for the students during the day to tutor when necessary. These teachers, one of whom is the QUEST advisor, approach teaching like coaching. They build team focus, commitment, and energy. Teaching students to use study groups is an important component of their approach, and their classrooms have a "one for all and all for one" spirit about them.

When brought to the board, though, the proposal hit a snag. Board members immediately recognized that this was a valuable resource that should be available for *all* students. And so it was approved as a course open to anyone interested and prepared. The teachers did not object. They simply and systematically recruited students of color for Pre-Calculus. It has worked exceedingly well because of their determination and hard work.

Pre-Calculus has been so successful in preparing students and in building their self-confidence that we have introduced another bridge class to assist and accelerate students moving from Algebra I to Geometry. My role as superintendent in QUEST, student clustering, and summer bridge classes has been nothing more than taking others' good ideas and finding the right political strategy and resources to make them happen. A lot of intangibles have fallen into place that help teachers feel free to create and approach the administration. Establishing dialogue in a variety of venues about race and achievement is a component of energizing faculty to take responsibility for offering systemic solutions.

Project Excite

One final initiative that is making a significant difference is a program known as Project Excite. An idea brought by a Physics teacher, also race-based, took hold through hard work, a collaborative partnership, and determined political negotiations. Project Excite is a partnership among ETHS, our elementary feeder district, and Northwestern University in Evanston. Every year, a cohort of approximately 30 third graders of color receives exciting lessons in math and science during the school year at the high school (the program intends to stay with each cohort group through 12th grade). This is followed by summer enrichment activities at Northwestern. The result has been a doubling of students of color in seventh-grade Advanced Math. I needed to play a role selling the idea to my elementary counterpart and to the dean of the Education School at Northwestern. The big sell was, of course, about resource commitment on the part of the university. They have seen the value and have been wonderful partners in this endeavor.

The Lessons Learned

Of course, lessons learned come from the "Monday morning quarterback" perspective, accumulated and shaped by personal reflection and by a myriad of interactions with colleagues, associates, and friends.

An Evolutionary View of Change

With board support, I established closing the achievement gap as a priority 14 years ago at the start of my superintendency. Yet we have only begun to see student outcome results over the last 5 to 7 years. In 1999, gains in the percentage of students of color attending four-year colleges began to emerge as a first indicator.

Substantive reform simply takes a long time. In order for change to be sustainable, the culture has to evolve, first, by people becoming receptive to entertaining the conversation about the achievement gap; second, by their committing to doing something about it; and finally, by their resolving to do something about it as a community. We are fortunate that we had the kind of patience it takes to "stay the course."

Consistent, Focused Leadership

Throughout my time as superintendent, we have maintained a sharp, coherent focus on closing the achievement gap with staff and community. Although we have obviously had to respond to other issues, we have not let them distract us as a system from this important goal. We have viewed academic equity and excellence for all as nonnegotiable and have always tried to act decisively to protect them—for example, in our new mission statement. One benefit of this approach is that when I have visibly challenged the status quo, it has empowered others to be risk takers. Teachers have felt freer to come forward with their own bold ideas.

As the process has evolved, I have tried to always keep the larger goal in mind and know that not every initiative is essential. Part of my role is to test the political waters and to build constituent support by assessing reactions of key influence makers to new proposals. I have learned that I need these same people for a series of battles, not just one. On occasion, I have reshaped initiatives—for example, by delaying implementation of the new graduation requirement in math—in order to gain a toehold for change.

With goals clear, I see myself as a coach trying to take a group of disparate individuals and interests and build a team with similar commitments and complementary behaviors, to reduce and to eliminate the inequities that have existed.

Creating a Context for Change

We have worked throughout to create the conditions for a diverse staff and community to engage with the complex issues of race and achievement. Without this long-term effort, the recent acceptance of race-based programs would not have occurred. Our early staff development efforts and community conversations raised racial awareness, sensitivity, and understanding. We learned that adults need to engage in honest, open dialogue about race and achievement in a safe setting. We also learned that historical, institutional racism does not fade from memory easily and that we, as leaders, must acknowledge its impact in order to establish trust.

By engaging staff and community in dialogue, we created a context in which people not only acknowledged the problem of academic inequity but also accepted responsibility for it and developed the will to confront and to solve it.

Creating a context for change not only involved internal work but external outreach as well. The MSAN has broadened the perspective of board, staff, and community. They know now that we are not alone in struggling with this problem. Our leadership in the network builds morale and renews energy. People realize that we are national leaders in this effort. Our participation also increases openness to new learning. Teachers return from network conferences excited about new ideas to implement. In confronting a problem, people here often say, "How are they dealing with it in the network districts?"

Building Capacity

Effectively reducing the achievement gap demands not only new attitudes but also new knowledge and skills for all of us. I learned how staff development, for example, could become much more effective. As my story illustrates, in the beginning, our staff development program involved didactic, occasional, one-shot presentations by outsiders. Over time, it became much more coherent and comprehensive, blending the expertise of outside experts with our own internal resources, and much more focused on student work ... the real work that we are doing. My consciousness about how to support effective staff development also evolved over time as a result of professional reading, listening to teachers and others in the organization, and personal learning activities.

We have also built capacity through personnel changes. New hires in math have made key contributions to instructional improvements. New administrative hires have helped us create a communal ethos that makes us more effective. Our efforts at confronting poor performance by teachers with systematic documentation and honest feedback have also paid dividends.

Structural Reforms

Essential changes in how we do things have occurred as the culture has evolved. The board and I have established new policies and administrative procedures that align with the equity commitment in our new mission statement. With faculty support, we have also initiated several important program and schedule changes—double periods, semester math courses, common planning periods, looping—that better support classroom efforts. We have also initiated new programs aligned with our equity goals—including the summer bridge programs and the peer-mentoring program.

Creating the context for change and reshaping the culture has involved everyone and has had an effect on everyone—including our students. They have been able to see adults working and struggling together to confront entrenched assumptions and an obstructive milieu, so as to make opportunities available to all. We are now seeing student investment in this challenge as well, not only academically, but also behaviorally. One healthy sign of the culture change is that we have begun to hear more student voices taking part in our ongoing conversations through their involvement with programs like MSAN. It is heartening to experience the difference that student as well as faculty and community commitment to equity can mean.

I trust that this commitment, now evident on all levels, will sustain a continuing effort at ETHS to avoid complacency and will continue to remind us of our responsibility to expect the best of all our students.

References

Bowen, W.G., & Bok, D.C. (1998). *The shape of the river: Long-term consequences of considering race in college and university admissions*. Princeton, NJ: Princeton University Press.

Johnson, C. (1998). *Middle passage*. New York: Simon & Schuster.

Hearing from our different authors clarified for us that leadership styles are a combination of tacit beliefs, experience, and personal qualities as much as conscious decisions about approaches to work, and are as varied as people are. What emerges as a common factor contributing to success is authenticity—consistency of words with actions—that enables the development of trusting relationships. Larry Leverett tells his story of one leader with one leadership style who moves between two different school districts with very different cultures.

CHAPTER 4

A Tale of Two Cities

PAUL KELLEHER WITH LARRY LEVERETT

In Greenwich now for 3 years, Larry Leverett is making the transition from a career in urban schools to educational leadership in a suburban environment. This chapter describes his recruitment to the position, his personal struggle about leaving urban for suburban education, his adaptation to Greenwich, and the surprises, controversies, and resistance he has confronted as he tries to persuade the community and the school organization to focus on the achievement of underperforming students.

This chapter resulted from collaboration between Paul Kelleher and Larry Leverett. Paul interviewed Larry and produced a transcript of that dialogue for joint review and revision. In writing the chapter, he consulted other sources like local newspaper reports and board minutes. He and Larry then discussed and revised the chapter. As much as possible, the chapter presents Larry's story directly. His words are in italics throughout.

Two Districts

Travel from Plainfield, New Jersey, to Greenwich, Connecticut, is only about 60 miles and takes just over an hour by car, but other facts provide a more accurate measure of the distance between the two communities. Plainfield is a poor, urban school district. Ninety-eight percent of students are African-American or are Hispanic. Approximately 70% are eligible for free or reduced-price lunch. Greenwich is an affluent suburban district. Only 20% of its students are minorities, mostly Hispanic. Only 8% are eligible for free or reduced-price lunch.

When Larry arrived in Plainfield in 1995, he found what he describes as a "challenging situation" in which he faced low expectations for students from both staff and community, and a culture of apathy and complacency. With a concentration of poverty in the community, he not only had to fight for resources but also for community engagement.

From the outset it was clear that the superintendent's hand had to be present in organizing efforts to mobilize the district to improve student performance. The state of New Jersey had established minimum levels of proficiencies (MLP) on achievement tests to be at the 25th national percentile in reading and mathematics. Districts were in compliance with state requirements when 80% of the students reached the MLP. I was outraged by the acceptance of such a low level of performance and knew that performance at this level would only result in graduates being grossly undereducated. It was my moral responsibility to proclaim loudly that this was unacceptable and that our children and staff were capable of much more. The celebration of minimum levels of proficiency had to end, and we had to reset our sights on higher levels of performance for our students.

In Greenwich, however, he found a vastly different situation.

The consistency of wealth and advantage, social capital, community investment, unbelievable resources provided for children by their families, the school district, and community, and consistent high expectations for most students were grossly different from anything I had seen in my personal or professional life. I had some ideas about the gap between poor communities and affluent communities, but my eyes had never seen the difference portrayed so vividly.

I'll never forget the experience of my first school visits just prior to becoming superintendent. I went to several elementary schools—the "hail and greet" visit. "Good morning, boys and girls. This is Dr. Leverett." I can recall being in third- and fourth-grade classrooms. Children would put their hands out, shake my hand, look me in the eye, "Welcome, Dr. Leverett. We're so pleased to have you visit our school today."

These kids were not "outliers." This happened with consistency. The confidence, the social capital, the mastery of language and nuance and what is right in a situation blew me away. Right then and there, if I didn't know I was in a different game before that, I did then. These kids were being groomed to rule!

Equity Warrior: No Alibis, No Excuses, No Exceptions

Larry's mission and passion as an educator were very clear in Plainfield.

I approach my work with a sense of urgency and have never really been reluctant to tackle problems that interfered with the mission of educating kids. I am specifically passionate about driving schools to improve performance of kids that have been historically underperforming, and my career has been focused on improving outcomes for low-income children of color. Plainfield was my kind of place! I really have a passion for education as a tool to advance the cause of social justice. Acting on my passion demands that I not treat my time as superintendent as a mere job or career enhancer, but rather as a place to push the educational system to do what is right for ALL students. No alibis! No excuses! No exceptions! This perspective is not necessarily informed by something I read in grad school. It's a perspective based on seeing schools fail to educate fully my cousins, nieces and nephews, friends and children of friends, and others marginalized by race, social class, and neighborhood boundaries. For me, being an educator is not business, it's personal—it's who I am! Who I am and what I do are inextricably linked.

Over his seven-and-a-half years in Plainfield, Larry built a collaborative team, including staff, parents, and community members, who believed in and acted on the belief that all children can and should achieve at high levels.

The Plainfield experience was particularly special and rewarding because of the development of a strong team of people who shared my passion for education as a tool for social justice. They became equity warriors, people who regardless of their role passionately led and embraced the mission of high levels of achievement for all students, regardless of race, social class, ethnicity, culture, and disability or language proficiency. They often acted outside their assigned roles and served on cross-role teams that valued contribution and commitment more so than hierarchy and job assignment. These equity warriors were risk takers, communicators, coaches, models, advocates, problem solvers, and barrier removers. In every sense they modeled their values, beliefs, and behaviors for others to emulate.

I loved our tough, no-fat mission: "The Plainfield schools, in partnership with the community, shall do whatever it takes for all students to achieve high academic standards. No alibis. No excuses. No exceptions."

If you were to cut me open, I would bleed my commitment to this mission, whether in Plainfield or Greenwich . . . In Plainfield, I enjoyed going into classrooms and children would know parts of the district mission. Every administrative meeting began with a recitation of the mission. We were very mission oriented. It was a unique, special period. And we got results.

As almost always happens to superintendents, changes in board membership bring new political challenges. Board members that chose the superintendent leave, and others who may not have the same commitment to mutually shared beliefs or the same personal loyalties replace them.

I had a wonderful six- to six-and-a-half-year run in Plainfield before the political climate changed. The board became more interested in jobs and contracts. I had fended off the pressure from the political machine telling me whom to hire for either teaching and learning positions or what contractors to work with for years. Eventually the board became stronger in their resolve to make the school district a job mill and to hire people not on the basis of qualifications but on the basis of relationships. A powerful local assemblyman successfully ran board candidates and threatened several incumbent board members who were employed by the town. The nepotism and patronage mounted and it became increasingly difficult for me to do my job. I became virtually impotent. I was being forced to leave or to play a game that ran against my ethics. I wanted to continue leading the mighty band of mission warriors, but it became clear to me and them that the board was no longer interested in what was best for teaching and learning.

The inability to secure the appointment of a principal confirmed for Larry that he could no longer be effective in Plainfield.

A major turning point was the board's failure to confirm my recommended candidate for a troubled middle school. The candidate—a young, white Harvard graduate—was denied because his age and ethnicity did not fit the profile of a majority of the board. More and more the board's action had to do with adult interests and biases and less to do with what is best for children.

If it's really about the children, then it should not matter who or what a person is. The questions must be centered around that person's ability to add value . . . My failure to secure appointments and other recommendations eventually caused me to lose faith in my ability to lead change in Plainfield. This reality cut deep and was hard to accept; my "spirit" was broken.

Greenwich Recruitment Initiative

First Impression, First Interview

Although his diminishing effectiveness left Larry feeling disenchanted about Plainfield, he had no plans to leave until his contract ended in 2004, and he had no aspiration to apply to Greenwich.

I never had any interest in working in a high-wealth community such as Greenwich. I didn't see myself fitting the profile of Greenwich and in all honesty, I never would have thought to apply there. Urban education was my passion, and working in an affluent school district was simply not on my career radar screen.

The Greenwich board, however, had other ideas, and they undertook an unusually methodical and board-directed recruitment initiative.

They found me . . . the board chair found me as a result of an extensive investigative effort. The board built a dossier using Internet searches, networking with professors, talking with people in professional associations, examining state report cards, mining the Plainfield website. I was not identified by a search firm or anything like AASA or the state organization.

Larry was flattered but not initially receptive to the invitation from the consultant to the Greenwich search to become a candidate.

What do people talk about in places like Greenwich? . . . What is that conversation like? I was intrigued . . . Why are you calling me? Don't you know Plainfield, New Jersey—urban, poor, free and reduced-price lunch, African-American, Latino, gangs, everything? . . . Do you have the right number?

Larry's first experience of Greenwich gave him a glimpse of the enormous social capital there.

I was invited up for an interview. I arrived at the new and spacious Greenwich Public Library in the midst of a very heavy afternoon rain storm and had to circle the library's large parking lot three times to find a parking place. I recall thinking . . . public library? Tuesday afternoon? Heavy rain? No parking? Students in school? There's something different about this town.

I knew that the library was not being used as a refuge for large numbers of people without homes during bad weather. The meaning of this scene became immediately apparent. This is a community whose residents place a high value on knowledge and information.

Larry liked how the board had structured their search.

The board hired a consultant. Actually, two consultants—one from a private sector executive search firm and the second, an independent consultant who did searches for CEOs for international corporations. So that was very different. And I'm enjoying this now because this way of searching for a superintendent was very different from my earlier experiences with more traditional education search firms.

More important, he felt he had nothing to lose.

My attitude in the interview was very casual. I'm here and it will probably be the only time I visit. It's a nice library and community. I'm glad I've had an opportunity to visit for the day.

I talked in very plain language, professional but very plainspoken about my work . . . I talked about accountability. I talked about mission and commitment. I shared my passion for closing the achievement gap and using education as a means to advance social justice. I recounted our efforts to be accountable through accepting collective responsibility for the welfare of Plainfield children.

What the Board Was Looking For

The board and its consultants certainly learned about Larry's direct communications style in this first interview, but he also learned about their leadership expectations and found them similar to what leadership in Plainfield demanded.

The interview process was structured to tease out the behaviors, strategies, and attributes that are part of the candidate's encoded repertoire, that are traits embedded in the leader's style . . . It's interesting because a lot of the same strategies—to jolt the organization, to challenge the status quo and create disequilibrium, to push the conversation, to organize for action—are similar to what Plainfield was looking for.

I think the board was looking for leadership. They were looking for a certain amount of willingness to do what's right . . . They were looking for someone with an outsider perspective on the organization. They were definitely looking for someone who had not only talked about change but led change and had a track record of improved measurable outcomes in terms of student performance.

His Conflict and Struggle

The board continued to express interest in Larry, inviting him back for a second interview. He, however, felt ambivalent about pursuing the Greenwich position because of his commitments to urban education and to urban students.

I had a . . . personal struggle. I talked to my wife, my son. I talked to friends. I talked to colleagues. I even reached out to a minister in my church to explore my moral dilemma. I could not get comfortable with the idea that I would sell out and leave children with very great needs to go to this very wealthy community where all the streets appeared to be paved with gold. I was abandoning my personal mission to pursue a career opportunity in a perceived "cushy" job. That made me feel cheap and made me very conflicted—deeply conflicted about "What am I really about? . . . You talk one way and then you're going to do this. You must be full of it . . . What's driving you? Is it career goals and climbing up some proverbial career ladder? Are you a hypocrite that espouses empty rhetoric regarding your passion about the education of low-income children of color? What are you really about?"

I had never really thought about those questions before because my career choices were fully compatible with personal commitment to equity and social justice. I only did the work for which I had fire in my belly. So I wrestled. I wrestled. I wrestled. And I couldn't get settled. So I just resolved to go through the second interview.

The second interview involved an intensive day of dialogue between Larry and various configurations of board members.

I'm now at Indian Harbor Yacht Club. I had never been in a yacht club before. They're very nice . . . I met with groups of two or three of the eight board members in one-hour structured interviews. Each group probed a different aspect in a behavioral interview focused on extracting information about my leadership traits and behaviors, my disposition . . . my organizational skills. Then it concluded with a cocktail hour and dinner with the full board. By then, I knew that I was being seriously considered for the Greenwich superintendency. How is this happening? The events of the day didn't seem to add up in my head . . . the Greenwich Board of Education was actually interested in me becoming their superintendent. This is not a picture that I ever envisioned in my wildest imaginations about the direction of my career as a school superintendent.

Key Question: The Fit

In Larry's recollection, the most dramatic moment of the day occurred after he realized that they were serious about him as their next superintendent, and he decided to raise his concern that he did not match the Greenwich profile.

I ended up asking the board . . . around coffee time, "Look, this is serious. How are you going to sell an African-American male, urban educator, with some track record of improving student performance but, in my opinion, nothing to write home to mother about . . . How are you going to sell this person to your community?" One by one, and all eight members spoke. They said, "That's not your problem. When we find the superintendent that we want for our schools we know what to do. We know how to sell things, and whoever you are and wherever you come from does not matter. We know what we're looking for, and if you have it, you don't need to trouble yourself with how we're going to sell it. We know how to do that."

I mean that was supposed to be my "in your face" question. And they just put me away. And I knew that this was a school board that knew what it wanted in the next superintendent and would not be bound to the stereotypical image of the superintendency in high-wealth, high-performing communities.

Mutual Commitment

Larry's strong positive impressions of the search, and of the board reaching out to both him and his wife, overcame his lingering self-doubt about "selling out."

Then came the offer, and they invited my wife and me to have dinner with the board chair and the search committee . . . We had a lovely evening. They made my wife feel real comfortable, a real part of the process. Actually talked to her initially more than they did me because they were making the commitment to us. That was beautiful . . . and I just sort of said, "These are really good people. I think that if they want me, I'm gonna take a shot at this."

His Appointment

Larry's concern that he did not belong in Greenwich, however, continued—at least through his appointment.

It never really stopped. I mean I can remember on December 22, 2002, at 8 A.M. in the morning when I was appointed—how different everything was. No one who looked like me other than my Dad and one of my sons. It was almost like an out of body experience being in the midst of such wealth, privilege, and homogeneity. I was still wondering, "What the heck am I doing here and why am I here?" Actually, I had been praying the Prayer of Jabez. In this prayer, Jabez called on God saying, "Oh that Thou would bless me indeed, and enlarge my territory" . . . and God granted him that which he requested. Standing in the boardroom I reflected on what had been granted. My territory had indeed been enlarged in ways that I never imagined. I pondered, "What have I gotten myself into here."

But the welcome he received assuaged these feelings.

It was such a wonderful honeymoon. The community embraced me. This is not what I expected. Staff, parents, and town officials treated me with acceptance and regard. The appointment occurred 3 days before Christmas and the board president introduced me as the "best Christmas gift we could give the children of Greenwich." It was a wonderful and special day.

Getting Started

First Surprise: Incompetent Management

From the interview process, Larry knew of board concerns with the effectiveness and efficiency of budget management and other operational areas, but the extent of the management problems he discovered in Greenwich surprised him.

Just gross incompetence in several cabinet level positions—business operations, budget director and human resources. The leadership of business operations had little command of the district's finances. They were weak stewards of the taxpayers' resources.

Larry's predecessor had completed a management study 2 years earlier that had identified some of the issues, but the recommendations had not been implemented. The delay exacerbated the negative view of school management held by elected town officials, whose approval was required under Connecticut law for any school funding, including the annual budget.

We were hemorrhaging. We had no credibility with town hall . . . We were viewed as an ineffective management team. They were reluctant to fund major capital projects because they were convinced that we wouldn't know how to manage the resources effectively and efficiently. And they were right.

These management problems created a special challenge for Larry. Although he had had a superintendent's normal oversight responsibility in developing, presenting, and implementing the budget in his previous districts, he had no hands-on, direct experience in administering day-to-day business and finance operations.

My immersion in the business side of the district was deeper than I had experienced in earlier superintendencies. I always knew my budget because you've got to know the budget, but I had the good fortune of working with capable business administrators. I had come to see myself as a "teaching and learning" superintendent who was involved in the business side enough to meet fiduciary responsibilities.

His first priority as superintendent became making the personnel and operational changes necessary to improve the operation of the district.

We cleaned up the business challenges during the first 14–16 months and began to see changes in how the district was perceived. The political leaders took note and gained confidence in our capacity to be effective and efficient in managing the taxpayers' resources. One hundred percent of our capital budget request was funded this school year. We're building a new $27 million elementary school and have gained approval of a major renovation of another elementary school . . . The budget I recommended to the school board was adopted by the board and the town's governing officials.

He did not, however, fulfill his hope that during his entry period in Greenwich he would establish himself as an instructional leader.

That was my hope. I would be an instructional leader. I didn't touch instruction for more than a year. I felt like a fish out of water without a lead role in shaping the direction of the district's educational program. I remember sharing my frustration at a district leadership council meeting where I publicly announced my concern regarding my isolation from the core teaching and learning work. I was concerned about having lost the connection to work that I had a passion for. I went to Greenwich to elevate my knowledge of curriculum and instruction, to do some things that I didn't have the opportunity to do in my other jobs . . . to really challenge myself in a different way.

He gained some "elbowroom," however, in the currency of increased credibility, especially among parents and community members.

Overall, we put together a strong management team and the board and community appreciated the changes in management of the district. The investment in shoring up the business side of the district was viewed as an important prerequisite to advancing the instructional agenda. I didn't like my role in this work, but accepted that the district had been hemorrhaging in these areas for quite some time.

The staff reactions to Larry's efforts to gain fiscal credibility with town fathers, however, were more ambivalent.

The level of funding for public education in Greenwich is amazing, particularly arriving there after nearly 8 years in one of New Jersey's 30 poorest school districts. We had to fight for every nickel we got in Plainfield and the money and resources behind each learner paled in comparison to the money spent in Greenwich. Inside the district I was actually viewed as too conservative in my requests of the town and was occasionally criticized by staff for not waging budget wars for higher levels of funding.

First Controversy

Larry's "honeymoon" did not last long. In less than two months, he found himself in the middle of a community brouhaha. When he arrived, he inherited an elementary principal vacancy at Cos Cob Elementary School and a search process for a new principal that was well underway. In fact, this search was the second one for the same vacancy. A search in 2002 had ended when the previous superintendent's choice turned down the job. Instead, the vice principal, who had been an internal candidate, was given the role of interim principal for the 2003–04 school year, and a second search was launched. The vice principal reapplied for the position, and as a letter to the editor of the local newspaper noted, "Her support among parents is overwhelming" ("Letters to the Editor," *Greenwich Citizen*, May 30, 2003). Her roots in the community, however, ran even deeper. As Larry describes it, she was

Born and raised in Greenwich—actually born and raised in the center of the school neighborhood—graduated the local high school, and taught for many years in the Greenwich School District.

Larry, however, felt that the search had produced a stronger candidate, an experienced principal from a New York state district.

I find this fabulous candidate . . . and I was here like 6 weeks, 7 weeks. The search had started prior to my arrival and preliminary interviews had been completed. I became involved and participated in narrowing the field of candidates. And—long story made short—I didn't appoint the internal candidate. My predecessor came to the same conclusion during an earlier search and life went on without major disturbance. I made the same decision and all hell broke loose . . . I started on March 31 and all hell broke loose on May 22.

The morning of May 22 did not begin well. When Larry announced his decision to the faculty at the school, several staff members booed him, and the *Greenwich Citizen* reported that half of the faculty rose and walked out of the meeting to protest his decision. One teacher's reaction was reported this way: "She felt 'blindsided' by the decision . . . she had to wonder why someone with 'identical' qualifications was chosen over someone familiar with the school." Another teacher said, "With such an enormous outpouring of support, Leverett shouldn't have made such a quick decision" ("Cos Cob Parents, Teachers Rally to Support Petrizzi," 2003).

By that evening's board meeting, of course, the word was out among parents and in the community. According to the newspaper, "Nearly 100 parents crowded into the cafeteria, in hopes that their collective presence and speeches . . . would be enough to overturn the decision that had already been made. But the group of supporters (of the interim principal) could not change the minds of the board or the superintendent."

When Larry made his recommendation, again according to the paper, "Many politely clapped . . . but most people shook their heads in disappointment and complained to each other that 'their voices weren't heard'" ("Cos Cob Parents, Teachers Rally to Support Petrizzi," 2003).

Despite the political pressure, the board voted unanimously to approve Larry's recommendation for the outside candidate. The paper reported the audience response:

"A sentiment held by many in the community—'this is unbelievable' could be heard throughout the proceedings. As the audience filed out... [the chair of the board] asked, 'Please leave quietly.' The audience responded with chants of 'no, no, no' " ("Cos Cob Parents, Teachers Rally to Support Petrizzi," 2003). As that response forecasted, the community's negative reaction did not subside quickly. Over the next several weeks, Larry endured intense criticism.

A community meeting where I stood alone for $2\frac{1}{2}$ hours in the school gym tested my ability to remain calm in the eye of a storm. Over the following weeks there were Freedom of Information Act requests for the recommended candidate's personnel file from her present district and the contents of the internal candidate's personnel file. There were several dozen letters to the editor of the local newspaper and literally hundreds of emails lambasting the board and me for the selection of the external candidate. Several parents organized a demonstration in a park adjacent to the school, and more than a few dozen people gathered with placards, balloons, and chants to "Fire Leverett" blurting from a bullhorn.

I thought I was D.O.A. Gray hairs started popping out like crazy. Here I am, brand new in town, no Connecticut connections, in a different element altogether than anything I've experienced personally or professionally. And then between March 31—whoa, golly—and May 22 I'm in this predicament. It was the ugliest experience in my whole career.

Larry also sensed the racism underneath the veneer of public outrage, and he felt afraid.

I was quite concerned. I did not feel safe. Forget about job security. I'm not talking about that kind of thing... I starting feeling that I was not going to be physically safe. I was frightened. People didn't know me and I didn't know them. "What does he know about our community? He needs to go back where he came from. He doesn't know this type of community"... All of that was code being used to mask other feelings some had.

His candidate, now the board appointee, also felt the ugliness that Larry describes, and she decided that she would not accept the position. In a press release issued on June 10, Larry announced her decision to the community. He attributed it to "the current negative environment in the community" and stated that the "intrusive measures that were taken to second guess her appointment" provided "evidence of distrust" that led her to feel that she could not be successful.

Despite his fear and discomfort, Larry remained clear that he was going to find the best possible principal for the school. He says he told the leaders of the opposition when he met with them:

I told them, "Look, you're gonna do what you're gonna do. But I've got to tell you and tell you straight, the internal candidate is not going to be appointed principal here. I'm not going to move from that. The board hired me to recommend the best prepared people for employment and that's what I am going to do."

His June press release also stated that the internal candidate "has expressed her intentions to pursue other options within the district and will not be pursuing the position." He was of course criticized for his directness and firmness. In a letter to the editor, for example, an "outraged" resident, the husband of a Cos Cob teacher, deplored "a badly mishandled situation" and criticized Larry for excluding the internal favorite from any further consideration ("He's Outraged by Cos Cob Situation," 2003).

Because of their positions as elected officials, Board of Education members felt the brunt of public criticism at least as much as, if not more than, Larry throughout the controversy. After all, they knew many more community residents than Larry did at this point in his superintendency, and many more community residents knew them and contacted them. Nevertheless, the board remained solidly supportive of Larry's decision. Their support made all the difference in his weathering this storm.

My school board did not waiver in their support, not even an inch. You can make tough decisions when you have that support.

As an experienced superintendent, Larry knew the importance of communicating with the board early and often, and of helping them to prepare for what was to come.

I didn't make the principalship decision in isolation. I checked in with the board and made the case for my recommendation to hire an external candidate. I knew that it would be controversial and put an end to my honeymoon.

But I had no idea about the intensity of the pushback I was to experience. Doing what was right even when it is not popular was something the board knew about me, but neither they, nor I, expected to have such a vivid example so early in my tenure in Greenwich.

Despite the surprising intensity and ugliness of the reaction, Larry and the board worked to establish a dialogue with the disaffected parents, teachers, and community members. As early as June 10, in his press release announcing that his candidate was not coming to Greenwich, Larry invited members of the Cos Cob community to e-mail or to phone him. The press release also announced that he had "already established and met with a planning team" of parents, teachers, and community members whose objective was to "provide the optimal educational environment for Opening Day 2003." The town hall special meeting that Larry described above took place on July 1 and seemed to have a cathartic effect. Board minutes note that

Over 200 people were present and over 20 people addressed the board expressing either agreement or disagreement with the board and superintendent's actions . . . Issues that were addressed were the timeliness of communication to the staff and the public, the issue of where the line is drawn insofar as the dissemination of interview information and its contents, and the lines of authority as far as the decision-making process . . .

Dr. Leverett also thanked everyone for their input and agreed that the communication with staff and parents was less than what he felt it should be on this issue. He vowed to work with the community and staff on improving communication and on healing and moving forward.

The negative community reaction began to soften, at least a bit. The letter to the editor from the outraged faculty husband, for example, also stated that, "Acknowledgement by Dr. Leverett and the board of their failure to communicate went a long way toward reassuring me that the board will be more forthcoming in the future" ("He's Outraged by Cos Cob Situation," 2003).

During the summer of 2003, working with the planning team he had established, Larry drew on his collaborative skills, developed in his earlier superintendencies, for reaching out to and genuinely including faculty and community members.

So, I started . . . That summer we worked. I got an outside facilitator to work with a group of opposition leadership, one or two staff members, parents, and me. And we got to a better place even though I had stated my position and kept working the issue . . . Then the goal of this committee, whether they liked it or not, was to make sure that the school opened as best it could that September as a place that was focused, to the extent possible, on the kids. "No matter how you feel about me or what I've decided, September's coming. We've got this interim principal. She's going to be here. The kids are going to be here. The faculty is going to be here. There are splits everywhere. Now we've got to do something about that. We've got to do it together." We had external support and were able to open the school and calm the waters.

On August 1, the planning team itself had a letter to the editor printed in which it summarized its activities in getting ready for the school year. Signed by all members of the team, including Larry, the letter described the team's efforts to dispel rumors, to plan for introducing the interim principal to the school community, and to examine current issues in "a productive and positive environment" ("Letters to the Editor: Cos Cob Prepares," *Greenwich Citizen*, August 1, 2003).

Two other events over the summer helped the healing that Larry vowed to undertake. The first was that he found a credible and effective interim principal.

We were fortunate to identify an interim principal who was of impeccable credentials. The interim, an experienced and respected elementary principal, was looking for a one-year assignment in Greenwich and had a reputation for building community. I got a really solid person that I could put in the school. The interim stayed for the year and helped enormously.

The second was that the internal candidate was appointed to a principalship over the summer in a neighboring district.

In the fall of 2003, Larry developed a collaborative and inclusive search process for a new permanent school principal that was substantially different from the one he inherited the previous spring.

I had the opportunity to do more front-end work with staff, parents. Engage them in the development of a profile. I personally . . . remained involved throughout the search process and worked closely to clarify roles and responsibilities of all shareholder groups. Transparent communications were key to building credibility and repairing the breakdown in trust. Everything was overcommunicated. Everything was overly transparent. I was completely accessible. The school community and I knew that we had to work together for the good of the school and we did.

From the discord and rancor that characterized the previous spring's process, Larry created and implemented a search process that produced a consensus candidate as the new principal.

Reconnecting to His Passion

From his first day in Plainfield, Larry felt the urgency to act as instructional leader. The low level of student performance and the widespread acceptance of it evoked his social equity beliefs and passions. Among other steps, he immediately established a community-wide strategic planning effort.

In contrast, Larry felt disconnected from his passion in Greenwich. The principal controversy and management problems consumed his time and attention. Moreover, the instructional needs were less apparent.

There are few districts that can boast of the aggregate performance of our students on a variety of measures, including SAT scores, AP participation and performance, and admission to highly competitive colleges and universities. The high school's enrollment in Advanced Placement courses more than doubled in the past 6 years with a very minimal reduction in the mean score from 3.8 to 3.7. SAT1 scores are the highest they have been in the past 16 years.

As an urban educator throughout his career prior to Greenwich, Larry was sharply attuned to, and quickly discovered, achievement differences among racial and ethnic groups in Greenwich.

Greenwich does an outstanding job educating 80% of our students. However, 20% of Greenwich students have not historically achieved similar levels of success. For these students the story is quite different—these students are mainly Hispanic, African American, English Language Learners, or students from families of all backgrounds who were eligible for free or reduced-price lunches. The district's lack of success with these students was masked by very strong aggregated performance results. Our mission calls for success with ALL students and leaving 20% behind was incongruent with the excellence that defines our district.

This knowledge helped him to reconnect to his passion.

I found my passion and mission at the same time. Closing the achievement gap became my clear mission. The Greenwich improvement mantra, "Closing Gaps—Accelerating Performance—Maximizing Achievement for All Students" became the battle cry and I was out to enlist the entire Greenwich education community to rally in support of this work. There was work for not only the superintendent, but for all members of the school district community. I was eager to provide leadership and move out of the role of a business-oriented superintendent. Moving toward the instructional leadership role was a bit more complex than I assumed.

Addressing the Gap

Engaging the Conversation

Larry found that his passion for closing this achievement gap and his impatience for action was not immediately shared by many people in the Greenwich education community.

In a place like Greenwich, it's difficult to put an issue like closing the achievement gap for low-income, Hispanic kids, primarily, on the top. Early on it was very, very lonely and uncomfortable because changing outcomes for the 20% of students who were not receiving the benefits of a Greenwich education was not a "front burner" issue in the school community. The district did focus on accelerating the achievement of students, but somehow changing outcomes for underperforming students did not get equal billing.

I have always had difficulty in my work because my passion feeds a sense of urgency that is often more immediate and demanding than the norm of most schools or districts. I was honest with the Greenwich board about my interest in closing achievement gaps wherever they existed. The board also believed that the district needed to do a better job with all students. This belief was not as uniform within the district. We continue to deal with belief systems that align with Murray's infamous book, The Bell Curve. *Views that intelligence is innate and that low-performing students need a diet of basic skills and remediation until they are ready for access to rigorous academic content are frequently voiced. Low expectations were and continue to be a major barrier to getting the job done for all students.*

As the first African-American superintendent in Greenwich, Larry felt that some people interpreted his interest in closing the achievement gap as a *disinterest* in the 80% of the student population who were excelling on numerous measurements. Critics quietly complained that a focus on the lowest-performing students reduced the emphasis on accelerating the performance of the highest performing students. They dismissed his concerns for the 20% on the basis of his personal background and urban experience.

I am the superintendent for all children, high performing and low performing, rich and poor, black, white, Hispanic, and Asian. I know that America has the best chance of fulfilling its potential if ALL children are educated to reach a high standard. Closing gaps and accelerating the performance of all students is my professional and moral responsibility. I raise the issue of underperforming students vigorously and know that Greenwich cannot set the standard for public education unless we improve outcomes for every student . . . Good instruction across the board not only closes gaps, but accelerates learning for all.

Culture of Autonomy

With instructional challenges masked by the advantages that come with affluence and with access to tremendous social capital, a culture of autonomy prevailed in the Greenwich organization.

Everything was believed to be fine, and there was no sense of urgency to make major changes in how teaching and learning was implemented. A large majority of students were meeting or exceeding performance expectations.

Central office supported the culture of autonomy.

Central office served as little more than a caretaker without a major role in leading systemic instructional improvement. Schools functioned as individual fiefdoms. A career Greenwich principal candidly shared his perspective about central office. He said, "Look, if you are from central office and I am doing fine with my parents and staff, then you can't touch me. If you are from central office, and I am having problems with my parents and staff, you can't help me. So I'm going for myself." That's been the prevailing culture for a long time.

Instructional practices were predictably varied, and the central office played little role in developing more coherence and consistency.

Elementary schools had three different math textbooks when I arrived here. Every elementary school claimed to be doing balanced literacy, but I couldn't find two schools that had similar interpretations of the components of a balanced literacy program. There were six or seven different literacy consultants selected by schools advancing their own ideas for a balanced literacy framework. I went from School A to School B and could not find significant similarities between the approaches. That was the situation across the curriculum and across the elementary and middle schools. I attributed much of this to the minimal expectations of the central office as a unit charged with promoting consistency and comparability across district schools.

The staff did not expect nor did they initially embrace instructional leadership from the superintendent or the central office.

Raising questions about the "do your own thing" modus operandi didn't add to my popularity. After all, most of the schools had good test scores and those that didn't, well, they were not expected to do so well because they served lower income students and had higher concentrations of English Language Learners.

Principals saw their domains threatened by my interest in launching a systemwide approach to instructional improvement. It took a lot of persistence to move away from this history. Many other staff members had a hard time accepting that the superintendent actually had a strong opinion about the role of the district working systemwide on common instructional directions. Often I had to take hard-line positions to communicate that I was serious and do what was required to push for system wide instructional improvement and alignment of efforts at all levels.

Some teachers and administrators viewed Larry's systemwide orientation to curriculum and instruction as inappropriate in a suburban context.

I heard a lot of chatter about the superintendent using an urban approach in a high-performing school district. Using the same textbooks for math, a consistent, balanced literacy approach, coordinated professional development across schools was viewed as educational heresy by some staff who enjoyed the autonomy to make these decisions within their schools.

Larry argued strongly that systemwide instructional improvement has a higher probability of success when there is alignment across schools in the areas of curriculum, instruction, assessment, and professional development. Best practices make sense in all school districts whether they are high performing or low performing, rich or poor.

Evidence-based elements of comprehensive school reform helped frame our work in Plainfield . . . teachers who more deeply implemented the elements of the whole school reform model had statistically significant higher learning gains. In Greenwich, I couldn't accept "I think" or "This is the way it has been here" as a replacement for what I knew worked to improve outcomes for learners. I questioned why suburban schools could not benefit from application of the same research base that proved effective in successful urban schools. I believe that good practice is good practice and can work anywhere.

Pressure and Support

Larry is pushing the culture of the Greenwich school district organization from autonomy to centralization around issues of curricular coherence, instructional alignment, and reallocation of resources through healthy doses of pressure and support.

All support, no pressure—no change. All pressure, no support—no change. You've got to get a balance of pressure and support . . . I knew that district staff needed to change if we were to have a chance at moving from a system of schools, to a school system. Central office needed to become much more proactive as the locus of both pressure and support. Asking people to work differently without providing the resources and building capacity creates a hypocritical basis for systemic instructional improvement. We had a lot of work to do to repurpose the leadership role of central office as an agent for systemwide instructional improvement.

In order to sharpen the instruments of pressure and support, Larry is trying to change the role of central office, from benignly supportive to authoritatively directive. He encourages central office administrators not only to visit schools but also to visit them purposefully through focused walks and structured walk-throughs.

I started raising questions here in central office. Beyond the business office, the cabinet was competent in their roles as they were defined. The board was heavily oriented toward micromanaging and the staff was oriented toward compliance with board wishes. Content area supervisors, while not in agreement with board-directed curriculum initiatives, did not have the resources to question the direction of the district. In general, the district staff was not proactive in expecting consistency in instruction and assessment across the schools.

Through his own perseverance and with board and central office support, he sees progress.

Whether I was going to be there for a day or a decade, I insisted on an agenda that would promote coherence and congruency. Thank goodness, the Greenwich cabinet responded admirably and is now an important leader in the conversation about teaching and learning. Thank goodness, that the board of education has shifted its focus from controlling the means to monitoring the outcomes. The board has made a tremendous difference in how our work is perceived by the schools. We are on the same page and everybody knows it!

Transfer of Agency

Larry believes that authority and responsibility for change must become broadly shared if it is to be institutionalized.

I want to transfer the agency as quickly as possible from me to the organization . . . leadership for making good things happen requires that the leadership be distributed and responsibility be shared.

Although he sees progress, Larry acknowledges he has had difficulty developing a shared sense of mission and purpose, especially within the organization, that will enable transfer of agency.

Getting to a shared reality regarding the need to improve instructional practice has been hard. It has been difficult to get the voluntary investment that the mission warriors of the Plainfield days were so eager to make . . . I have not been very successful in transferring ownership for this work. Right now, the collaborative style that characterized our work in Plainfield is not as systemic in Greenwich. Admittedly I have been more top-down and pushy than I like. My work must continue to evolve toward a more collaborative leadership approach if changes are to be planted deep in the organization.

The good news is that parents are already signed on. The board is signed on. Most town elected officials are signed on. More and more staff and most principals have signed onto the team. Over time, I hope that we are successful in efforts to move from politically correct compliance to complete acceptance of moral responsibility to do whatever it takes to escalate the performance of all of our kids.

Board of Education Support (Also Known as Political Cover)

As Larry tackles his organizational challenges, the board has provided him with key support in different areas.

Enacting a Social Justice Agenda

The board, first, embraced the achievement gap goal.

The board was clear from day one that improving performance for all students was its goal. Their selection of me as superintendent was a step toward challenging the system to do better.

The board has also put money behind their commitment by lowering class size in its lowest performing school.

The Hamilton Avenue School is in the least affluent section of Greenwich. For several years the school had been plagued by outbreaks of mold, indoor air quality challenges, and numerous other structural and building system problems. These problems were treated only when a crisis occurred. A comprehensive study of the facility recommended against long-term use of the school. The board committed to building a state of the art elementary school that will house pre-school programs, limit class size to 15 in pre-K through grade 1 classes, and incorporate features to support a community school design. Board support for the school serving Greenwich's most economically challenged and ethnically diverse school signaled, in what I believe were heroic terms, a commitment to doing whatever is required to serve all of the town's children.

Rethinking Governance

In November 2003, the board made Larry one of the most powerful superintendents in Connecticut, if not the nation, when it gave him what the local newspaper described as "full authority" to hire school administrators. "The move will eliminate an old policy that requires the board to approve appointments to principal or other top positions" ("Leverett Given Reins to Hire Administrators," 2003).

The board has moved from attempting to manage the district to a system of policy governance. Policy governance clarifies the role of the board to make policy and establishes the superintendent as the board's sole employee. The board is moving toward monitoring my performance based upon the extent to which the district is in compliance with outcomes-based policies. I know what my board expects of me and am held accountable for complying with their expectations. The policy governance model has resulted in the superintendency becoming a more powerful position. For once, the rules of engagement are clear.

Policy governance has resulted in the board being much more focused on board work and far less involved in efforts to control the management of means and reduced tendencies to engage in micromanagement. This system requires me to be more accountable to the board than I have ever been. However, it always has provided me with the freedom to do the work without the need to look over my shoulder.

I have responsibility and control over the means, and the board sets up the ends. That's cool. I like this arrangement and welcome the accountability that comes with it.

Plain Talk: Being a Truth Teller

When the board announced Larry's appointment to the community, the chair praised Larry's "straightforward communications style." Larry prides himself on his direct, clear, and honest talk.

I think it's important, for me, to name the things that are concerns of people or that hinder our performance. This makes these issues more visible, tangible, and transparent. If we say we're doing differentiation of instruction, and it's invisible to the human eye, then I'm not going to stand before parents and say we're doing this. If there are issues with local curriculum assessments that are based on multiple choice and testing discrete bits of knowledge, I will name local curriculum assessments as problems that must be addressed. Transparency is a necessary ingredient to build trust and credibility.

His willingness to name problems directly and publicly have won support and respect from a parent body that can be demanding.

People, really good friends of mine, colleagues and even family, were concerned about my accepting the Greenwich superintendency. "I really don't want you to go there. I'm concerned you're not going to be able to deal with the parents. You know how pushy and demanding those parents are. They want what they want, and they're just going to drive you crazy. You don't have any patience for that so you better not go there."

We have more than our fair share of high maintenance moms. However, I have experienced parents to be an important constituent group to support what I thought needed to be changed to address instructional improvement. Oh, they push and have the ability to organize for special interests at the drop of a hat. But I have found that plain talk and consistency between "talk and walk" have earned me credibility and greater encouragement. Anywhere I've been, parents as a body provide me with a lot of cover as the educational leader to do the job.

Objections From Faculty

Faculty expectations are different. Some look to a superintendent not for direct and public acknowledgment of problems, but for protection and buffering from parents and community.

Let me give you an example, a recent example. Hispanic parents group ... Greenwich High School ... So I talked about the performance of low-income ... or Hispanic students in general ... I started with the performance of Hispanic students in terms of access to honors courses, AP courses. The performance of Hispanic students on the CMT [Connecticut Mastery Test], CAPT [Connecticut Academic Performance Test], and the absence of representation in higher level courses. I learned that many of the 30–35 parents present did not know how the district tracked students into higher and lower courses. Unfortunately, they didn't understand that many of their middle and high school students were in the lower level courses and their performance, as a group, was much lower than the average Greenwich student. They said, "This is the first time we are hearing this" ... The parents asked, "Why is this happening?" I responded, "Your children are not being taught." That comment was printed in the local newspaper and angered many high school staff members.

Despite the negative reaction, Larry sees benefits to his "truth telling" to the high school Hispanic parents.

Upon reflection, I should not have said it quite that way, but I wanted to communicate my assessment of the situation that resulted in lower levels of achievement. I believe that if learners are effectively taught, then they will learn. If there are barriers, then it is our job to get rid of them. The reactions to my comments about ineffective instruction, while not well received, have stimulated the conversation on our responsibility. Since then there have been meetings with groups of teachers, communication with the union leadership, and other forums to move us toward a shared reality about teaching, learning, and our responsibility. Our beliefs about students and their capacity to meet high academic outcomes shape our action. There are two things we must believe to make good things happen for all of our kids. First, we must believe in their ability to be successful. Second, we must believe that we can do what it takes for each student to be successful. Our present reality is that these two beliefs are not uniformly present in the system.

The Lessons Learned

Urban and Suburban Best Practices

It is critical to explore with staff the belief that good practice is good practice in *both* urban and suburban districts. The transferability of strategies to strengthen curricular coherence and instructional consistency from a low-performing urban setting to a high-performing suburban district raised new questions for Larry and his staff to explore.

The idea of all the elementary and middle schools embarking on the journey to instructional coherence and consistency was very foreign. Actually, there were times when I really questioned whether my ideas about systemwide change were appropriate here. Were the principles of comprehensive school reform only intended for low-performing schools and districts? Should the district be pushing for coherence, consistency, and comparability if test results were high? I decided that urban or suburban, rich or poor, high performing or low performing, good practice is good practice and that evidence-based, systemwide approaches to instructional improvement made sense as a means to improve outcomes for all the district's learners.

Shared Realities About Data and Its Meaning

Larry has learned the importance of investing time in the thoughtful engagement of the schools' various constituencies to get to a shared reality about the data and its meaning to the organization. Otherwise, people can look at the same data and interpret the facts differently.

The frequent recitation of disaggregated performance results did not result in hundreds of staff members signing on to end this pernicious condition. Rather, it encouraged faultfinding, blame, assignment of responsibility to others [like] *families, SES status, absence of pre-school, etc.*

In both Plainfield and Greenwich we got to a shared reality and acceptance when we were thoughtful and methodical about how we engaged people in conversation and learning. Beating people over the head with data does not make them more ready to accept hard truths about the system's failure to perform. Helping the school community to accept ownership requires varied approaches: framing and reframing of challenges and issues; multiple approaches to data sharing that are clear and concise; increased knowledge of the current situation; professional learning; sharing educational research and documented best practice; and site visits to schools that were effective with similar student populations.

Doing a Few Things Well

Although Plainfield and Greenwich differ enormously, they are alike in their limited organizational capability to handle multifaceted reform.

School districts and schools learn better when investments are made to support capacity building to do a few things well. Both Plainfield and Greenwich had a lot of catch up to do relative to their stated missions. However, the capacity to manage a multifaceted reform agenda was relatively low in both districts. We learned that doing a few things well was far more preferable than diffusing the focus of the organization to fix every problem with immediacy. The "mile wide/inch thin" change approach may look good on the surface and signals lots of activity. The reality, however, is likely not to produce the expected outcomes. A narrow focus that is supported and sustained over time is much more likely to result in changes at the level of schools and classrooms. The temptation to fix all that is broken at the same time can result in little change in the places that matter most.

Governance Makes a Difference

The Greenwich board's policy governance model has proven empowering for Larry, providing him with the authority to act as the chief executive officer of the district. He is more accountable to the board than ever before, yet he enjoys the benefits of clear delegation of authority to operate the district.

It really helps me to do my job when the board and I are clear about roles and responsibilities. I never wish to return to work in a district in which the board and I are struggling with ambiguity about roles . . . We occasionally differ on interpretation of policies . . . but the great thing is that the conversation is grounded in policy-oriented discussions rather than blame and fault-oriented battles that fuel conflict and the breakdown of communications.

The politics of operating the school district have also changed.

The board speaks in "one voice" and there are very infrequent intrusions of the board in the administration of the school district. Staff and community know that the superintendent is accountable for policy implementation and attainment of board-adopted performance targets. They also understand that going to the board to address their grievance is no longer acceptable and "end runs" on the administration are not acceptable to the board. The dynamics of how we work has reduced conflict and backdoor approaches to getting things done through informal channels of communication.

Build Capacity of People to Work Together in the Change Process

If we want people to work differently, then we must provide them with the tools required to do so. Simply mandating new ways of working will not result in a more productive district or school. We must help people to develop the skill set necessary to support and sustain the relationships, respect, and communications that are characteristic of high-performing organizations.

To make change happen, a renorming of school culture to support a systemwide instructional focus must occur. The hard work of system-wide instructional improvement will not be successful if separate silos within the central office and across schools remain as the preferred arrangement for doing the district's work. Schools and districts that have enjoyed the norms of considerable autonomy must embrace the norms of collaboration and must learn the skills to work effectively together across department or unit boundaries.

Mobilization for systemwide instructional improvement requires that the staff at all levels develop skills to work outside of their comfortable "cocoons." Central office has a leadership role to use integrative work processes that facilitate interdepartmental collaboration, negotiation of resources, and proactive strategies for problem solving, communication, and conflict resolution.

Conflict as a Route to Change

Conflict is an inherent component of any major change effort. Providing leadership in the development of tools to help staff resolve them is essential.

The African proverb, "While the elephants fight, the ants are crushed" illustrates the importance of building district and school capacity to manage the challenges and conflicts inherent in systemwide change initiatives . . . Social emotional learning is now being described as the missing component of instructional reforms. Students and adults both can benefit from learning and incorporating these skills. Conflict is an inevitable part of the change process, and we need to do a better job working with school- and district level staff to equip them with a repertoire of tools and techniques to increase their capacity to facilitate the change process.

Know Thyself

At times, in both Plainfield and Greenwich, Larry has struggled to restrain his drive to get everything that needs to be done accomplished. He continues to work to find the right amount of organizational stretch that is appropriate to the capacity of the district and its schools to handle a fast-paced, multifaceted systemic change process. He is, for example, comfortable and tolerant of ambiguity, but others around him want clarity and order in change management.

I have come to realize that a high-powered visionary leadership style can be a bit much for the district. I am impatient and aggressive, and these tendencies sometimes work against the established goals. I foster a "push back" culture in which my colleagues are encouraged to rein me in when the stretch is disruptive to our shared goals.

I believe we all pretty much have a "strong" side and a "weak" side. My strong side is when I am an emotionally intelligent leader. My weak side is when I resort to a more harsh, "take no prisoners" approach to my work. I am a much better leader when I stay on my strong side and fairly disastrous when I resort to the weak side to make my point. I know that my effectiveness is compromised, and I must continuously assess and self-assess my leadership approach to become the leader I must be to help my district achieve its full potential. The responsibility to lead in an emotionally intelligent manner is mine.

Passion and being impatiently patient are strengths that leaders need to promote systemic change. Our work as superintendents takes place in the context of varied time zones. The board has its sense of time, the public and staff another, and parents yet another. We are under pressure to make change happen at a rate and speed that aligns with the pressure of internal and external stakeholders. I am most effective when I don't allow my passion to lead to a hard-driving impatience that is inconsistent with my organization's capacity to manage.

REFERENCES

Cos Cob parents, teachers rally to support Petrizzi. (2003, May 30). *Greenwich Citizen.*
He's outraged by Cos Cob situation. (2003, July 11). *Greenwich Citizen.*
Letters to the editor. (2003, May 30). *Greenwich Citizen.*
Letters to the editor: Cos Cob prepares. (2003, August 1). *Greenwich Citizen.*
Leverett given reins to hire administrators. (2003, November 28). *Greenwich Citizen.*

Superintendents often mourn the "good old days" when they were educators and did not need to worry about the managerial and political aspects of their districts. Linda Hanson shows how effective a superintendent can be in the role of educator as she and her reading staff help their school board understand the implications of a mandatory graduation test.

CHAPTER 5

A New Superintendent Embraces the Role of Teacher

LINDA HANSON

Most superintendents find themselves arguing against their boards' wishes at some time during their tenure. However, I did not expect to find myself in this spot at the very beginning of my superintendent career. During my initial interview for the position, several board members had talked about their high expectations for students, and they told me that they had passed a board policy requiring students to undergo a reading test to graduate from high school. My antennae waved mildly, but I was so eager to obtain my first superintendent's position that I did not probe this issue. I was delighted to be named the new superintendent of a district that consisted of one high school of 1,600 students (not unusual in Illinois) in a predominately blue-collar community in the suburban Chicago area. The district had over 20% minority population, mostly Hispanic, with many second-language speakers. At the time, in 1990, Illinois had not enacted any uniform measures of standardized testing, and most schools selected their own norm-based, standardized tests. High schools were usually compared with one another by ACT composites. Our school was average.

The scathing education report issued in 1983 by a task force on U.S. education, titled *A Nation at Risk*, was still reverberating in communities the year I became superintendent. This report asserted that public schools were mired in mediocrity and that enormous changes needed to take place at the core of education. In other reports, U.S. students' educational progress was frequently unfavorably compared to students' progress in other countries. *A Nation at Risk* claimed that educational administrators were content with the status quo and were not holding students accountable in rigorous ways. The reputation of school administrators had been in steady decline for years when the board and I began our conversations about student learning and achievement. Board members had heard complaints repeatedly from the business community about how students could not read well, how schools were not expecting enough from students, how grades and curriculum had been "dumbed down," and how businesses were suffering because students were not adequately prepared for the workplace. Interestingly, local parents believed that their own children had received a good education and were well prepared by our high school, but felt that "other" children in the school system had not received a good education.

Unfortunately, the district had lacked stable administrative leadership for quite some time. The former superintendent had been gravely ill for several years, and when he died, the district had an interim for the year before I arrived. Our board was a solid group of people who wanted to do the best for our school district. They were buffeted by the nation's increasing criticism of schools, several uncertain years, and perceptions of the business community that the students graduating from the high school did not have sufficient skills for the world in which they would compete for jobs.

I certainly needed to understand the community and school better, so I set my entry plan into motion. I joined the Rotary, held coffees, met with parents and staff, and tried to listen more than talk. The issues that revealed themselves were both spoken and unspoken. The articulated issues were that the test scores were not high enough and that the town's business people felt that the school should be perceived more highly than it was. The unspoken issues were those that I had learned of over the beginning months in my position. They centered on an underlying competition with a neighboring town. Our town was predominantly blue collar; the neighboring town predominantly white collar. While our town struggled with effective programs for second-language learners, our neighboring community's minority population consisted mainly of children of Asian doctors and researchers from nearby pharmaceutical companies who did very well academically. When houses went on the market in the neighboring town, realtors' ads listed the school system as one of the advantages of buying a home there. The realtors in our town were silent in their advertisements about the attractions of our system. Mentally, I set one of my first goals—that realtors would someday feature our school district as an incentive to buy a home in our town.

As I spoke individually to each board member, he or she talked of the need for our high school to rise to the next academic level. The board members collectively believed that raising the reputation and status of the school was necessary for the good of our students and community. They clearly wanted higher student achievement and more rigor in the curriculum. During these individual meetings, no board member specifically mentioned the reading requirement that they had recently passed. Effective in three years, this requirement would bar students from graduation unless they received a 10.5 grade equivalency in both the comprehension and vocabulary sections of a particular standardized test.

Next, I talked to staff members and listened to their concerns. First and foremost, the teachers expressed concern about the morale issues that were deeply imbedded in the culture of the school. The school had been run for many years in a top-down style that reflected a lack of trust in teachers. The superintendent had expected the principal to carry out his orders with few questions asked. When teachers left school for lunch, they were required to sign out, noting their destination, and sign back in when they returned. A person monitored the door in the morning to determine which teachers were tardy. The teachers did not feel respected, and they knew they were not an important part of the decision-making fabric of the school. They responded to such constraints by simply closing their classroom doors to be left alone to teach their students to the best of their abilities.

During my conversations with teachers, a few raised concerns about the reading requirement that had been briefly mentioned in my interview. They described their understanding of the policy to me, explaining that effective in 3 years, all seniors would be required to pass the Gates MacGinitie reading test with a 10.5 grade equivalent in both vocabulary and comprehension, or else they would not be allowed to graduate. My interview with the board replayed in my head, and I realized that I dimly recalled having heard something about this requirement, but I was quite sure that the teachers must be mistaken about the specifics. However, the principal confirmed that his understanding was the same as the teachers'.

The Superintendent and Board Dynamics

The school board was comprised of six men and one woman. All were college educated and very committed, and all expressed that they enjoyed their roles on the board. Without strong superintendent leadership, the board members had taken over some of the traditional roles of the superintendent. They had led the school based on their own successful experience as business people, but without the benefit of educational research, knowledge of best practice, and an understanding about how effective change occurs in a school organization. They seemed to feel ambivalent about turning the reins over to me when I arrived as their new superintendent.

I telephoned the board president for clarification about the reading policy, and he confirmed the teachers' understanding. He told me to speak specifically to Don, the board member who had spearheaded the drive to pass the policy. Don was a senior member of the board with over 20 years of service. He was a highly educated man with an Ivy League degree who had immutable opinions on student learning. He was also the board member who was the least supportive of my appointment. I had been hired on a 6–1 vote, with Don being the dissenting vote.

Don and I met. Our conversation quickly evolved into a discussion of our beliefs about teaching and learning. I talked about providing students with authentic and meaningful experiences, moving students forward academically, involving teachers in designing and creating lessons with high interest for students, teaching students not only to know the names of the state capitals but also why we have state capitals, and fostering a climate of learning that encourages and nurtures students. I told him about my own experiences for many years as an art teacher and the kind of classroom that I believed best supported and helped students grow.

Don believed that the best educational foundation for students was being in possession of many facts, usually mastered through rote learning. He thought that the best instructional technique was an interesting and powerful lecture. He believed all students should have a classical curriculum of study consisting of Latin, possibly Greek, mathematics, and a reading syllabus including the books he had read as a freshman in high school: *Antigone*, *Silas Marner*, and *Great Expectations*. Knowing that I was a former art teacher, he expressed his belief that the visual arts were unimportant for high school students. He believed that negative consequences and fear were more motivating than positive feedback. Most of his understanding and thinking had been based on his own personal educational experiences.

As Don and I talked, we realized that our definitions of "high standards" could not have been more different. Our approaches to learning were diametrically opposed. And, sadly, neither of us seemed to respect each other's point of view. Where Don advocated memorizing a large body of facts, I believed in learning less material, but learning it more deeply. He believed that fear of failure motivated students; I believed that their successes and accomplishments motivated them. He believed that the curriculum should be uniform for all learners with little deviation; I thought that curriculum should be varied based on students' developmental needs and should allow for student choices.

He was proud of being the originator and author of the new reading policy. The policy summarized what he thought was the right way to educate young people. For me, it symbolized what I believed was wrong—the idea that more testing would improve the final product of student learning. Don ended our conversation by telling me that he would outlast me; he had "seen superintendents come and he'd seen them go." The implication was that I might be going sooner than I anticipated.

I began to understand that working and finding a common ground with individual board members were critical to my success with the board as a whole. Clearly, my greatest challenge would be Don, who thoroughly enjoyed playing the role of rebel. He was well educated, well read, and occasionally outrageous. If his vote would not actually affect an outcome, he would vote "no" on an issue such as the annual budget just to be contrary. Early on, he filed a Freedom of Information Act to attempt to require me to give him confidential information that another superintendent had shared with me. If he felt so inclined, he would give information from our closed sessions to the press. He imposed rules on others, but refused to follow them himself. The other board members treated him fondly and often said, "He has a good heart." When possible, they gave him his lead. When necessary, they would tell him "no." He was generous to teachers, but saw little value in administrators. He would donate rare books to the history department and would give money personally to support a student who could not afford a needed item. However, he would tell the secretaries they were overpaid and vote to keep their salaries at minimum wage. He would have liked to do away with administrators altogether. Where he amused the other board members, he frustrated me. Where they would say, "It's just Don," I would think, "It's *Don* again."

The stage was set for a struggle that would play out in terms of what we believed about learning, students, and motivation. As we were forced to examine our beliefs further, we found ourselves increasingly in opposition. I began to see clearly that I too was a person of immutable opinions about student learning. Ultimately, this struggle was one from which he and I would never recover. Throughout our time together, it was rare for Don and I to talk about anything without one of our tempers flaring.

Upon reflection, I now recognize that he was the board member with whom I had the most spirited conversations about teaching and learning. He was the person who loved to delve into these topics as much as I did. We were the two people who would debate endlessly about pedagogy. We would trade articles to support our particular beliefs. We would cite studies that gave proof of an opinion one of us had ventured. We worked to win the other over to our own point of view. Neither of us budged. He and I took umbrage with each other about small items; we bristled about unimportant issues. The other board members suggested that I take a more philosophical approach to Don, but I found myself annoyed and never amused.

The Wrong Policy for the Right Reasons

After speaking with Don, I told the board president that I had some concerns about the reading policy, and he suggested that we discuss it at the next board meeting. The principal and I had discussed our strategy, and we had decided that he would play a supporting role from behind the scenes and that I would be the person on the front line with the board.

At the meeting two weeks later, the board members explained that they had passed the reading policy when the interim superintendent was in place, just prior to my arrival at the district. In passing this policy, they felt they had sent strong messages to the community about raising the rigor of our school's curriculum and their commitment to high standards. They felt that they needed to "get tough" in order for our school to rise to the next academic level. The board defined its goal—to instill more pride in our schools by raising students' reading ability. The policy called for a reading pretest taken at 10th grade with a remediation plan to support poor readers with summer programs and in-school tutoring. The administration was expected to work out the details for success. The board did not want excuses why this could not be done. They reminded me that their policy had immediately created a favorable impression in the business community, and that the press conveyed the message that our board was modeling a tough educational stand for other boards of education. Parents had written letters to the newspaper editor praising the board's stand. The board members basked in the accolades they had received. I went to bed each night wondering how to solve this dilemma.

My unspoken opinion was that high standards were easy to establish and hard to attain. The board had set a standard that not every student in our school would be able to achieve. Among my many concerns was that the board had established the policy with no input from the principal or the teachers who would have to make it work. The policy put the achievement burden solely on the backs of students. There were no corresponding expectations for parents, teachers, the principal, the superintendent, or the Board of Education itself to define their respective roles in helping students attain the standard. The policy did not address teachers' instructional practices in each classroom that would need to be changed to put reading at the center of the departments' curriculums. All teachers would need to be educated in reading, and few teachers of subjects outside of English or reading understood much about the reading process or knew how to help students read strategically. Parents would need to play a supporting role from home by turning off their television sets and checking that their children spent time regularly with books. As a school, we would need to use varied measures of assessing individual students' reading progress. We would need to diagnose areas of difficulty and then recommend ways to help students meet the requirement. We would have to differentiate lessons for diverse learners and make curriculum revisions. Even if we could make all of these changes in the short time we were allotted, it was unlikely that every student would be able to pass the test at the required level.

Teachers' responses to the policy varied. A few teachers thought it was a great idea and that high standards are always a good thing. Others enjoyed turmoil and strife in the school setting and metaphorically rubbed their hands together with glee, waiting for the policy to implode, because the fallout would not affect them. Most teachers did not feel invested in the decision either way; they did not see it as touching their classrooms. The teachers who typically worked with struggling students were very concerned because they could name those who would not be graduating in three years. The reading teachers expressed concern about the policy because they felt that its concept was flawed at a foundational level, and they also felt the heaviest burden for achieving the desired effect. They had not been included in the decision making, and they believed that the policy did not reflect what the research said about reading achievement. These teachers questioned me about my views of the policy and what action I planned to take. I told them frankly that I saw serious issues with implementation, and I hoped that they would work with me as experts in reading to achieve the goals of the board. I further stated that achieving the goals might involve some method other than the policy the board had developed. I asked them if they thought they could create a reading curriculum that would raise the average reading scores of all our students, and they were intrigued by this reframed challenge, pledging to be helpful in any way that I thought was best. With this in mind, I had begun my series of conversations with the board.

At the next board meeting, I shared my broad reservations. Teachers and administrators had not been involved in the crafting of a policy that would depend on them for implementation. Measuring reading and comprehension with one test was not a reliable way to determine total reading ability. Fear was being used as the motivator for our students. Reading was a complicated matter that was not as simple as kids "trying harder" and our work needed to reflect this reality. Last, the district left itself open to serious legal challenges with the implementation of this policy.

The board listened to me with respect. However, they did not find my concerns compelling. They were not concerned that they had not involved teachers in the decision, because that had not been the way changes were historically made at the school. They thought that the test was a good one, and they were relying on the experts who had developed it to know more about reading than our staff. They were convinced that a high-stakes penalty was a better motivational tool than a "softer" one. They had not thought much about the legal issues; however, reading seemed pretty straightforward to them.

The board was convinced that our unique policy placed us on the cutting edge of finding ways to help students be more successful, and they held firm. They believed they had found the best way to increase our students' knowledge and skills for college, the workplace, and beyond. Representing the community, our board decided to keep the reading policy in place to assure high expectations and standards for student learning.

The stage was set for the classic tensions that often arise between boards and superintendents about the roles each should play. The board members believed that it was their job to set policies, and that the superintendent's job was to carry out those policies. I believed that effective policies needed to be written with the input of professional educators.

The board members expressed repeatedly that student learning was at the heart of their decision. They felt that they would have an awkward situation if they revoked a policy that was popular with the community before they even tried it. Unfortunately, they had enacted the "wrong" policy for the "right" reasons.

Working Through Dissenting Opinions

As I thought about the initial presentation of my concerns at the board meeting, I wondered about my lack of success in shifting the board's opinion in any way. I realized that we had no interactive dialogue at the board meeting—instead, I had simply laid out my concerns. As I prepared for the next meeting, I realized that I needed to engage the board more fully in the conversations and provide more details to support my concerns. As a result, I prepared legal, logistic, and pedagogical questions that I gave the board in advance for discussion at the next meeting. I asked that they also submit their own questions for us to discuss. As it turned out, they did not submit any questions of their own, but I posed the following questions to them:

1. What if a student has a "B" average throughout four years of high school, but achieves less than a 10.5 grade equivalency score on the test? Can his parents rightfully argue that we have provided four years of school reporting (through awarding grades) that allows them to believe that their son is in good standing and will graduate? If they challenged us legally, would their challenge prevail in court?
2. If a student who achieves an average 10.6 grade equivalency score is not allowed to graduate because one of his subtests is below 10.5, will we have a legal challenge and will we prevail?
3. What do we do about students who transfer to our school during their junior year and are below the reading level?
4. What does a high school diploma represent? Does it mean the same thing for every student who receives it? What does it certify?
5. Are we comfortable with one test assessing the reading level of students and determining graduation?
6. How do we deal with students who make good annual progress in reading, but who cannot achieve the benchmark?
7. If a student achieves a 10.4 grade equivalency, do we feel that this test is so accurate that withholding a diploma is warranted based on one-tenth of a point?

8. Do we believe that there are ways in which we can improve the reading scores of all students rather than just the struggling ones?

The board members agreed that these were issues that needed to be worked out. The conversation at our meeting was rich and thoughtful. However, they still believed that their job was to make policies, and they felt sure I could work out the details to implement the reading policy successfully. They reaffirmed their stand.

Although I did not achieve the goal of having the board reconsider their policy, the discussion around the table helped me to better understand their perspectives. I now understood that they believed that student achievement was mostly a question of motivation. If students tried harder, they would read better—and all students could achieve a 10.5 grade equivalency if they put their energy into reading. High-stakes testing, to this board, would in the end motivate students to succeed.

The board members clearly needed to learn more about reading and motivation. I suggested that in our next meeting, we invite several of our reading teachers to talk about how students acquire reading skills and how we assess them. My "honeymoon period" was in effect because I was still a very new superintendent, so the board members were willing to support me by hearing these reading presentations at our meetings, and they also agreed to attend a learning retreat. I asked the reading teachers to prepare a series of short presentations for the board's next meetings. I requested that the presentations model good instructional practices by being engaging, easily understood, interactive, and content-rich. At every opportunity, we wanted our board members to experience and eventually be able to articulate the elements of excellent instruction. The teachers were excited to have a chance to address the board. They were highly competent teachers, confident in their own skills.

The Teachers Present

The presentations of the reading teachers were excellent. The teachers organized important concepts in novel ways; the tasks were interactive and fun. The board began to look forward to the next presentations at our meetings.

In one meeting, the reading teachers gave the board members a short reading test and let them self-score it. They talked about reading for different purposes, the link between reading and writing, strategic reading, learning to read better by reading more, and reading for lifelong enjoyment. They talked about the purposes of good assessments:

(1) generating trend data that could be used to improve the curriculum; (2) diagnosing individual readers' strengths and weaknesses; (3) looking at long- and short-term growth in individual readers; (4) communicating results to parents, among teachers, and among grade levels; (5) and comparing instructional methods. They showed examples of different kinds of assessments, from standardized tests to teacher-collected data on each student.

One effective strategy involved a chart that listed specific reading goals and then detailed the multiple ways these goals could be assessed. The chart also detailed the extent to which standardized testing could assess these goals, and demonstrated that standardized testing served a specific assessment purpose, but was not useful for assessing many of the reading goals that we wanted our students to master.

In addition, the reading teachers told our own students' compelling stories to explain why scores might not ever reach the benchmark set by our board. These students were our own, and they were unique. One boy had endured extensive chemotherapy as an elementary student who battled cancer, and had consequently developed learning problems. His reading was below grade level, but he was the hardest working student in the class. Two years earlier, one of our students arrived from Mexico as a freshman with a third grade reading level. English was her second language, and she read poorly in her native Spanish. She was full of energy, loved school, and was making amazing progress. She had gained the equivalent of three-and-one-half years' growth in reading in a little over a year, but she was still far below her grade level. She would not continue in school if she did not receive her diploma. We believed we could help her bridge to a postsecondary experience that required a diploma, where she could continue to improve her reading while learning a skill to support herself as an adult, if she was supported appropriately.

These students had faces and names, and were the ones most likely to experience the negative effects of the new reading policy. The ground shifted slightly as these students became real to our board members.

In another session, our reading teachers asked the board members to read a two-page story and write several sentences about what they had read. After a short discussion, the teachers talked about how "summarizing" and "personal connections" were the most common responses to reading. They asked the board members to write again, this time making predictions, asking questions, and critiquing the author. This writing produced richer conversation that was more thought-provoking. The board members indicated that their own depth of understanding improved through the use of the varied responses to reading that our teachers demonstrated. It became obvious to them that a standardized test would not easily measure their improved understanding.

The reading teachers also presented an excellent assessment tool that required students to chart and set goals for their own responses to reading. In sharing this, the teachers pointed out that their goal in the classroom was not only to have students read well—they wanted their students to love reading.

Learning together strengthened our bond as a team. The board and I were not only working through a difficult issue, but we were setting in place the way we would approach difficult problems as a team in the future. The discussions, conversations, and mutual learning helped us develop mutual respect for each other's thinking. We learned the value of doing real work together as a method of team building. Trust began to cement our board–superintendent relationship.

We placed our learning retreat on the calendar and because of its success, it was eventually held several times each year. At the retreat, we asked the reading teachers to present content-rich material, once again reminding the board of the importance of modeling excellent instruction. The board members grew in their understanding of education, and over time became very knowledgeable about the issues and complexities of learning. I grew in additional ways as well. I began to understand that working with the board was all about the journey we took together. I was learning to value them as individuals and as a group. Together, we began to forge a team that trusted each other and had the best for students at the heart of our decisions. Even Don added his perspectives to the group. He was eager to take part in our retreat and learning sessions at the board meetings. He played the role of devil's advocate, and often posed questions that made us think in ways that we had not considered before. His questions added value to our team—but he still did not embrace our thinking.

Another Look at the Reading Policy

Don had crafted the reading policy, and now he feared that the other board members were moving away from it. He saw me as weak, and accused me of being afraid to stand up for high standards, telling me that he could not support me if I did not care about student learning. He talked to many community members and even wrote to our local newspaper accusing those of us on the side of eliminating the policy of not having high expectations for students.

After the newspaper published Don's letter, I attended a Rotary meeting at which several business people asked me why I did not want high standards for the kids. Did I really believe that a superintendent should be making student work easier, when everyone else thought that schools needed to be harder and more challenging? The topic had become so complex that it was difficult for me to answer the Rotarians' questions in a short, comprehensible way. This was not an easy time for me.

Initially, I had realized that there were two responsible courses of action that could be taken regarding the reading policy. The first was to inform the board of my concerns, and then implement the policy to the best of my ability. The second was to work actively to rescind this high-stakes policy by educating the board to understand that reading, in all its complexity, was not easily assessed with a one-shot test. I chose the second path because I believed that in the end, the policy would reflect poorly on the board, the school, and the community.

We continued to move forward in our discussions at board meetings and the retreat. The reading teachers drew parallels between the learning the board was doing and student learning in the classroom. They explained that the curriculum was "what" they wanted the board to learn about reading, and the instruction was "how" they used strategies to engage and to connect the board with the learning. In time, the teachers noted, they would discuss assessment—what had been learned, and how well. They wanted the board members to understand clearly that the way they were approaching the lesson plan for the board's learning was their everyday practice in the classroom.

Additionally, they wished to address "motivation" and its role in learning. Although the teachers acknowledged that different people are motivated in different ways, they began with the premise that, in most cases, positive rather than negative motivation leads to higher achievement. They posed this question: "Which is more motivating to you, the positive feelings that come with successfully mastering a difficult task or the negative penalties assigned if that same task isn't mastered?" Most of the board members agreed that positive task completion was a more powerful motivation than penalties.

The teachers then related research-based findings that suggested a loss of motivation when subject matter was too far below a student's level or too far above a student's ability for mastery. Achievement also declined in situations where students became overly anxious, a state we believed could be induced in our students by the potential penalty of not receiving a diploma. Exciting instruction, positive reinforcement, student-specific feedback, and support for mastering difficult concepts were given as examples of truly powerful motivators.

We posed this scenario for the board members:

A teacher comes to the principal and says, "I have a question for you that deals with motivation. I can legitimately give my student a grade of 'A' or I can legitimately give him a 'B.' Either is a fair grade. What will be more *motivating* to the student—to give him the 'A' and hope he will work to keep the 'A' next semester, or to give him the 'B' and hope that he will work to achieve an 'A' next semester?"

We asked the board members how they thought the principal should answer this question. Most of the board members said, "She should give the 'B' and the student will be motivated to achieve the 'A'." They also asserted that this was how the "real world" worked.

But when I asked them what they thought would most effectively motivate their own children, they all, with the exception of Don, chose the "A." Seeing the decision applied to their own children caused them to reconsider their answers.

We also asked the board to respond to this scenario: I put a $10 bill on the table and asked if any board members were motivated to earn this money quickly and easily—within a minute and with no particular knowledge needed. They were all agreeable. I held up a picture that had a background of black and white shapes. Embedded in the picture was a bearded man's face, also black and white. The background and the foreground blended together and the man's face was difficult to make out. I announced that anyone who could point out the bearded man's face in the picture would earn the $10. I also explained that we were timing this exercise, because we thought that those who could find the face more quickly were better learners, and the $10 would go to the first person to see the face.

Everyone tried, but after a full minute, no one had been able to pick out the man's face. I pointed it out. Most of the board members had an "a-ha" moment, because once they saw the man's face, they could not look at the picture without seeing it! Still, one board member could not see the face, and even an offer of $20 could not "motivate" him to see it. Motivation was not the key to this task; simple instruction was. When they were taught to see the picture, most of the board members could see it with ease. Even though the $10 bill "motivated" them, it did not translate into learning or achievement. Through activities like this one, the staff and board moved closer together on what we believed about motivation and its role in learning.

Picture Pi

As the board and I continued our learning sessions about instruction, assessment, and reading, several parents wrote to me. I shared the parents' letters with the board in our "Friday Weekly Information" packet. Parents who knew their children might not do well on the reading test were the most concerned.

One mother wrote that her child had had difficulties at birth. This girl had struggled throughout her years of school and had never had an easy time reading. Although she was not diagnosed as needing special educational services, her parents said she became overly anxious in testing situations and felt that she probably would not pass the test. The mother asked if there were waivers available, or if there were other ways that her daughter could complete the requirement. Another mother wrote to tell us that her son studied hard but still achieved only average grades. She believed that he did his best, but he was a slow and plodding reader. She said that he had never had much confidence in himself, and was feeling demoralized about his chances of receiving a diploma now that the reading test was a requirement. The mother felt sure that if he failed the test, her son would quit high school and never return. She told us that although he was a slow reader, he planned to go to the local community college—and she was terrified that our plans for higher standards might end his education altogether.

I did not hear from the majority of parents, who seemed not to worry about the policy—perhaps because they did not fully understand it, their children read well, or the future crisis was too far off. Several parents wrote and praised the board's actions in passing the policy. One letter stated the parents' hopes for my leadership as superintendent—that I would continue the work the board had so bravely undertaken, knowing that the only way students would achieve their best would be if we expected the best.

My fellow Rotarians had also expressed strong support for the board's actions. Early on, they were pleased that the board took the stand they had, and as business people, they wanted me to know they supported the policy. After a few months, I decided to ask if I might speak again at one of the Rotary meetings. I took the opportunity to talk to the group about my hopes for our high school, and how I believed that we could bring student achievement to a higher level. However, I admitted that I had some questions about the reading policy. I posed some of the same questions to the Rotarians that I had posed to the board, assuring them that I was committed to raising achievement levels for all students, not only the ones who were poor readers. The Rotarians were supportive. Most of them understood the complexities once they were explained in detail. I offered to ask one of our reading teachers to come to a meeting and address the group if they were interested, and they accepted this invitation.

The effect was somewhat different than I had anticipated. I expected impassioned questions about our standards and comments about the preparation of students for the world of work. After the presentation, few questions were asked. The Rotarians indicated that they felt confident that we knew what we were doing. They did not seem to be overly concerned that we were discussing the policy's viability. What we thought was going to be a huge hurdle was reduced to a speed bump, by taking the time to explain why we were examining our earlier decision.

In retrospect, I believe that by this point our board had generally come to the unofficial decision that they would abandon the policy. However, before making a final decision, they decided to take more time. They had begun to enjoy the stimulation of meetings where they learned about the reading process—where they learned about learning. The need was not yet pressing to make a decision on the policy, and they wanted to think of a way to disengage from it gracefully, believing it would be awkward to reverse a decision that they had so publicly championed.

We continued to investigate. We tested all juniors to predict what our failure rate would be a year later if the policy was in effect. The rate was higher than the board could comfortably accept. There was still some lingering sentiment that if we worked harder with these students, they could make the grade. However, now we knew that more students would not pass the test at this level than originally envisioned. Additionally, the teaching staff believed that many students who had difficulty reading had other special gifts that would enable them to be successful in life, and this sentiment was effectively conveyed to the board. We strongly believed that withholding high school diplomas when they had met all other requirements would have had a crippling negative effect from which many students would never recover.

Last, I contacted a representative from the company that published the Gates MacGinitie reading test. I explained the school's policy—that the test was going to be used to withhold a high school diploma from students who did not meet a particular standard. The Gates MacGinitie representative was knowledgeable and helpful, and understood the problem of using a norm-referenced test for such a purpose. He wrote a letter to our board explaining that the test was never intended as a one-time measure for graduation decisions. The letter also predicted the number of students that we could expect to fail every year with a requirement of a 10.5 grade level equivalent in both comprehension and vocabulary. He warned that even with Herculean efforts, we probably would not be able to bring 100% of our students to that level.

The board now agreed we should abandon the policy. The question they now confronted was how to accomplish reversing the decision without losing face. I suggested to them that one of the benefits of our long investigation of the policy's efficacy was that time had dulled the interest that had originally been shown by the community. I shared my Rotary experience with them and recommended that, based on our confidence in the reading teachers, we should shift our public focus to improving the reading level of "all" students. With this final piece of information, the board voted 6–1 to rescind the policy, with Don's being the dissenting vote.

The board asked the English Department to revise the curriculum to reflect an emphasis on improving reading levels for all students. The reading and English teachers were excited to take on this project, and set out with passion. Our excitement was very real. We talked to the press about the new curriculum we planned to create, detailing what we hoped to accomplish and offering an interesting series of stories to print about teaching and learning, using many of the examples that we had explored with our board. When the final story on the reading policy came out, it was as a footnote to the main story about the curriculum that we were developing.

Fast Forward

At the end of my third year, instead of administering a reading requirement that would have failed to award a number of students their high school diplomas, we had developed an English curriculum that had improved reading levels for all students and gained respect throughout the country. The Mid-continent Research for Education and Learning Education Lab (MCREL) featured our research-based English curriculum as a model in one of their documentaries. The same year that we would have denied many students a diploma for their reading scores, our high school won the U.S. Department of Education Blue Ribbon Award, largely because of the work of our principal and the teachers in the area of curriculum. And not long after, our realtors began using our school district as a selling point for home buyers!

What We All Learned

My stand on the reading policy had consequences. Don never again voted in favor of retaining me as superintendent. He found even greater fault with my thinking and decisions after the policy was rescinded. Our relationship remained contentious for the remainder of our time together.

However, if pressed, I do believe he would have acknowledged that he enjoyed our fiery debates and appreciated finding someone as passionate as he on the topics of teaching and learning. Perhaps neither of us understood that our passion and single-mindedness made us more similar than different.

Prior to becoming a superintendent, I had accepted the conventional thinking about board–superintendent relations. The literature suggested that the board should set the vision and create the policies related to the vision and the superintendent should implement the policies and run the day-to-day operations of the district. I realized rather quickly that, in reality, the issue of who leads whom is sometimes messy and gray. Superintendents often find themselves in situations where they must provide leadership to the board, and at times, even confront board members' inappropriate or unproductive behaviors.

Each board member sees their district in a different way. Some see it through the eyes of their own children, through a neighbor who is employed at the school, and perhaps through the eyes of their taxpayer friends who meet weekly for breakfast. The multiple perspectives of board members are similar to the story of the *Seven Blind Men*. In this story, seven blind men touch a different part of an elephant, and then each man describes the elephant from his own experience. One touches the tail and says that an elephant is a thin, ropey animal; another touches the tusk and asserts that an elephant is hard and sharp. Individual board members all see real but sometimes contradictory aspects of the district and its workings. They see things differently from fellow board members. Keeping the good will of seven people while bringing them to a collective view of the complete "elephant" is one of the leadership challenges of the superintendent. In order for the "whole" to be understood, each board member's perspective must be respected and treated as important. By putting the various individual perspectives on the table, the board can collectively come closer to seeing a whole they can share.

A superintendent must lead all board members both collectively and individually. I found that success in working through difficult issues with the board depended on the relationships we established. Mutual trust, respect, and credibility provided the foundation for us to feel comfortable talking openly with one another and expressing our respective points of view. While the superintendent works with the board as a whole, the relationships between each board member and the superintendent must be established individually. The ability of each of us to understand personal quirks, thinking, experiences, and passions helped us stay open-minded and respectful. We learned that when we were able to honor every person's viewpoint, even if we did not all agree, we gained each other's respect.

The leadership of the superintendent is more powerful when it is grounded in a strong vision of teaching and learning. In order to lead effectively, I needed to know what I believed and why I believed it. These core beliefs sustained me through the tough times. When I was not always sure of the outcome, I did know that what we were trying to accomplish was right for our students. My beliefs kept me focused and grounded.

Aspiring superintendents might consider that quality relationships come from working and solving problems together. Considering the superintendent and board as a "team of eight" rather than one superintendent and seven board members is the first mental model that new superintendents should put in place. Generally, everyone is eager to help solve a problem in a constructive way. In my case, there were people more skilled than I in the area we were studying. The teachers were more persuasive than I could have been in demonstrating the issues that the reading policy presented. They "opened" the doors of their classrooms to let the board see the day-to-day challenges of teaching their students. They made the work engaging so our board felt that the time spent studying the issue was worthwhile and interesting. Asking our teachers to be the teachers of our board was a tangible way for me to show my confidence in them. Using a format of ongoing study gave us time to let a complicated issue "evolve and get solved." Our success came from taking the journey together. We emerged with the positive feelings that accompany thorough work and sound decision making. Those feelings provided a foundation for us as we went on to tackle other important issues on our agenda.

There is no passion like that of a new superintendent. Now that I am older and more experienced, I realize how exceptional the journey was that our board members were willing to undertake. They were willing to learn—to suspend their beliefs and question their assumptions. Most importantly, they were willing to revise their thinking. It was a remarkable time for the board, our teachers, and me, as together, we learned and grew in our understanding of relationships, organizational dynamics, and the curriculum of reading. By working together, we were a powerful team that made a wonderful difference in the lives of our students.

REFERENCES

National Commission on Excellence in Education. (1983). *A nation at risk: The imperative for educational reform*. Washington, DC: U.S. Government Printing Office.

Most of us at some point in our career have to face the fact that we cannot control everything that happens in our district. As we mentioned in our introduction, we learn that even logical plans implemented skillfully can meet unexpected, uncontrollable obstacles. This can have serious consequences, from the lack of achievement for students to the loss of our jobs. Our anonymous contributor shares his courageous story of holding fast to what is best for children in the face of adversity, and ultimately having to make the decision whether to fight for his job or not. NSSE has never published an anonymous contribution before, but we agreed that "Juan's" story was too valuable not to share.

CHAPTER 6

The Importance of a "Good Fit"

PAUL KELLEHER, WITH JUAN MARTINEZ (PSEUDONYM)

The Sunnyside Independent School District Board of Education selected Dr. Juan Martinez as its new superintendent of schools by an unusually cohesive 7–0 vote in 2002. In describing the superintendent search, the local paper characterized the board as highly politicized and often divisive. So the board's unanimity in appointing Juan to their most important position was surprising. Board members said Juan's knowledge of both academic and budget issues impressed them. Perhaps most important, according to at least one trustee, was Juan's promise to stay out of politics.

Just over 2 years later, the board rejected an extension of Juan's 3-year contract by a 3–2 vote. Although the expressed reason was disappointing test scores, the paper reported that a majority of the board members were unhappy with Juan's leadership. Subsequently, the newspaper gave the board one of its weekly "Idiot Awards" for denying Martinez a contract extension, noting that he had made significant progress in dealing with parents and students and in stabilizing the district's finances, but recognizing that he had also, perhaps, disturbed the status quo by aggressively bringing accountability to bond projects and the like.

What happened in just a little over 2 years that such a promising partnership went awry? What turned fiscal accountability, as described by the media, into a negative? What connections did a political scandal involving bribery and voting fraud have to do with Juan's abbreviated Sunnyside superintendency? This chapter tries to answer those questions and others, arguing that the "fit" between superintendent and district is a critical consideration from the very beginning, and suggesting that Juan's mistake may have been his choice to accept the Sunnyside position in the first place.

Juan traced his journey from his triumphant arrival to his recognition of departure as his only viable option in a wide-ranging conversation with Paul Kelleher, volume co-editor, who produced a transcript of that dialogue for joint review and revision. In writing the chapter, Kelleher consulted other sources, including local newspaper reports and board minutes. As much as possible, the chapter presents Juan's story directly. His words are in italics throughout. His name and other details have been changed throughout the chapter in order to protect Juan's anonymity. Material from newspaper sources has been modified, and specific citations not included, to protect the identity of the principal figures in this article.

Sunnyside: The Political Context

Sunnyside Independent School District is an impoverished school district in the southern United States. Most of its roughly 12,000 students are Hispanic and economically disadvantaged. Many are English language learners. The schools have a history of poor achievement.

Deep-seeded and long-standing political conflict had an enormous impact on Sunnyside and on Juan during his tenure. For many years, the board had been chronically polarized between two warring political factions, with ascendancy determined by the annual board elections. Because of conflicts with the board, Juan's predecessor had resigned from the job before a scheduled retirement. At that time, the state education agency reprimanded board members for overstepping their authority and actually engaging in micromanagement of the schools.

In some ways, the most significant political event during Juan's tenure in Sunnyside occurred a few months after his arrival. The district attorney indicted a number of local officials who were charged with bribery and corruption. None of them were current board members, although one was employed by the district. However, the alleged head of what the local paper called a "political machine" had begun his political career on the Sunnyside board before serving in other elected capacities. Three of those accused had relatives who were current Sunnyside trustees, and were members of the political majority on the board after the 2002 election. According to the media, the "head" of the operation had maintained power by orchestrating his successors. The indictment included charges of bribery, breaking state election laws, and bid rigging of contracts, and included examples of the ongoing influence of indictees on the Sunnyside school board, as when board members were allegedly pressured to vote for certain contracts and project managers.

Juan, of course, had no involvement in or control over any of these events; they all occurred before his arrival. However, as this chapter will show, the scandal had a profound impact on the work he did, especially in facilities management; on conflicts he had with the board majority; and on his ultimate decision to leave.

A Triumphant Beginning: The First Summer

When Juan was interviewed for the Sunnyside job in mid-2002, he thought that the increased rigor of state accountability tests would mean that improving student performance was likely to be the board's top priority:

The one thing that I prepare for the most whenever I'm going for an interview in a school district as a superintendent is curriculum and instruction. That makes up three-fourths of my entire binder. In Sunnyside, it was about that much [holding his finger about 2 inches apart]. *I was very intimately knowledgeable about the kids' scores.*

Through the interview process, he learned that the board also had another urgent priority that he would need to address immediately:

The finances were what they sensed was the most pressing urgency. They felt they had a negative budget, a deficit budget of about $2 million. What they wanted was a balanced budget. And we had to work on that. . . . I mean we worked on the budget right away because the budget has to be approved [within a few months]. *We had to address that.*

When he began his superintendency, he was surprised to discover another, even more urgent problem: The facilities were in chaos.

But the other thing that hit me that I wasn't expecting was that we had a construction crisis where we had [the majority] *of campuses that were not going to be ready to open up and receive the students because they were all going through remodeling.*

The reason that the district was trying to remodel all its schools at the same time, and had not followed a more orderly plan, could be traced back to the controversial decisions about hiring an architect and project manager 3 years earlier.

It was kind of like the explosion that builds up in a volcano. . . . It was cumulative. It was building up from decisions that were made back in '99 that were not the best. . . . Instead of hiring three architects to handle $35 million or $40 million worth of construction, one was hired. Instead of . . . getting one from here, the neighborhood, the person was from [out of town]. *Also, instead of . . . three general contractors, only one got hired. Third . . . there was a project manager. But the project manager was essentially caught between a rock and a hard place because there were vested interests and connections to the general contractor and to the architect. I don't know if there were any to the project manager. They were all . . . in positions where they couldn't be effective.*

Because board politics—and, as the indictment alleged, possibly board corruption—determined the contract decisions, the crucial working relationships among the architect, general contractor, and project manager had become politicized.

There was infighting between the general contractor, project manager, and architects. . . . And the kids were caught in the middle. . . . It got in the way of getting the job done. And the schools were not going to be ready because if anybody made a movement, they would step on somebody's toes—including board members. . . . If one board member would criticize one individual, say the general contractor, the other faction, or the other group that recommended that person, they would be pointing the finger at each other.

Through hands-on, personal involvement, Juan gradually began to understand the political landscape and was able to neutralize inappropriate board involvement.

I didn't really know what had transpired, so it was naiveness that helped. And I started getting little glimpses and senses of that in the discussions of the folks around the table because I attended every construction meeting, every week on Mondays. If we had other critical meetings, I would attend them also . . . in addition to the summary meetings on Monday.

He came to see his political naïveté as an asset in this situation.

They needed to have the situation where someone came from the outside that didn't have any political ties, no baggage, no allegiances, didn't owe any favors or debts but could just tell the truth. And say, "OK, guys, you're messing up; you're messing up; you're messing up. You two need to work it out together." Which is essentially what I did. The architect was blaming the general contractor. The general contractor, the architect. I said, "You need to take care of it. We're holding each one of you accountable." And I would report to the board.

Personnel and political issues, however, were not the only challenges Juan faced. One of the area's rainiest summers further delayed construction work.

That summer we had a level of flooding that's supposed to happen only once in 100 years. It further delayed construction. What I figured out was that we had just about 4 or 5 weeks to get everything in order.... And everybody was just watching to see how I could handle it.... We sat down with all the stakeholders, essentially the construction people. I sat them all around, and I said, "Look, guys, I need to know whether we're going to be able to open up schools. If not, I have to develop a Plan B.... What I told them was, "I want you to put together a plan that tells me what it will take to get it done... in terms of human resources, in terms of money, in terms of time. If it means opening up Saturday and Sunday, if it means opening up late at night having access to the buildings, we'll do it".... So they came back with a plan.

Even though Juan had two administrators directly responsible for monitoring the construction, his personal attendance at construction meetings enabled him to employ his problem solving and conflict management skills as well as his executive authority to facilitate decision making and commitment.

Even though I had both people there, I was still there because whenever I needed to bring people together, get it to a resolution, get agreement, and summarize... at the end, I was the one who was doing that. But I would just let everybody do their part, and they knew I was there. And when I needed to come in, I would come in.

The construction work continued to the last minute, but all schools were able to open in part because of Juan's personal involvement, doing what he calls the "Giuliani thing":

The one that came the closest again was the high school. And we were there Sunday (before school opened). I was there moving furniture, putting little plates on electrical outlets on the floor and setting up.... With the custodians and the teachers. Bringing in tacos for the custodians... to continue working Saturday, Sunday. And we got it opened.... And everybody took notice. We were able to overcome it.

People recognized and appreciated Juan's visible and personal involvement.

The board noticed and they complimented me publicly. They liked the fact that the superintendent was there with the people and worked side by side. . . . The staff, the custodians, and the teachers, the union rep who happens to be there at Sunnyside High School, was very complimentary of the fact that we were there with them. . . . Being right there when the emergency needed to be taken care of. That was not the only time that they told me that.

In addition to overcoming political fractures in the construction operation, during this first summer, Juan had to confront the political divisions across the board in his first public board meeting. The controversy involved the board's inability to agree on a district insurance agent to write employee insurance policies.

One bloc, one . . . group on the board, the one that came in before I came to work . . . had just knocked out the previous insurance agent of record. They had just knocked out the previous one hired by the other board faction. The new group wanted to institute their own agent.

In the first meeting the other group, now out of power, tried to counterattack, saying that board couldn't have a new agent of record. Their gentleman didn't have a certain certificate. And I'm caught in the middle, and so are 700 teachers and 800 paraprofessionals. So you have about 1,500 folks that are caught in the middle because if insurance is not acted on there, there might not be enough turn around time to have new insurance . . . settled and agreed on—either continuation or replacement—by the time we start school in August.

Because of the consequences, Juan successfully risked mediating this dispute in a public board meeting.

So I had to mediate that . . . in a public board meeting—by making the appeal that we had to make a decision on something . . . that night because if not 1,500 employees would be without insurance. . . . I spoke out at the very end. And that's what made the board take action. Now the other matter about the certificate—that could be researched and investigated. But action needed to be taken on that night. So it happened.

Juan's action increased his credibility among the staff:

The other folks, like the employees . . . and also the executive team members, they felt that took courage and that it was very good. . . . I didn't see it as courage. I saw it as just the job that I have to do. And that it was very critical that I spoke up because the board needed to take action. And if someone else had mentioned it, maybe they wouldn't have done it. It made a difference also who it had come from.

Peace and Tranquility: "One Big Happy Team"

Juan's summer of triumph, a result of his visible, personal interventions in balancing the budget, getting the schools open on time, and resolving the board's insurance impasse, brought a period of unusual harmony among board members and the superintendent in Sunnyside:

I had a honeymoon of about a year and a half. . . . I only had one very challenging board meeting, and it was only the first one. . . . And after that meeting, the board became very peaceful, very collaborative.

Juan attributes board tranquility not only to the credibility that summer built for him, that but also to the work in board development that he undertook with the help of consultants from the state School Boards' Association:

I had mentioned in my interview that the very first thing we needed to know besides what are the three goals you want me to work on this year. . . . "What are going to be the rules of the game?" We play baseball in the backyard. What's the line that defines a foul ball? So they knew before I even came in that I was going to do that. So we did board operating procedures . . . goal setting, and team building.

And that helped the board set aside some differences. If they hated each other or disliked each other for something else, what they found out was that we were all there for the same reason, and that we all had something in common, which was the kids. We wanted the best thing for the kids. . . . When we went to [the state school board conference], six out of seven went. We were all a big happy team . . . I had scheduled it so we all could go have dinner together, all the board members and those of us who took our spouses; we had dinner with the spouses. So it was going great. It was going great.

Improvements to Curriculum and Instruction

In the fall of 2002, during this period of board harmony, Juan focused more of his attention to what he thought his role should be: that of instructional leader. At the time, the state already had one of the nation's most mature and fully implemented state accountability models. But in 2003, big changes were coming:

We were transitioning into a new state assessment. . . . We knew that the rigor was going to be higher and the extent of testing was going to encompass other skills . . . the level of thinking of the kids was going to have to be different, and the teachers needed to make those adjustments.

Juan wanted to improve the district's instructional delivery. Like many state superintendents, his vision was of a comprehensive school improvement model that strongly aligned curriculum, instruction, and assessment in order to improve student achievement. A key component of the model Juan sought to implement was the regular use of student performance data by teachers to diagnose instructional needs and to modify curriculum and instructional strategies:

Planning, aligning . . . data desegregation and item analysis of how the kids have actually done just prior to getting out of school. You take that information and you do your modifications, your adjustments, your tweaking for the following year.

Another key to this model was support for quality curriculum and instructional development work that teams of teachers would provide to improve programs continuously in response to ongoing student assessment. Put simply, strengthening how teachers actually did their work was crucial. In Sunnyside, a "curriculum collaborative" of teachers did most of this alignment work during the summer:

And the only way it was going to happen is if this collaborative changes—changes the teachers, the way that they do things. . . . My folks . . . felt that the collaborative had deteriorated [over time] and they were producing poor products. The quality was down. And also the quality of the folks generating the products was not there. . . . But the root of the problem was . . . the framework we set up in terms of how to do this curriculum alignment.

Juan and his staff strengthened accountability by changing the work culture of the teachers, rewarding them for the products they produced, rather than the time they put in:

I was after two things. I was trying to change the curriculum collaborative from being paid for time to being paid for product, from seat work to product. . . . We created a hierarchy or framework by which we showed how the product was going to be checked. . . . They had to be recommended and had to apply to be part of this curriculum collaborative team. We also instituted team leaders—to check the quality, do scope and sequences, concept maps, benchmarks assessments, and a resource guide.

They also improved the quality by making curriculum collaborative work more competitive:

The second thing that I was trying to do was to break away from what I call the "ball and chain" of getting only the teachers that are available in the summer to write. We paid a little bit less for curriculum collaborative than for the summer school. We had competition among our own programs. I thought we could . . . have them make a commitment in . . . the spring . . . April and May. Then, if they want to do summer school, they can as long as they turn in the product before they start summer school. . . . So we made it very competitive to the summer school. . . . I was changing also the model of how the work was being produced. They all agreed to it.

Although Juan reorganized the curriculum process and put strategies in place that were meant to lead to a stronger curriculum, more accountability for teachers, and more rigor, and presumably better student achievement, the results were not immediately apparent in the first round of the new testing program in the spring of 2004. Because of the higher standards, some of the elementary schools that had previously achieved "exemplary" status from the state, based on aggregate test scores, fell a notch to "improving" status. This drop mirrored a pattern that occurred throughout the region and the state. Nevertheless, this drop in scores ultimately became the justification for the board decision to refuse to extend Juan's contract.

Winning the Support of Principals

Juan's organizational initiatives did not just focus on teacher accountability. A major organizational change that he initiated strengthened principal accountability as well, by incorporating review of a school's student testing results into the principals' annual evaluation:

We . . . look at their data from the prior year and then look at their data for the ongoing year in terms of the benchmarks.

In spite of the extra work, in his first year, Juan also took the unusual step, in a district the size of Sunnyside, of evaluating each of his principals personally. In his work with them, he clarified his belief in the importance of instructional leadership:

I put a straight line from all the principals to me. . . . And they knew my philosophical stand and my belief that the most important thing for that principal to do was to become very knowledgeable [about curriculum and instruction] *and that I valued that. I didn't want them delegating that to an instructional assistant. They needed to be in there. They needed to know what direction their department, their groups of kids, their campus needed to go instructionally.*

So I shared . . . when I felt there was a weakness in one of them, I let them know that I wanted them to get stronger.

Where he saw weaknesses in principals' academic knowledge, he tried to build capacity by encouraging them to attend professional development workshops:

Because we knew we were going to be looking at curriculum in the summer, I sent my middle school principals . . . to "Curriculum Boot Camp" because I felt that my secondary were the ones who needed the most help.

Juan also took an active role in hiring principals, looking for those who could provide leadership in curriculum and instruction to their faculties:

When I chose my principal for one campus . . . I chose an instructional principal for that high school, a "test score queen." Also, when I made my selections for the elementary, they knew I didn't look at color. I didn't look at gender. I looked at what their knowledge was in curriculum. That was my biggest thing. They knew it because when I asked my questions, they were all centered around curriculum and instruction.

Although these steps heightened performance expectations and increased accountability, Juan found the principals to be responsive. They appreciated the greater access to him that their new reporting relationship provided. They also appreciated that their relationships with other central office administrators, their former supervisors, changed.

Also the other folks were now supportive, rather than, as they call it, "cracking the whip." There was only one person who could "crack the whip," I guess [laughing].

Juan did not meet strong resistance from principals to his organizational changes. Instead, he developed a deeper rapport with them:

They respected me a lot. . . . I can think of two reasons. One is leadership style. That I'm very participatory. I hardly ever say, "You have to do this." Or, "You're required to do that." It's very rare that I don't give them options. It's only when we don't have an option, or I feel very strongly that it needs to be done.

Then the second thing, I think . . . they respected the knowledge base that came from experience. That I have walked in their shoes. That I had been at all levels and so they respected also that I was knowledgeable in curriculum and instruction—not just management of the organization, not just finance, maintenance, and operations.

His staff, both principals and central office administrators, recognized that Juan was a different kind of leader from what they had become accustomed to in Sunnyside:

I heard several times before I left, it was the first time that they felt like they could talk to somebody that would know, understand what they were talking about when they were talking curriculum. That hadn't happened before. And I think it has a lot to do with generations, and decades, and types of folks that had been there before who were athletic directors and maintenance and operations people.

They would follow me to the end of the earth. . . . That's how they felt. Some of them wanted to follow me to wherever I was going. But, you know, those things you don't control.

A Confirmation of Success

Most of the press coverage that superintendents receive focuses on the negative—a controversy in which they are protagonists or criticism by the public or staff. At the end of his first 6 months in Sunnyside, the local paper published an unusually positive, highly flattering feature about Juan, which described his active, hands-on, visible work style, personified by regular visits to schools and classrooms. It commended his accomplishments, including his personal involvement in opening schools on time. More significantly, it quoted others praising Juan; principals, union representatives, and teachers all had highly laudatory things to say about both his work and character.

The article also described the ongoing fraud and bribery investigation and Juan's support of ethics training for the board, noting his expressed commitment to doing "the right thing." The piece concluded with the observation that the board had a "mixed reaction" to Juan's style, noting that it was possible that the board had heard Juan's commitment to staying out of politics as a confirmation of "business as usual."

The Three Milestones

Juan points out three milestones—conflicts with the board—that ended his honeymoon and led to his departure from Sunnyside.

The Bond Parent Advisory Committee

The first situation occurred late in 2002, about 2 months after the grand jury's indictments in the bribery and corruption scandal were handed down. This conflict with some board members involved the control of the management of construction work, including the awarding of contracts for the new bond issue, passed just before his arrival.

So we had a second bond for about the same amount—$35–40 million. Because I had just had to clean up the spilled milk from the earlier bond, I knew that we had to do this one differently.

Juan wanted to give effective control to a cross-role group, including parents, who would oversee the work.

One of the things that I strongly believe ... is empowering the stakeholders. My first conflict ... with the board president was in setting up a Bond Parent Advisory Committee. Let them handle the construction delivery phase, the selection of the architect, the selection of the general contractor, and determine if a project manager was necessary, and the delivery method of the construction ... But there was an opposition of philosophy between the board president and myself. So that was the first test.

Because he felt strongly about the importance of this change, despite the board president's opposition and the heated discussion they had privately, Juan went ahead and put the proposal on the board agenda for public discussion and decision. At the board meeting, one of the other board members argued that the Bond Advisory Committee was a good idea. The board president said nothing, offering no rebuttal, and the motion passed unanimously. However, Juan felt that the president and the board majority resented that he brought this issue forward for a public discussion and that his action, in effect, did "freeze the funds."

We put it on the agenda and let the board decide. So the board decided to let the bond parents handle it. But essentially what that did was change the way business was done in that district in terms of parceling out contracts.

That was a turning point to change the culture of the organization.... Our board was clean and straight those three years because we placed that power in the parents' and the community's hands. You had three board members there (at Advisory Council meetings). You had two from the majority and one from the minority. But essentially, the reality was that rarely did all three appear ... because they knew that it wasn't going to make a difference. The parents were in total control.

It changed the dynamics of how election contributions were procured because the recommendations came from parents. The parents weren't going to be looking for political contributions. So there was no money in it anymore ... I just wanted to make sure that we had a clean school district operation whenever it came to giving out contracts.

The Direct Intrusion of the Grand Jury Indictments

The second milestone conflict occurred the following spring, and centered on the indicted district employee. Juan felt that the school district should take some action:

It was the fact that he was on camera being taken downtown and that's not something that you want kids to be exposed to as with someone who continues working and going into schools.

He sought legal counsel in finding an appropriate course of action:

I had the advice of legal counsel, HR, and another firm that we have on retainer. I don't do things in isolation. I always involve folks. Because it was a very delicate matter. Their advice was that I could have terminated the employee.

Even though he had the legal authority to fire the employee, the board's legal counsel advised Juan against termination because the attorney did not think the board would support it:

But our own school legal counsel told me . . . that they [the board] probably would reverse it. When he [the employee] filed a grievance, because that would have been the next step for him, file a grievance against the superintendent, and then my decision would be reversed and the employee would be reinstated.

Juan then decided on a temporary suspension and a reassignment.

What I did with him is no different than what I did with another person who got suspended for breaking board policy. . . . So we just did the suspension for a certain amount of time. What we were doing was waiting out . . . the legal process.

Although Juan also had the power to enact the suspension, some board members objected:

There was a feeling, again, on the part of the same board member, the first board president that I started out with . . . that I shouldn't have suspended that guy even if I had legal advice from their own attorney, and the other attorneys who at that time were also doing retainer work for us on personnel matters.

The employee in question then filed a complaint against Juan and the district with the Equal Employment Opportunity Commission (EEOC), alleging discrimination. In the spring of 2003, the board went into executive session to discuss the suit with both Juan and their legal counsel. Even though the employee had not filed an actual lawsuit and had made no claim to financial damages, the board proposed to reach a financial settlement with him. Juan and the board's attorney recommended against any settlement:

We felt that, the legal counsel also, that it was too premature because there is a process that is gone through by any entity, whether it's the EEOC or the OCR [Office of Civil Rights]. *It doesn't matter. Everything goes through a process. There had been no investigation done about whether there was a valid claim of discrimination or not by the employment office . . . nothing.*

The board disregarded this advice and decided on a settlement. They chastised Juan for suspending the employee and ordered him to write a letter of apology, and voted to award the employee approximately $25,000 for damages and legal expenses. Ironically, according to the local paper, the motion to approve this settlement was made and seconded by those board members who were closely aligned with other indicted officials.

A Legislative Audit: The Proposed Tradeoff

The third milestone conflict—a state audit—occurred the following year, and was a result of the decision to approve the settlement for the indicted district employee:

The reaction of . . . the minority on the board was to report the board about . . . the fact of that gentleman that got a settlement. . . . The result of that incident prompted the feeling in one of the board members or two to report to the [state education agency] *what they felt was inappropriate.*

They talked to the [paper] *that same night or the following day and it was in the* [paper]. *But it didn't stop there. I think there was a call made to the state. . . . I don't know whether it was* [the state education agency] *or a state representative . . . to request that there be an audit. . . . We got notice of that in the spring.*

It was announced that the legislature had ordered the audit because of constituent complaints about district finances, in particular the recent $25,000 settlement. The board majority, predictably, wanted to fight the state audit. They proposed filing a lawsuit to prevent it, and they asked Juan to support such an effort.

I was asked if I wanted to go along with filing a lawsuit against a state representative or against the educational agency. I would not go along with that. . . . We had nothing to hide. There was nothing wrong with the [budget people] *coming in and doing an audit of what we were doing and whether there was anything we needed to improve on. I didn't think it was right to file a lawsuit against someone that had made a recommendation to audit our school district.*

The board president, according to Juan, suggested putting Juan's contract extension up for discussion and approval at the same meeting where they would discuss taking legal action to stop the audit with Juan's support:

They wanted to know . . . if I would be party to a legal action. And at that time, also, the mention of the contract extension or renewal was brought up for the following week. . . . It was at the same time that we were talking about the audit, and there was a special meeting taking place the following week. . . . They said, "We can go ahead and also put the contract on."

Juan felt that proposed timing of the two actions at the same special meeting was not a coincidence. He refused to support any legal action, and told the board that they could consider his contract extension later in the year:

Had the recommendation about the contract been separated out, I would not have had a problem. But I saw it very clearly right there—an opportunity to trade. . . . That just goes against what I stand for.

The audit of the district did take place despite board opposition. Ironically, the evaluation did not find financial irregularities, perhaps because of the Bond Advisory Committee that Juan established. The audit, however, did find that the board was failing at providing appropriate leadership for the district, in the process minimizing the superintendent's ability to accomplish stated district goals and objectives.

The Final Decision: "Just Let It Go"

In a split vote, 3–2, the board did not approve an extension of Juan's contract when they considered it a few months later in the summer of 2004. Their decision essentially gave him close to a year's notice, until his 3-year contract was actually over. Juan's key decision at this point was whether or not to try to rally support and pressure the board to reverse its decision. Some of his staff and some community and board members offered to support such an effort:

They found out that—at the end of the second year, the summer—that I was just going to be able to run out the clock and spend the last year there. They felt very bad. Because of the fact that we were doing well in all areas, it just didn't make any sense to them. The principal ranks, the central office ranks, a couple of the community, and some board members also. They asked what is it that they could do to help, what is it that I wanted them to do. And I said, "Nothing." Because I felt like I didn't want any people to get caught in the crossfire.

Juan also felt that making a fight out of it might not be the best decision for his career:

They were ready to do it, demonstrations and walks and whatever. But I said, "No. Just let it go." Because I'm of the belief that if people feel that you're good, that you can do a good job, then you find another place. I said, "I'm not place-bound." If I put up a fight, and then I happen to win, then I'm only good there. I can't go anywhere else. If I happen to put up a fight, and I lose it, then I'm not going to be able to go anywhere else. So I said, "Leave it alone." They did; they respected my wishes.

Political Crossfire

It's incredible the things that happen when you have politics get involved in the education of children . . .

Juan came to Sunnyside pledging to stay out of politics. As this story illustrates, his apolitical stance helped him to effectively manage the health insurance crisis he faced in his first board meeting and the facilities challenges of that first summer. In spite of his efforts to remain politically unaffiliated, and to be fair and impartial in responding to all sides, the political vortex of Sunnyside eventually sabotaged his tenure.

I got caught in a crossfire. Because I was asked from the very beginning to take sides. . . . And I had just learned . . . that you can't do that. You have to treat everybody the same. They all represent community. . . . So I didn't take sides . . . and . . . by not taking sides, I, too, took sides. It's one of those ironic things in life because I wanted to treat everybody the same. And I did.

Because, by not going with the majority and being inclusive of everybody, I actually took a side of treating everybody the same way. And I didn't side with them. I sided with the general population . . . everybody. . . . I decided not to neglect them just because they weren't in the majority. Whatever we did with two thirds of the district, we did with one third of the district. I could not, I would not neglect them. It's a matter of principle, I guess.

As he looked back on his tenure in Sunnyside, reflecting on the three milestones leading to his departure, Juan saw his values and beliefs at stake in each situation:

I could have done something different at any of those, but, when I go back and think about it, I don't think I could have or should have. I would not change any of those. It would violate what I stand for and what I believe. I believe in empowerment—that's the first milestone. Second one—doing at least what is the minimum that's required when someone has done something that really is not appropriate as an employee of a public school district. The third milestone—I just didn't feel I could support going after someone that had heard from a constituent or someone in the community to do an audit of us. I think . . . you're going to get some criticism . . . but you always can benefit from the audit.

The Lessons Learned

Even though he does not see himself acting differently if he faced those three milestones again, Juan learned some important lessons from his Sunnyside experience that have import for educational leaders in general.

Do Your Homework

Juan characterized the summer chaos of the facilities and buildings as the first surprise of his Sunnyside superintendency. However, he actually had an earlier surprise about Sunnyside when it was announced that he was a finalist for the position. That earlier surprise resulted from what he now sees as his failure to do his homework thoroughly:

I was one of the finalists. I had already done the headhunter interview, the first tier. It was narrowed down to just three or five of us.

My own newspaperman from [Juan's previous school district] brought me a folder full of newspaper clippings of all the things that had happened that I was not aware of, like that [the state education agency] had had a monitor in there, in Sunnyside. They had done investigations. That they were on probation when I got there.

I focused so much on studying the district to prepare for the interview. I focused on the academics; I focused on the community, the business side, the performance, the finance.

One piece that I didn't do my homework on was the board politics. I didn't study the board like [I should have]. [With my previous position, I had] interviewed quite a few folks that had lived there or had a relative there or had worked there. So I did very good homework about that dimension of that board. And I took it with my eyes wide open. But I didn't repeat that with Sunnyside until I had already been asked to interview.

In the excitement of successfully competing for a public position like superintendent of schools, it is easy for a candidate to forget that the board's choice to offer the job is only half of the process. The candidate's choice to accept it is equally important. An informed candidate choice requires careful and systematic homework on all aspects of the district before accepting a position.

Wait for the Next Bus

In 2002, Juan had decided that he wanted to leave his current superintendency for a bigger, more challenging system. While at the time taking the first position offered made sense, in retrospect the lesson learned is to wait, if necessary, for a position and a setting that is a better "fit":

And then the other thing, even if you're in a desperate position, wait . . . even if it's pouring, even if it's raining, wait for the next bus to come to that stop. I could have, I might have, with that information, maybe held back. . . . When I applied and I got picked and . . . my newspaperman comes in with a file . . . I could have then waited a little bit longer for another bus to come by. At that time, I was looking at two or three other districts to consider around the area. But I didn't. I pulled out my name from two of them and went for this one.

Turning down a job offer is difficult. The appeal of its certainty can obscure its disadvantages when compared to the hypothetical advantages of other, only possible, job alternatives.

Learn the Skills of Political Leadership

It certainly seems that there was little that Juan could have done to overcome the turbulent and corrupt Sunnyside political history. One of his mentors, a colleague in the area, confirmed that judgment for Juan:

He doesn't believe that there is a person yet that can do away with 30 or 40 years of dysfunction. . . . He says, "Don't knock yourself down that you did anything wrong or that you could have done anything better."

Juan does wonder if he might have been more successful if he had taken a less demanding political challenge, perhaps in a smaller district, in order to strengthen his skills in political leadership—skills that only experience teaches:

I became superintendent [in my early 40s] and went into a small school district from a large school district working in central office. I don't know if it would have made a difference to have another intermediate step that was maybe not 12,000 students but was maybe 4,000 or 5,000, somewhere in there—to hone your skills of being a quasi-political figure. That's the only dimension that when we go from central office to the superintendency, we don't have experience in. Because we're not politicians; we're not trained to be politicians. . . . You're kind of just thrown into the water, and you have to learn it. I learned a few things that I needed to do to work with my [previous] board. And I applied them to Sunnyside. But it wasn't enough for me to be able to coalesce the group.

Even when pledging to stay out of politics—that is, avoiding partisanship—a superintendent still needs political astuteness and skills. As Juan suggests, experience is probably the prime teacher. But preparation programs can also strengthen their support for this learning, perhaps through on-the-job mentoring.

Build a Strategic Team

As he considers his own experience and that of his colleagues and mentors, Juan feels that in his next superintendency, he will work longer and harder with the board, at the beginning of his tenure, on team building, positioning himself as an essential member of the team, with strategic planning as the vehicle for his efforts:

One of the things that I am planning on doing, which I didn't have the opportunity to do in Sunnyside. . . . But you have to have the board commitment. A lot of working together opportunities at the beginning, in strategic planning, creating this plan whereby with the board, you're a critical, essential part of it. You make yourself essential. The board feels that if you're gone, the plan can't be followed. It's just a feeling, because in reality, a good strategic plan can be continued by new leadership.

Whether through strategic planning or other joint, long-term planning, developing a mutual commitment to a vision for the future and a strategy for reaching it is essential entry phase work for any superintendent. These activities not only clarify direction, but also build trusting relationships.

Watch Out for Political Blind Spots

A new superintendent who is unfamiliar with a new district may face political blind spots, not seeing that certain actions and attitudes of board members may be solely motivated by politics—for example, a reelection campaign, or the ambition to be board president:

There are behaviors of the board and of members that are up for election every year that happen starting from November, political season, through May. Really, as a superintendent then, you almost have to look at the political year and then [understand] *the time that you . . . have to do things.*

Just listening to my office personnel who have gone through two or three superintendents: "Oh, Dr. Martinez, this is going to happen." Or, "This is just happening because of this." So you start seeing a cycle, and you start seeing a pattern. Then, as a superintendent, you start having to work within that cycle in terms of when you can get things done.... They could even predict who was going to be the next officer.... The following year, that person's turn was up.

Office personnel, especially a loyal and politically unaffiliated secretary, can be important sources of essential political information. During the entry phase, any new superintendent has to find multiple sources, especially of institutional memory, to map as completely as possible the political topography of a district in order to eliminate blind spots.

Conclusions

The broader lessons from Juan's experience in Sunnyside include, first, that aspiring superintendents, and not just the board of education, have a choice. As Juan says, sometimes it may be better to "wait for the next bus." In making a decision about a school district, candidates should realize that districts need to "fit," just like a suit of clothes. You can make minor alterations, but you have to pick out the right size. If a school district has values, beliefs, or norms of operation that are inconsistent with a candidate's, then no amount of alteration or modification is likely to make the fit right.

A second important lesson is that candidates should do their homework about a school district carefully. Information about demographics, academics, and finance are codified and relatively easy to find. Crucial information about district politics exists in less explicit form within networks of relationships in the district and is much more difficult to obtain, especially for an outsider. Regional and state superintendent professional groups can be a valuable source for some of this information. Newspaper articles, and even board of education minutes, can also provide some inkling of the political landscape.

A third and final lesson, especially during the first few months on the job, is that a new superintendent should work systematically to clarify expectations with the board of education—expectations about district direction, board goals and procedures, superintendent goals, and behavior. For example, how much of the public limelight do board members want and expect? How much of the public limelight does the superintendent want and expect? Both state and national school board associations have resources that can be helpful to this process. The more mutual understanding and agreement there is about expectations, the stronger the board–superintendent relationship will be.

Currently serving as a district administrator for another school district, Juan believes that his experience in Sunnyside has taught him critical lessons in leadership that will serve him well in the future, and those lessons provide food for thought for both aspiring and current educational leaders.

And for me right now this is a wonderful break, a wonderful reprieve that I think is going to reenergize me, give me some new tools, get updated with curriculum, and work with a very challenging population in a very challenging school district in terms of all the barriers that they have to overcome. And when I get into that position again, I think I'm going to be that much better prepared and have more wisdom, I think, and handle the board politics a little bit better.

We found the enactment of democratic ideals to be a common theme throughout all of our authors' stories as they describe their work to transform their districts. Becky van der Bogert shares her joys, struggles, and lessons learned that surround a deep commitment to trying to model democratic ideals in her leadership style.

CHAPTER 7

Democracy During Hard Times

REBECCA VAN DER BOGERT

My superintendency has been like a good marriage. Both the school community and I feel blessed to have had a true partnership built on mutually held beliefs and convictions, and to have had an opportunity to dream and make our dreams come true. Like most marriages, however, it has been a tremendous amount of work as we have discovered how difficult it is to bring our dreams to fruition. There have been rocky moments when our beliefs were challenged both externally and internally, and even times when I questioned if the relationship was the best for "the children"—the students of the district. At the foundation of everything, though, there has been an incredible opportunity for growth and learning about the human experience—what it means to stay united at times of joy and sorrow, and how to accept one another's frailties and celebrate our strengths.

I am about to share a series of snapshots of my superintendency beginning with our romantic engagement around democracy and the way members of our school community challenge one another to live by our democratic beliefs through our deeds. There will be some theoretical discussion, which risks oversimplifying the ongoing struggle we have experienced as we try to move from theory to practice. To keep us reality-based, you will see a snapshot of a successful process in which democracy worked in its truest sense, and another snapshot in which we failed in both our commitment to democracy and to each other. Lessons that we have learned about democracy and negotiations will be shared, along with the questions that remain. As the foundation of all of these lessons, you will find my ongoing exploration of a lingering question I have always had: How do I let myself feel the pain that comes with the territory of the superintendency, learn from it, and grow, rather than taking flight?

Let us begin with the setting.

The Winnetka Public Schools

Located just north of Chicago, Illinois, the Winnetka Public School District is comprised of five schools that serve approximately 2,100 students from grades pre-K to 8. Relatively affluent, the town is known for the quality of its schools. Many previous residents have moved back to the town so their children can attend the same schools they did; newcomers have moved to the town because of the schools. Considered by many as our greatest shortcoming, student racial and ethnic composition is fairly homogeneous with only 5% of our students representing other ethnicities.

The schools were founded by Carleton Washburne, a superintendent who worked closely with other well-known progressive educators such as John Dewey, Francis Parker, and Perry Smith Dunlap in the 1920s to create schools that were based on the principles of progressive education. These leaders also founded the Progressive Educators' Association and conducted some of the first major research in the country on teaching to the individual child's abilities and interests. Many of their founding principles are deeply rooted in the district today; a belief in the importance of creating an environment in which our children live and learn about democracy and social justice, and a commitment to child-centeredness and developmentally appropriate education. These principles are visible in the schools and articulated in our current vision statement.

We are a dynamic community of learners committed to respecting childhood, challenging the intellect, nurturing creativity, fostering reflection, encouraging action, and exploring possibilities for the future. We believe that a developmental, child-centered approach to education is the most effective way to meet the needs of our students and the high level of expectations we set for them. We are guided by a set of beliefs embedded in a culture that honors tradition, reflects on transitions, and makes choices about transformations.

The Marriage: A Commitment to Democracy

I was recruited to become the superintendent of the Winnetka Public Schools because of my beliefs—beliefs about democracy, beliefs about child-centeredness, and commitment to the principles of progressive education. I had been working as a superintendent in a district in New England based on a similar philosophy and had written about democratic leadership and consensus building.

Like most superintendents, my passions and beliefs come from my formative years, years when I was expected to be invisible as a student and when I privately developed a commitment to provide otherwise for the next generation. Like most of us growing up in the 1940s and 1950s, I was to ask no questions, do what authority demanded, and sit quietly while adults had conversations. In school, I was the good little girl who did exactly what I was told and got good grades, and no one really knew what I was thinking inside. In fact, I was not really challenged to think.

Fortunately, I was blessed to experience an alternative graduate program that awakened me to the power of pursuing my own learning, my involvement in democracy in various student organizations, and my commitment to social activism. I was part of a pilot program in which we developed our own reading list and syllabi based on our personal interests, then graded ourselves, and we were challenged constantly to analyze our own learning.

Filled with a passion to provide an environment in which everyone has a voice and we strive to live by our words, the only thing that has been in the top middle drawer of my desk during all of my leadership roles is a laminated copy of James Beane and Michael Apple's (1995) conditions that are the necessary foundations of "the democratic way of life."

- The open flow of ideas, regardless of their popularity, that enables people to be as fully informed as possible
- Faith in the individual and collective capacity of people to create possibilities for resolving problems
- The use of critical reflection and analysis to evaluate ideas, problems, and policies
- Concern for the welfare of others and the "common good"
- Concern for the dignity and rights of individuals and minorities
- An understanding that democracy is not so much an "ideal" to be pursued as an "idealized" set of values that we must live and that must guide our life as a people
- The organization of social institutions to promote and extend the democratic way of life (pp. 6–7)

Given my commitment to and interest in democratically run organizations, I knew after my first visit to the Winnetka Public Schools that it would be a good marriage, as well as a learning laboratory for me. An effort to "extend the democratic way of life" has been an explicit part of the vision for the Winnetka Public Schools for the last 80 years and is still strongly stated in our district's current philosophy.

Education in a democracy, said Alexis de Tocqueville, "is an apprenticeship in liberty." It promotes the attitudes, values, and skills needed to live in freedom. Democracy is not inherited. It is constantly learned and experienced. We create freedom, sustain it, grow from it, embed it in our families, communities, and institutions, and claim it as our heritage.

Yet, there is no guarantee that democracy will prosper unless our words combined with our deeds allow it to be so. Thus, we believe that communication, the interchange of knowledge, ideas, criticism, and advice in all of its diverse forms, is the bond that holds the fragile elements of democracy together.

As a superintendent, I review these words often and challenge myself as to whether we are providing opportunities for the interchange of knowledge, ideas, criticism, and advice in all of its diverse forms. As a community, our staff and board members remind one another often that it is our deeds as well as our words that are important.

We have many community and professional forums and are always creating new ones that seek to include all interested voices, provide processes for hearing diverse opinions, and develop the skills of reaching consensus or comfort in living with what we have come to call "healthy tensions." Teacher committees develop curriculum frameworks and have the autonomy to make their own professional decisions about appropriate materials and strategies and the readiness of their individual children. District-wide grade level released days are scheduled regularly for teacher-led discussions about such topics as curriculum initiatives, implementation strategies, and the development of integrated units. Our Winnetka Teachers' Institute and Professional Growth Fund are in-house, teacher-run staff development programs, funded by the school board and run by teachers for teachers. Our teachers are introduced to the district during a 3-day overnight New Teacher Retreat organized by veteran teachers. This retreat supports new teachers in learning about our philosophy and culture and concepts such as integrated learning, child-centeredness, and developmentally appropriate learning.

Underlying the creation of these forums are a few basic assumptions.

- We are all leaders and learners. This means that I, as superintendent, am creating environments for others to lead and am very often "leading from the back of the room."

- We play different roles in the district, all of equal importance.
- When a decision is to be made, if at all possible, everyone affected by the decision will be involved in the decision-making process and have a voice.
- If problems arise, we are all on the same team working together to solve the problem.
- Different opinions are respected and useful to the process.

As outlined, I would like to move now from this theoretical discussion of our commitment to democracy to the reality of trying to live it through our deeds. Let us first look at a snapshot of a process that worked democratically, and then one that broke down.

Democracy in Action: Rewriting Our Philosophical Document

One of the successful examples of democracy in action was the rewriting of our philosophical document. I arrived in Winnetka in 1994 at a time when the district's philosophy was being challenged by a group of citizens and a couple of school board members who felt that there should be more focus on test scores, exit exams at each grade level, a curriculum that provided the same core body of knowledge to everyone at the same time, and grades for primary students rather than narrative assessments. They wanted less of a focus on democratic principles of shared decision making, and more "rigor" as opposed to child-centeredness. The board members who were leading this charge represented themselves often as the "voice of the community," and it was true that they represented a group of citizens who were attending school board meetings and were very vocal in the community.

Toward the end of my first year, we decided to set up a structure that would give staff, parents, board members, administrators, and residents an opportunity to take a close look at our philosophy and to provide feedback as to their perceptions of the implementation of our philosophy. At the same time, we committed to take a look at our philosophical document to see if it needed any revisions. This "opening up" of the process made some of my biggest supporters on the board uneasy, but I had been hired because of my ability to listen to all constituents and find consensus. I decided to take a risk and follow one of Apple's necessary foundations of "the democratic way of life." I placed "faith in the individual and collective capacity of people to create possibilities for resolving problems."

Carefully Structured Process

Our director of curriculum spent many thoughtful hours creating a community process that would honor all voices, carefully gather information from all stakeholders, and enhance dialogue among diverse opinion holders. It involved a task force, the hiring of an outside researcher, focus groups, the development of a survey for the community, careful analysis of data, and recommendations to the staff for further study. The goal was to reach consensus, but in the event we did not, the decision-making process that we would use to complete our recommendations was well articulated.

All voices. To assure that all voices were heard, the process was lengthy. It began in the fall of 1995 with a task force of 54 people—teachers, administrators, school board members, and parent and nonparent residents. We reached out and invited the leaders of those who were challenging us. We wanted their voices heard, and trusted that, as part of a democratic process, we could discern how representative their voices were and also stretch our own thinking about our philosophy. At the first meeting of the task force, the process was outlined for everyone in detail, discussed, and agreed to by everyone as fair.

This task force worked with an outside researcher who held focus groups, culled the issues of concern, and put together a 17-page survey that we sent to all residents of the community and to the teaching staff. The purpose of the survey was to help us understand whether the community understood our philosophy and if they felt we were living by it. We also wanted to know their perceptions of what we were doing well and what we needed to address.

After analysis of the survey data by our researcher and her presentation to the task force and the full teaching staff, a consensus was reached as to what recommendations staff needed to explore further. This consensus was developed on the basis of both majority and minority opinions. As one school board member stated, "The results yielded something for everyone. For the skeptics and nonbelievers, the survey indicated areas that the community felt needed discussion or improvement. For the believers, the results constituted a broad endorsement of the schools by the community. For everyone, the survey indicated an unarguable need for more and better communications" (Fead, 1998, p. 20). For this particular board member, "The survey put into perspective the most strident voices in our community while revealing areas ripe for growth and improvement—or clarification and communication" (p. 20).

Mutual Problem Solving Based on Solid Information

With this strong response from community and staff, and a thorough analysis by our researcher, we took the data and recommendations to another task force group called Winnetka: A Community of Learners (WACOL). WACOL was comprised of teachers and administrators whose task was to study the data and recommendations and rewrite our philosophical document as a team.

To engage the rest of the staff, they decided to plan a summer institute that covered the major topics that emerged: democracy, the arts, and teaching and learning. Three days after the close of school in June of 1996, the majority of our staff voluntarily stayed to listen to panels of guest speakers and Winnetka teachers on these topics and then discussed them in relation to our district.

During the following school year, the WACOL task force engaged in many hours of shared reading, discussions, and the writing and rewriting of our new philosophical document. Throughout the year, they asked for feedback from the whole staff at faculty meetings and an Institute Day, and a draft of the new philosophical document was offered for feedback to the board and administrative team as well.

After two years of study, our document was completed and mailed to all Winnetka residents, along with a history of the process and a thank you for everyone's involvement. To this day, there is true ownership in the document and I hear it quoted often by teachers, board members, and residents.

Democracy Struggling: A Less Successful Story

A far less successful story of democracy in action was the teacher negotiations that took place during the school year of 2000–01. Events over the previous 4 years had set the stage for what we all knew would be a difficult bargaining process. The enormous increases in health insurance costs in the last two years of the contract left some teachers with less take home money at the end of the settlement than before. Everyone acknowledged that our teachers were behind in terms of compensation. No one knew, however, that this had the makings of a perfect storm.

The board was extremely supportive of teachers. Many of them were parents in the schools, and had worked hard on the teachers' behalf to get both facilities and operating referendums approved. However, the board was feeling external pressure because the community had just passed tax cap legislation by a 5 to 1 vote, which limited our revenue to the Consumer Price Index. They knew the town would be watching the negotiations more closely than usual and they were not sure if taxpayers would pass the next tax referendum if it appeared to be a "salary referendum."

Denial Despite the Cues

I moved forward playing the same role I had played in bargaining sessions of years past. I met separately with the leaders of the teachers' negotiating team and the members of the school board to begin preparations. I made the false assumption that the process would be difficult but filled with the same good will as our previous negotiations. The board was aware that the salaries were behind and that teachers expected and deserved to have a relatively high settlement.

I wrote a memo for the new members of the board explaining that bargaining can be an opportunity to build relationships and enhance what we do for children. The following quotes will give you a flavor of what I hoped to convey.

Teacher bargaining marks a significant event in the life of a school district. Although it is a difficult time, it can also be an opportunity for everyone to renew their commitment to the district, reflect on what the district stands for, and enhance ways in which we are all going to work together on behalf of children.

It can be a fruitful time for us to reflect on our hopes for the future direction of the district as well as the implications of our vision for both the process and the anticipated results of bargaining.

As we prepare for bargaining, we all need to hang on to the challenge of holding in front of us, as we always do in Winnetka, our common goal of doing what is best for our children. With this goal made explicit and stated throughout the process, we can all stay on high ground together.

In keeping with the philosophy of the Winnetka Public Schools both the process and product are important. Members of the school board and the superintendent need to work to shape the results of the bargaining. Equally important is thinking about the process itself and how it will positively impact the culture and ultimately the teachers and students of the district. (WACOL Task Force, 1999)

After reading Fisher, Ury, and Patton's (1991) *Getting To Yes*, members of the board felt prepared and believed that things would go smoothly. They decided that they would share their long-range financial plan openly with the teachers, discuss tax caps, and work with the teachers to determine the highest possible increase for teachers that would pass in a referendum.

Previous to this preparation, I had been meeting with the president and vice president of the Teachers' Association on a regular basis to discuss any concerns in the district. The teachers surprised me at one of our regularly scheduled breakfast meetings when they told me they were bringing a representative from the Illinois Educators' Association (IEA) to the bargaining table. They explained that they had put together a team of teachers who had never bargained before, and they felt that they needed additional advice. I expressed my discomfort about having an "outsider" at the table, because we had never had anyone but teachers and board members participate in negotiations. The teachers were clear and adamant that they wanted to have someone there.

I spoke with the board about this shift, and they decided against bringing in an attorney. They believed it would only escalate the "sides" mentality and felt that, once we all got to the table, we would use our mutual problem solving skills and find a settlement that was fair to everyone.

A week after these discussions, a member of the teacher's negotiating team stopped by my office, as he did frequently, and with a smile he remarked, "Becky, I hope we are still friends when this bargaining is over because I am going to take it all the way to a strike on you." I smiled in return and responded that I was sure that would not be necessary as we had a very reasonable board. As he left the office, I can remember thinking that democracy and the wisdom of the group would prevail. I opened my desk drawer and reread one of Apple's necessary foundations: "faith in the individual and collective capacity to create possibilities for resolving problems."

Even if this particular teacher believed what he said, the rest of the negotiating team would be reasonable and we would work it out. I had *so* much faith in both the teachers and board members as problem solvers, and in the tenets by which we lived, that I missed the cues and kept right on going with preparation for interest-based bargaining. I assumed, as had happened the last time we bargained with this method, that everyone would honor one another's interests, gather facts and figures together, and resolve differences mutually.

The Bargaining Process

At the first bargaining session, everyone at the table, including the teachers, board members, our business manager, and I, agreed on interest-based bargaining as our process. It was also agreed that the business manager and I would play a neutral role as we had in previous bargaining, by providing information and advice for either party upon request. I left with a feeling of relief and a belief that things would work out.

The second session was when I began to develop some concerns. The teachers came in with a double-digit request for an increase in salary for the first year. I knew this was higher than the district could afford for all four years put together. The board members were stunned. One of the board members had been involved in interest-based bargaining before and had expected to begin by presenting the long-range plan and showing the teachers the money that was available. The board members continued as planned, hoping that once the teachers understood the financial situation they would work with the board to find a realistic settlement.

I later learned that the teachers who had not been trained in interest-based bargaining had legitimately thought the presentation of a proposal was the appropriate way to begin. In fact, they had spent a great deal of time preparing their proposal, and felt disrespected because the board was not prepared with a counter proposal. This was the beginning of the teachers and the board members, both well meaning, speaking to each other in two different languages. They were engaged in two different processes without understanding what the other was doing. There was so much misinterpretation on the part of both teachers and board that trust and the willingness to try to work together seemed to disappear. I found that my suggestions to teachers were greeted with suspicion. I was dumbfounded.

In the past, the bargaining process had been kept relatively separate from the school day and little was communicated to the staff at large until there was an agreement. A few months into this process, principals were reporting that they were seeing signs of discontent among the teachers. It started slowly with uncomfortable glances between teachers and administrators and then escalated to teachers gathering and walking out together in a line past the principals' offices in picket fashion to come together in unity outside the schools. Board members and members of the administrative team heard stories of teachers dressed as board members and parents dressed as injured teachers without health insurance for Halloween. During the fall open house for our parents, it became clear that teachers had been given a script, because most parents came out of presentations with the same information: that the board was being disrespectful of teachers and the teachers were not even going to get health benefits out of the current negotiations.

When the board heard of the discontent and concluded that the teacher members of the negotiating team were not hearing them, they decided it was time to bring in an attorney to assist them. Still committed to bargaining, in keeping with our culture, they found the most "win-win" attorney they could find. In response, the teachers brought in an additional person from the IEA who was trained in interest-based bargaining. The attorney and the IEA facilitator tried to bring us back to mutual problem solving, but too much misunderstanding had already taken place. They were able to engage everyone in mutual problem solving over nonmoney issues, but as soon as we entered discussions about money, the process became adversarial again. There was one agreement—everyone concurred that we had brought this additional help into the process too late.

Four months into negotiations, there was consensus that we needed to enter into mediation. The attorney was advising the board not to get involved in a public dialogue and I was advised not to have conversations with teachers about bargaining for fear of being accused of unfair labor practice. Communication at this point was minimal and filled with distrust. Some members of the negotiating team accused the board of "hiding" money. The board felt as though the teachers would never understand their need to be accountable to taxpayers. All of our usual ways of working with one another dissolved. Frankly, we were all like ducks out of water.

To the teachers' credit, they seemed determined not to have this impasse affect the children, and other than a handful of teachers discussing it with their students, we believed teachers remained committed to their teaching during the day. The first I heard of the process potentially affecting our students was a rumor that the middle school teachers planned to provide minimal comments on student report cards. The district had prided itself in providing very thorough narratives for parents, instead of grades, through grade six and then continuing to provide shorter narratives in grades seven and eight along with letter grades.

After consulting with the attorney, he suggested that I alert the teachers about fulfilling their obligations. I was concerned about how teachers would perceive any intervention on my part, particularly around any judgment of their role as teachers. I invited three of the leaders of the negotiating team from the two middle schools for lunch and I chose my words carefully. I explained that they were still to do what was best for our students and that grade reports were a part of their commitment. I also shared that this would reflect poorly on the teachers in the eyes of the parents. Two of the teachers readily agreed and returned to advise their colleagues to complete grade reports as they always had. The other returned and portrayed the conversation in a very negative light to his colleagues. The majority of teachers did the report cards; only a handful made a minimal effort.

The Infection Spreads

At this point I realized that I was being portrayed by some of the members of the negotiating team as unsupportive of the teachers. I found this extremely painful, as the reason I had entered administration was to create an environment in which teachers had a voice, were a part of the decision-making process, and felt valued. I believed, however, that I needed to put my feelings aside and take the positive approach. The next time I met with the leaders of the Teachers' Association for breakfast, I asked them how I could help the situation. They were clear that they did not want me to intervene in the bargaining and that my role was to get a funding referendum passed once we had a settlement. I understood then why the teachers were not listening to the board about the need to respect the taxpayers' concerns. We had always passed referenda by large margins and the teachers assumed we would continue to do so.

I also asked at the breakfast if I could count on some help, after a settlement was reached, to dispel some of the misinformation being spread about the board and about me. I expressed that it would be important for us to work together on behalf of the children. The teachers seemed to suggest with their responses that what happened in bargaining was separate from the rest of the time in the district, and that we would all go right back to our positive working relationships when things were settled. Once again, I was dubious and also deeply hurt that they could be so cavalier about our relationship, which I felt had been an important contribution in terms of how we worked together on behalf of students and a significant reason as to why we were able to accomplish all that we did.

Things escalated over the next month, with teachers organizing outside of schools each morning, demonstrating at board meetings, and meeting with parents. This, of course, inflamed the board even more. Board members finally sent a letter to the community because they felt it was important to explain the situation, and this communication further angered the teachers.

It appeared to many of us that we were headed to strike. The board received a formal letter of intent to strike on a designated date if we had not settled. Teachers prepared with their picket signs, and had their phone trees ready on the evening before the designated date. As we bargained through the night, some parents appeared with candles and sang outside the school, and cameras from every TV station were outside waiting.

At this point I was deeply saddened, but the sadness was overridden by adrenoline. I truly believed a strike would tear at our culture and I was not sure we would ever be able to repair it. I can remember listening to the board for hours as they deliberated throughout the night over each proposal. In the beginning I said little, in hopes that they would decide to settle. It was not until the end, when there was a 3 : 3 vote and we were waiting for the last person to vote, that I spoke up. I advised them that settlement was the right thing to do, but I would respect whichever way they went. With many tears, the board agreed to the settlement at 6:30 a.m.

The four board members who voted in favor of the settlement did so because they felt a strike would destroy the culture of the district and we might never recover. The three board members who voted against the settlement did so because of a fear that passage would convey a message that this is the way we do business in Winnetka, and they also expressed concern about the possibility of passing the next referendum. No votes were based on the quality of the settlement, and the room was filled with emotion, conflict, and ill feeling.

Even though we had settled, I knew we had a lot of work ahead of us. Our usual way of relating to one another had dissolved during this process. Little if any mutual problem solving took place, the teachers had placed me in a hierarchical role by portraying me to the rest of the staff as unsupportive and on the board's "side," and inappropriate power had been used by the teachers. I believed all of this would be destructive to the culture we had fostered.

At my next breakfast meeting with the leaders of the Winnetka Education Association, I expressed concern about the possible impact of the bargaining on the culture that we had nurtured and that was so important to us in Winnetka. They believed strongly that the process of bargaining was "separate" from the rest of their work in the district, and that the way we related to one another in negotiations was, by definition, bound to be different from the way we related in other situations. Although I had no proof at that time because it was too soon, my belief in a holistic approach to organizations left me with the sense that anything as powerful as this could not simply be "disconnected" from the rest of what we did. I knew some of the principals, the board, and I had been wounded and believed it would be difficult to separate this from our future interactions.

I wanted to take flight. In fact, I did take flight emotionally, but my passion for the district and what it stood for, and my regard for the teachers, administrators, and board members with whom I worked, kept me grounded in the daily tasks of running the district. The year after the settlement was a peculiar one. As the leaders of the association had suggested, we did return to our mutual problem solving around children, to grade level discussions about curriculum, and to other professional conversations.

However, there was a stark silence around the topic of negotiations. A couple of teachers reached out to me about their discomfort with the process, sharing that they had been admonished not to discuss it. I tried continuing business as usual, attending grade level meetings, touring the buildings often, and engaging in conversations about what is best for children.

I felt as though I was living a divided life. When I was with the teachers, I felt there was a genuine respect for one another and we were functioning in a positive way around what was best for the children. But sitting deep in my stomach was a knot that created a certain numbing effect on all of my other feelings. We were all tiptoeing and cautious with one another. The negotiations had become nondiscussable or, as referred to later, our "elephant in the living room."

I met with consultants, fellow superintendents, and some teachers who all had the same advice: at the right time, I needed to open the conversation and provide forums for all of us to have the conversation together about the negotiations. It would be necessary to share my own feelings about the process before the two-way discussion could take place. I struggled with these suggestions for several reasons. I was still hurt, and still trying to separate the bargaining from the rest of our interactions. What would happen if I started to share my true feelings?

The truth of it was that I did not know where or how to open the discussion in a way that would be productive.

The Healing Begins

Fortunately, for the next 2 years, I was a part of a series of "Courage to Teach" retreats in which I made my way back to a healed state and found a way to open the conversation. During these retreats, with the supportive help of many colleagues, I was able to explore my original reasons for entering the profession, my beliefs, and my sense of integrity and identity as an educator. I came to realize that I did not have to silently hold full responsibility for what had happened, and I came to forgive myself and everyone else.

Much of the work in the retreats had been done through poetry, in a totally safe setting. The strategies I learned in the retreats also provided me with some of the tools for talking about the bargaining in a way that was honest and constructive, rather than blaming.

Once I had developed an approach, I decided the most captive audience I had was going to be on the opening day of the new school year. So, less than a year after the settlement, I stood before almost 200 teachers with heart pounding, voice shaking, and opened with:

The story I'm about to share is about leadership: my leadership, your leadership, and our leadership.

I can still remember finding my way to Winnetka as though it happened yesterday. I was sitting at my desk in Lincoln, Massachusetts, intently poring over budget documents, when the phone rang. After a lengthy conversation with a search consultant . . . actually it was the third conversation . . . I agreed to visit Winnetka to see if it was the match he thought it was. As I hung up the phone I quietly whispered to myself, "Only if I think I can bring ALL of who I am to the position and the district will benefit."

I made the visit as agreed and after spending a great deal of time learning about the inner workings of the schools and the culture of the district, I too felt it was a match. It was clear that Winnetka already had clear and deep philosophical roots, and a highly intelligent and committed staff with a strong set of values. I sensed that the district needed someone who could work with others to help strengthen the roots, to continue to clarify what we believe in for children, and to cultivate the kind of democratically shared leadership that would preserve the roots long after any one person's tenure. I felt it was a match and I could bring "all of who I am" to it.

I too had a clear set of beliefs that I'd held passionately for decades. I believed that children benefited when educators could bring all of their authentic selves to their teaching and learning. I believed that we all teach who we are and therefore attending to the heart and soul of those interacting with our children is a large part of providing the best for our children. I believed that the role of a leader is to contribute to such an environment and to model bringing all of their beliefs and passions to the job. It was part of my being that if all of this were to happen, we had to make a concerted effort to have a democratically shared leadership in which all voices were heard and everyone's growth was nurtured.

I made the right decision. As the years passed, I knew I had found a home here; a place where we all could grow together, have passionate dialogue about what we believe is best for children, and engage all constituents in meaningful leadership roles. I never felt so whole, challenged, and passionate about my work.

Then during our past negotiation process, we experienced what I *thought* was an unraveling of what we had built. As the superintendent, I felt that I should somehow have been able to move the process along without our breaking down into "us" and "them." I'd always been able to do so in the past. I went through a great deal of pain . . . the pain of feeling like a failure, the pain of not being perceived as a supporter of teachers when I'd committed a lifetime to doing so. The pain that comes from fear—the fear that I might have been responsible in any way for the tearing of our culture. I was even questioning my beliefs and if I'd been true to them. I pulled back from philosophical conversations about shared leadership on a national level, and I certainly avoided my critical friends who had been on panels with me throughout the years, questioning whether shared leadership could work.

Fortunately, I have many long-term soul mates who reminded me that when one's heart breaks, it creates a wide opening. If one can leave it open, it can be an opportunity to be more vulnerable than ever to learn from the human experience, to grow, and deepen connections. I have been blessed to be surrounded by other educators, board members, and friends who not only supported me so that I could keep that wound open, but also challenged me and joined me in my journey to learn in many ways through the healing process.

I'd like to share one of my greatest lessons that came to me while I was sitting in a circle with a group of friends and quietly reading a poem written by Vaclav Havel. It went

It is I who must begin

Once I begin, once I try—

here and now,

right where I am,

not excusing myself

by saying that things
would be easier somewhere,
without grand speeches and
ostentatious gestures,
but all the more persistently
—to live in harmony
with the voice of Being, as I
understand it within myself
as soon as I begin that,
I suddenly discover,
to my surprise, that
I am neither the only one
nor the first,
nor the most important one
to have set out
upon the road.
Whether all is really lost
or not depends entirely on
whether or not I am lost. (Havel, 1988)

While quietly reading this poem, it struck me like a bolt of lightning! I felt all was lost in the district because I was lost. Not lost because I failed, but lost because I'd forgotten that I was neither the only one nor the first, nor the most important one to have set out upon the road . . . the road of preserving what we have here in Winnetka. How arrogant of me to think that I needed to hold the responsibility alone.

In my heart, I have always felt a "we." I also knew I had many colleagues who were trying to sort out what happened. But in my head, I thought it was "I" who should have made it work. Part of my healing process has been to understand and feel otherwise.

I've always believed that a true democratic leader needed to be somewhat invisible so others could take the lead: providing the resources, protecting the democratic processes, encouraging others to lead, and thinking about how to weave it all together.

I've learned that it may not be enough to be in the background if others don't understand why you're there or if I feel I need to bear the burden and privilege of responsibility alone.

If we are to share leadership here in Winnetka, then the quality of leadership throughout the district is dependent on our relationships. It requires a deep understanding of one another and how we might best work together on behalf of children. I share what I've learned with you this morning in the spirit of deepening that understanding.

I closed by sharing a poem called "Shoulders" by Naomi Sahib-Nye, which expressed our need to hold one another on our shoulders like precious cargo and saying

I am no longer lost. I stand here before you to say that I believe in shared leadership, I am neither the only one, nor the first, nor the most important one to have set out upon that road. Our sensitive cargo is our unique culture here in Winnetka and together we must be willing to do as the poem says, "what he is doing with one another." May the school year 2003–2004 be one of gaining deeper understanding of how we can support one another in caring for our sensitive cargo.

Back to Open Conversations

When I wrote my opening day address, I honestly did not know how it would be received. There had been indications throughout the previous year that the bargaining process and related events were disturbing to many. During a workshop with an outside facilitator, the teachers listed bargaining as a "nondiscussable," and several teachers had approached me about what could be done before the next negotiations. But I had learned not to assume that the thoughts of a small group of teachers were representative of the whole. My confidence had been shaken and for the first time in my professional career I was questioning my instincts. Perhaps the majority of teachers were fine and believed no damage had been done. Perhaps I was feeling it far more deeply than others. Was I projecting my own feelings on them?

Finally my instincts took over, and my belief in the wholeness of organizations told me that what went on during negotiations still had to be very much with all of us. I felt that if we did not discuss it, it would affect us in major ways down the road. As frightened as I was to open the subject, I found that doing so ultimately opened the door for many future discussions about our commitment to democracy and bargaining. There was a sense of relief expressed by many teachers during the days following my address.

The principals reported that it was the topic of conversation in every one of the buildings and it finally freed others to discuss the unhappiness they felt about what we might have lost. One of the teachers who had been on the negotiating team called me and said it was one of the most courageous and risky things she'd seen a leader do. I knew things had been well received in the corners of greatest concern when the president of the association called me that day and referred to my words as "right on target."

Lessons Learned and Unanswered Questions

It is with humility that I share these lessons learned about democracy, bargaining, and working through the pain of our jobs. The humility is because many of these lessons seem so obvious to me now as I write this piece. Often, as superintendents, we are scurrying so quickly on the treadmill of *doing* that we do not have time to reflect on what we might learn from what we have *done*. I offer these lessons not because they are profound, but in the spirit of trying to be helpful to anyone who might be currently on a similar treadmill.

Lessons About Democracy

Leadership in preserving democracy. The strongest lesson that keeps coming back to me is that democracy does not just happen without a clearly defined structure and a means to monitor the structure. I mentioned earlier that one facet of my leadership is about creating environments for others to lead, which often involves my stepping back and leading from behind. During this bargaining process, I felt I would be interfering, seen as controlling, and violating my commitment to democracy if I intervened. I kept waiting for "the individual and collective capacity of people to create possibilities for resolving problems." It had always happened before in our district under my leadership.

I realize now in hindsight that, unlike most processes that take place in our district, the democratic process for negotiations had not been clearly defined. The ground rules about listening to one another, honoring different perspectives, and working together to find a solution had not been agreed to. At some point in the process I should have intervened and pointed out that we were not living by our usual democratic principles. Paradoxically, I learned that there are times when a leader must be dogmatic to preserve democracy.

Lessons About Bargaining

Preparation in service of a common language. The lesson I learned about democracy related naturally to our bargaining process. In preparation for our recent 2004 bargaining sessions, the president of the association, the president of the school board, and I had a series of meetings together. We discussed a variety of topics, including the composition of the negotiating teams, the process we would use and what that meant, the information we should mutually gather ahead of time, and what kind of training we should all have. We even discussed and agreed on the specific trainers. It was decided that the teachers would have a representative from the Illinois Education Association and the board would have an attorney skilled in interest-based bargaining and committed to being fair to all. The trainers worked with all of us together and taught us the elements of interest-based bargaining. After a series of team building exercises, we developed agreements as to how we were going to work together.

Because of this preparation we did not have inadvertent misunderstandings about what the other person "meant." In fact, we found it to be a bonding experience, sharing jokes about certain vocabulary words and anecdotes about how we were using what we had learned with our children, in purchasing a car, and even with our partners. We also began every session by going around and asking each person how they felt, their hopes for the day, and if there were any elephants in the room. We closed each session similarly, and strove to be sure that everyone had a voice.

Know the people at the table and their history in bargaining. Hindsight is always 20–20. In trying to analyze what happened, I did some research on the history of bargaining in the district. I discovered that one member of the negotiating team had, in fact, been involved in bargaining before I arrived in the district, so long ago that the younger members of the team hadn't known, and the model had been a traditional, adversarial one. Had I done my research before we started, I would have been able to shift gears and have very different discussions earlier in the process.

Do not assume that others perceive you the way you think you should be perceived. This may sound like such a basic piece of advice, but I continually need to remind myself to try to look at things from the teachers' eyes and to remember that they do not all see things the same way. I felt such a deep sense of passion for the teachers and the district, and an even deeper bond around our beliefs, that I assumed we would bring all of that to the bargaining table. I forgot that there were many younger teachers in the district who did not understand our culture yet, and even some veteran teachers who did not have the same perceptions of how we work together in the district. They believed that the way to accomplish things was through the use of power.

I was devastated when I heard of parents being told that I was not supportive of the teachers and did not value or respect them. This was perhaps the most personally painful part of the learning process. I realize now that no matter how hard I work at trying to break down hierarchical barriers and support teachers, individuals in an organization bring their beliefs and assumptions about authority from a lifetime of experience. I have also come to realize that some teachers used this accusation as a strategy because they knew how important it was to me to be viewed as a supporter of teachers. Most important, I have learned to listen to feedback and challenge myself as to whether I am doing the right thing by teachers and students regardless of the perception or misperception.

Lessons About Walking Through the Pain

Walking through the pain. A single day in the life of a superintendent is filled with many strong emotions: pride, joy, sadness, anger, and yes, pain. Some moments are exhilarating and fill us with energy to move to the next level. Others pull us down. One of the things I have been trying to learn over the years is how to turn those painful moments into opportunities for learning. Most psychologists and learning theorists tell us that the most painful experiences provide us with the greatest opportunity to learn.

I do not have any easy answers as to how to walk into the pain and turn it into learning, but I have learned some things along the way.

Share the pain with others. Very often, the source of the pain is a dynamic at work that makes it difficult to share with others, for example, board or administrative team issues. In addition to this, we have been conditioned that pain is a sign of weakness and that leaders should be "strong."

I have learned over the years that sharing my pain with others in an appropriate way and at the appropriate time has been helpful to the organization as well as to me. It has not been viewed as a weakness—quite the contrary. I have had times when I shared with parents, board members, and even teachers how painful their words or actions have been. Inevitably, their response is that they had no idea of the impact of their actions, and it opens a conversation about how we can work together more effectively on behalf of the children. A willingness to express feelings and work through difficult issues conveys a tremendous commitment on everyone's part.

Do unto yourself as you would do unto others. I am pretty good at helping the members of my administrative team when they are in pain because of an angry parent or a mistake they have made. When I am in pain now, I have learned to step back and remind myself of how I ask others to put things in perspective. The one angry parent is one out of how many thrilled parents? The mistake is how large, with respect to the whole picture? I have learned how to "self talk" with the same advice I would give others.

Accept a lack of perfection. All organisms have weaknesses. I was devastated when we came close to a strike in our district. I had written a great deal about democratic leadership, teacher support, and other progressive ideals, and to be totally honest, I was embarrassed that this failure had happened on my watch.

I have come to accept that school districts, like all organisms, have times when they are frail. No district has the immunities necessary to protect us from the times such as I have described, and no superintendent is without mistakes. I have come to believe that accepting frailties as a natural part of any organization is helpful in responding to them in a constructive manner.

I believe our district is stronger today for having lived through this experience, and we have more immunity than we did before as a result. All of us who lived through that time are much more vigilant about protecting what we have. We have also developed a greater ability to work through difficult issues.

Let others support you. The members of my administrative team have taught me this and I am forever indebted to them. During this bargaining process, I was trying to protect them so they could continue to be neutral in the buildings and to keep the positive relationship they had with their teachers. I thought I was hiding my pain well until I arrived at one of our weekly meetings and found they had written (and proceeded to sing) a song about me that was very touching.

There were many times in the subsequent weeks that I gained great strength from their gesture and the district was stronger for my having been supported by them. They taught me that when I say that I hope we will all grow together that it means *me* too . . . It is okay for the leader to have needs too. And they also taught me that it is not selfish to let others support you; it is actually good for the district as well as the soul.

Build a repertoire of things that comfort and provide you the courage to work through the pain. I have learned that it is one thing to know what would be helpful during painful times—it is another thing to actually practice it in the middle of a painful situation. This takes a retraining of habits and an explicit effort. Over the years, I have built a repertoire of things that remind me to use the resources I have in difficult times. This repertoire is probably different for everyone. For me it is turning to friends, meditation, spiritual readings, quiet walks, and exercise. Such comforts need to be a part of our routine so we can reach for them easily when needed.

I would like to close with a reading that was sent to me by a dear friend. I received it shortly after the experience I have described here, when I was struggling about whether I should remain in Winnetka.

Belonging has everything to do with coming out of hiding; making yourself visible to the world, and giving up any sense of immunity. One of the deep understandings of life is to understand that existence is just one humiliation after another . . . There's a lovely root to the word "humiliation." It literally means "of the soil." It's from the word humus, meaning soil. When you're humiliated, you're literally returned to the soil; to the ground of your being. And any abstract ideas you might have had about yourself disappear.

The astonishing thing is that with your feet on the ground of your being—in the territory of your own life—the possibilities are much greater than you had built with those ghost-like abstracts of a person you thought you should be in order to live out your life.

There's something about the innocence of humiliation, of finding yourself anew, of having been shriven. Having been released from a kind of encasement of a self that we might have spent years building, but was actually a barrier between ourselves and reality rather than a bridge to it or a meeting place to it. One day totally exhausted, humiliated by the exhaustion, and returned to the ground of myself, I looked to a friend, a former Benedictine monk, and asked, "Brother David, say something about exhaustion. Speak to me about exhaustion."

Brother David responded, "You know, the antidote to exhaustion is not necessarily rest."

I asked, "What is it?"

He answered, "The answer to exhaustion is whole-heartedness . . . When you're not whole-hearted, the world can't actually have a real conversation with you."

(Whyte, 1996)

References

Beane, J.A., & Apple, M.W. (1995). The case for democratic schools. In J.A. Apple & M.W. Beane (Eds.), *Democratic schools* (pp. 1–25). Alexandria, VA: ASCD.

Fead, K. (1998). In the eyes of one parent. In S. Karaganis (Ed.), *The search for common values in Winnetka* (pp. 17–22). San Francisco: Jossey-Bass.

Fisher, R., Urv, W.L., & Patton, B. (Eds.). (1991). *Getting to yes: Negotiating agreement without giving in* (2nd ed.). New York: Penguin Books.

Havel, V. (1988). *Letters to Olga: June 1979–1982* (P. Wilson, Trans.). New York: Alfred A. Knopf.

WACOL Task Force. (1999). *Winnetka: A community of learners philosophical document.*

Whyte, D. (1996). *The house of belonging.* Langley, WA: Many Rivers Press.

When superintendents gather in private conversations, it is likely the question "What's your board like?" will be raised. Becky Hurley speaks eloquently from a board member's perspective about the steep learning curve that she experienced and how she developed a productive working relationship with her superintendent and with other board members.

CHAPTER 8

Learning on the Job: The Education of a School Board President in Shared Leadership

BECKY BAIR HURLEY

This yearbook is written by and about superintendents and the superintendency, but the superintendent for my school district (one of the editors) suggested a board president's perspective might help shed some light on one of the superintendent's most challenging jobs: successfully working with a board of education. Why is it so challenging? Certainly because in our current culture of accountability boards can be more demanding than ever, but there is another more important reason. If you believe as I do that shared leadership makes for a stronger school district, it must start with the relationship between the superintendent and the school board.

There is no doubt that the relationship between our board and superintendent has been very strong during the 4 years that I have had the honor of serving as a board member. That relationship not only makes our respective jobs easier, but I believe it is the firm foundation for healthy democratic decision making throughout the entire school district. When the board and the superintendent work together with the same values and goals in mind, they create a culture in which those values and goals are more secure. As the board, superintendent, administration, staff, parents, and taxpayers embrace and reflect those values back to each other, the values are further reinforced. I think of this process of reflecting and reinforcing values among the constituents of the district as "360-degree learning."

How have we achieved what I have come to understand is a difficult balance? Was it the inevitable result of fortunate circumstances—or was it the result of intentional shared leadership work initiated by a wise and tireless superintendent and nurtured by a board that, rather than believing it must have all the answers, is truly open and eager to learn? Maybe you can guess the answer, but I invite you to look through my eyes as I recall the last 4 years and reflect on how I have "learned on the job" here in Winnetka.

The Winnetka Public Schools

The Winnetka Public Schools, a K-8 district in the northern suburbs of Chicago encompassing five schools and about 2,060 students, is a fortunate district. We have excellent schools that have been well supported by the residents, both philosophically and fiscally. We have had a strong history of commitment to progressive public education here ever since renowned educator and author Carleton Washburne arrived in 1917. Washburne's writings in the 1930s and 1940s made "the Winnetka Way" known across the country.

Winnetka also has the benefit of traditionally great school boards, nonhierarchical in their thinking, open to learning, and patient with "messy" thinking. One reason for this is an unusual "town meeting" type of local political system known as the "Winnetka Caucus," which brings very talented citizens into local government service without requiring them to mount a campaign or engage the support of political parties.[1] This does a lot to improve the type of citizen drawn into public service—citizens who agree "the secret of leadership is to think of your position as an opportunity to service, not as a trumpet call to self-importance" (Walters, 1993, p. 1). Or as it was phrased when the Winnetka Caucus was established in the 1920s: "The job seeks the man, not the man the job." The idea, if not the gender, remains as valid as ever.

The six other members of our current board comprise a wise and thoughtful group, and so as I admit how long it sometimes took for the light bulb to go on, I speak only for myself. We are blessed to have on the board some highly intelligent, highly principled people with incredible business and community leadership experience. But even more important than the board members' intelligence and expertise is a wonderful spirit of mutual respect and openness to learning. While all of these board members have areas of expertise, we never seem to fractionalize along those lines. We discuss as equals any issue facing the board. I think that says a lot about our respect for democratic processes and about the undeniable fact that these board members always, always, put aside personal interest in favor of the interests of our children and our schools. In every dealing with my fellow board members I come away wiser than I was before. They and past boards have been a real force in preserving the district culture and my hope is that our board will be able to pass along that learning to future boards.

With all this going for us in Winnetka, is it not inevitable that the superintendent and board would have a high-functioning relationship? The answer, I'm convinced, is "no." It is not inevitable, even in the best of circumstances. In most circumstances, it is not even very likely.

After 4 years on the board I have realized that this exceptional board–superintendent relationship was not nearly so strong in the recent past. More importantly, I have begun to appreciate how our current success is the result of deliberate and careful work on the part of our superintendent and board members. In Winnetka we say we are "A Community of Learners" and it is true. Together all of us—administrators, board, parents, teachers, and community—have worked to build a culture of shared leadership and together we have worked to explore a few important concepts:

- First, that the simple answer is usually the wrong answer (I think of this as the "siren song of simplicity" and tend to visualize school boards shipwrecked on a rocky coast). Instead, we must allow Winnetka to be a "messy" place where we can tolerate paradoxes and be patient with ambiguity.
- Second, that Winnetka is committed to using democratic processes in its decision making, so any change must be considered and developed by everyone affected.
- Third, that growth takes time—and despite the impatience many people will have with the process, in most cases taking our time is a very good thing.

Can what has worked here work in other very different districts? Can it even work here in different times and circumstances? I do not know. I know we have had bumps in the road ourselves, and those bumps demonstrate that a democratic culture can be lost, and lost very quickly. Keeping up that culture takes constant work, vigilance, and leadership. "Unfortunately," we have a superintendent who made this very complex work look deceptively natural and easy, and so it was some time before I realized just how important and difficult such work is.

My Perspective

To explain what I have observed and learned during my board service, I need to say something about my perspective. (If I am going to ask you to see things through my eyes you ought to know something about how I see.) Like many board members, I have no background in education. My background is in business law, practiced in a large traditional law firm. The culture of such a firm is businesslike, but tempered by the traditions of the law profession and an overlay of collegiality. And so when I arrived on the school board I *half* expected the board would issue mandates to the superintendent for her to follow and report on. I believe a number of board members who come from the business world arrive *fully* expecting that to be the case.

The ease and creativity with which educators discuss values and community also took some getting used to. Lawyers are a pretty straight-laced group. We were slow to come around to "business casual" dress and are not very good at talking about feelings and community. It was not long, however, before our superintendent had the board talking about values, vision, and what we want our schools to be. I distinctly remember being at one of our Summer Institute meetings (I will describe these more later) with teachers and administrators, and finding myself in a small group using pipe cleaners, cardboard, and brightly colored feathers to create a sort of performance-art piece representative of our district's values. I have to tell you, that was a mind-bending experience for a lawyer. The point I am trying to make is that many board members often do not come naturally to the types of conversation around values and community that I believe are more common in education, and that our superintendent has used so successfully in building relationships in the district.

However, because of my legal background I did bring a healthy skepticism of simplistic answers to my service on the board. If anything eschews the simplistic and embraces the contradictions of "messy dilemmas," it is common law, that is, the law based on court decisions handed down over hundreds of years. Some might think, for example, that the answer to the question "Isn't killing someone wrong?" is easy. But over the years the courts have looked at real cases involving real people, and then refined the law of murder to make it just. Considerations such as intent, mental state, age, and the need for self-defense acknowledge the complexity of the real world. Educators, faced with their own complex dilemmas, are often confronted with simplistic thinking from the public and, sadly enough, from policymakers. I think being skeptical of such thinking helped me look beyond simple answers and be more open to learning about the complexities facing our schools.

A Look Back

One candidate publicly committed to "reining in" spending and to increased testing ran against the candidates slated by our Winnetka Caucus system and won. He did not come to the board ready to learn, but with his mind made up, ready to implement change. He saw his job as one of oversight of a subordinate—the superintendent—and so naturally was not very open to learning from that subordinate. Others on the board resisted such a hierarchical view of the board–superintendent relationship and struggled to protect the philosophy of the district.

The board was divided, but more importantly, it was dysfunctional. This new board member was particularly difficult—obstreperous, demanding mountains of paperwork from the superintendent and business manager, unwilling to abide by majority decisions, unwilling to agree to customary or even mandated state policies—and to be honest the effect is still felt in the district 10 years later. Managing the board and its demands became an overwhelming burden for the superintendent. Meanwhile, the behavior of other board members was affected. They did not want to appear critical, and so sometimes felt constrained about raising questions, but on the other hand they were afraid of abdicating their responsibility to speak out when necessary. This breakdown in communication crippled the ability of the district to engage in thoughtful and democratic decision making. During this period of discord the very philosophy of the district was questioned. The board and the district as a whole seemed to be at a crossroads.

Let us stop for a minute and consider what happens when the board and superintendent do not communicate openly and honestly. First, each party feels constrained because there are things they want to ask but do not, things they want to learn but cannot, or things they want to say but will not. There are two results from this: ignorance and annoyance. Then those two results breed a third: mutual distrust. A board member's suggestion feels like criticism to the superintendent, and a superintendent's unwillingness to adopt the suggestion feels like a rebuff to the board member.

Here is an example from early on in my board service. When e-mail first began to be widely used, parents began to call for its use in communicating with teachers. Frankly, to many of the board members (myself included) it seemed like a simple idea and easy to implement. Our superintendent hesitated to pursue the change, knowing that some teachers would resist it and some parents would abuse it. Here is where trust comes in. A board member who distrusts the superintendent could conclude that the superintendent is not willing to accept ideas from the board, or that the board is being told not to meddle in district operations, or that the superintendent thinks the board is just too ignorant to understand the ramifications. A superintendent who distrusts the board could conclude that the board is trying to unilaterally impose its will, without studying the idea thoroughly or going through a time-consuming democratic decision-making process. I am sure all those thoughts briefly flitted through all of our minds.

Luckily, we were able to talk about the idea, and when the superintendent created committees at a couple of the schools to study the suggestion further, they identified the issues (Would the teachers respond promptly? Would privacy be compromised?) and a wise e-mail policy was gradually, if slowly, adopted. The board was very happy with the process, respectful of the outcome, and glad to have learned more about the issues involved. (It was also learned, once again, that growth takes time—and that is a good thing.) Most importantly, the board and superintendent realized that everyone had their hearts in the right place and were sincerely interested in doing the right thing for the district. Such experiences add to the level of trust and make future conversations easier.

Here is another, more difficult example. When I first came onto the board, during some dark days that I will describe in a minute, the time came for the board to write the superintendent's annual evaluation and district goals. The poor communication between the board and the superintendent had not completely resolved itself, and the turmoil of some very difficult teachers' contract negotiations made things worse, so the board had used the evaluation format to put in writing a number of questions about the district and the superintendent's philosophy. The superintendent, shocked to see a lengthy evaluation laced with critical input, felt unjustly criticized, and felt that the board was trying to play "gotcha." Because I was not familiar with the norm in terms of superintendent evaluations and because I did not fully appreciate how badly hurt all the parties had been, I simply did not understand all the fuss.

To me, the board had given a glowing evaluation, and was simply asking sincere questions about the district as necessary to fulfill its oversight obligations. I could only see one side and did not know any of the history behind the critical comments. After a number of healthy conversations, however, the board and superintendent came to understand each other better. We discussed the type of evaluation document that would best convey the board's interests and concerns, the superintendent came to see that the board was basically acting out of a positive intent, and communications improved. Here is the lesson, though: The following year, the evaluation was no less glowing but no less rigorous either, and the superintendent was better able to hear the board's critical input and respond to it. When you have a healthy board–superintendent relationship characterized by open communication and mutual trust, each party has more freedom to give critical input, and is more able to hear and accept that critical input. This goes both ways, and is essential for "360-degree learning."

A similar lesson applies every day in the relationship between a superintendent and the board president. The better the communication is between them, and the greater the mutual trust, the better each person will be able to "hear" the critical input from the other, and the more they will both learn.

Back to that divided and dysfunctional board. Our superintendent was sought out and hired by that board to replace a retiring superintendent, and it was clear that one of her first challenges would be to focus on the board and the district culture. Characteristically, her efforts were not "top down." Instead, she decided to allow the community to define the district culture for itself. She took the risk that, through a properly structured process, the community would reaffirm our traditional roots in democratic processes and progressive education, and help those calling for a fundamental change in the district understand that they were in the minority. After creating a forum in which all voices (parents, board members, everyone) could be heard in a nonthreatening way, the community did just that. The resulting document, a revision of the district's mission statement titled *Winnetka: A Community of Learners*, showed that the village understood the district philosophy, was generally supportive of the schools, and supported growth in important areas. Just as importantly, it reaffirmed that the community did not want the district to suddenly cast off its democratic processes for growth, as messy as they can be, and become a hierarchical place where change is dictated from the top. That gave wonderful support to the majority of the board, who had worked so hard to preserve the district culture.

With the core values of the district enunciated, our superintendent continued to work closely with the board to create new avenues for board members to become better and more educated members of the school community. Over time the obstreperous board members' terms expired, another teachers' contract was negotiated without controversy, the district passed several referenda, and the board again developed a strong reputation in the community. The superintendent was able to spend more time working on educational matters and less time managing the board. The district's ship looked like it was sailing on calm seas.

Then in 2001, another storm hit—and again, it was in contract negotiations. Our superintendent explains more about this in her chapter (van der Bogert, chapter 7, this volume), but I just want to outline what I see as its impact on the board. Board members began the negotiations meaning to use interest-based bargaining techniques, but the faculty, stung by what they felt was an unfair expiring contract (the inflation-adjusted contract had not kept up with the market during a surprisingly low-inflation period and employee health costs had skyrocketed), turned to traditional bargaining. Negotiations dragged on and a parent group, calling itself "Teachers First," became active and publicly blamed the board for the lack of progress on a contract. The board, determined to keep bargaining at the bargaining table and believing that a public fight would only damage the district relationships in the long run, responded in a limited way and did not rebut many of the charges made. Public outcry grew and became personal. The board members, who had enjoyed a strong reputation in the community, felt deceived and vilified. They felt that they had shared leadership with their partners in the community and with the faculty, only to have some of those partners go from dialog to slogans, from mutual respect to personal attack. A strike was scheduled, families were upset, and the press had a heyday. At the 11th hour, the strike was averted by a predawn settlement. This kind of discord is not uncommon elsewhere, I know, but it was a sudden and heartbreaking turnaround for our district.

The Board I Joined

This is where I and two other new board members entered the picture. One evening in November 2001 we sat in the audience and watched a tearful and dramatic board meeting that focused on the settlement. Going down the line, each board member quietly discussed how he or she had weighed the competing considerations for and against the contract. You could feel each person searching for the proper balance point, the proper conclusion. Certainly this was an expensive contract. Would its cost substantially harm the district? Would it give rise to another community backlash or endanger the passage of the next referendum? Would the salaries put us permanently ahead of the market, or would salaries elsewhere continue to rise? How much should the board be willing to pay to avoid a strike? What would happen to the future of decision making in the district if the board was perceived to "cave in" to community and staff threats? It was clear that all these questions had been considered by each board member. The vote was 4-3 in favor of the contract. The emotion in the room was palpable, but the feeling I came away with was incredible sadness.

Five minutes later the board turned over. The president read the impressive accomplishments of each of the three retiring members and the board passed resolutions of appreciation. What a way for these hardworking board members to leave their positions after many years of hard, unpaid work. We three new board members were then seated. It was a dramatic and tearful meeting, and I for one wondered what had happened to the uncontroversial board I had planned on joining.

Here was the situation, as it appeared to me. The superintendent, the administrators, and the board were completely dispirited. The faculty and parent groups had each split into camps, with those supporting Teachers First jubilant and empowered, and the others either horrified by the campaign and its tactics or outraged at the cost of the contract. Our little community had realigned itself into opposing teams.

The problem with "team" politics is that they are necessarily simplistic: Our team is always right; your team is always wrong. I knew from negotiating transactions that when two parties do not reach agreement the fault rarely rests entirely with one side. I was amazed that members of the public, privy to very little of the information being discussed in the negotiations and having heard from only one side, could honestly conclude that the Teachers First "team" was entirely right and the board "team" was entirely wrong. It seemed intellectually dishonest; it seemed to pander to emotionalism. But in emotional times it is particularly hard not to succumb to the "siren song of simplicity." It is no surprise how often good ships end up on those rocks.

Now I ask you to look through my eyes again, and put yourself in the place of a new board member in a strange (and emotionally charged) new world. I had been asked to come onto the board as vice president, which first of all tells you something about the enthusiasm the more experienced board members had for the job. So in that role I joined our superintendent and board president at monthly agenda-setting meetings. Like the other new board members, I felt a responsibility to help our battle-worn colleagues, and I realized we had some important work ahead of us. I knew that the board turnover could help the board get a fresh start in the community's eyes. I knew that the community needed to see and hear from board members (particularly the new ones) so it would be harder to cast us as the faceless "bad guys" gunning for the well-loved and well-known "good guy" teachers. And I knew we needed to blend those teams together and reunite the district in the eyes of the community if we had any hope of regaining community confidence. These were fairly concrete objectives. I was not yet as concerned about the district's culture as our superintendent and the other more experienced members of the board seemed to be. Maybe the lawyer in me felt like everyone would just have to get over it and move on. Or maybe I just did not have a clue yet. Here are four things that had me particularly stumped.

First, I did not yet know how to add my voice. The board members and administrators who had gone through the negotiations were still wounded and I did not want to do anything that could further damage them or the district. As a new member who did not know the culture very well yet, I watched what I said for a while. As it turned out, it was a good thing to listen to experienced board members so I could begin to understand the culture a little better. I did not, however, sit quietly for long, because I believe that all members of the board must be active and engaged in the group's deliberations and decisions.

Second, I had heard about the tradition of democratic or shared leadership in the Winnetka schools, but what did that mean? To me (and maybe to others from the business world) it was unfamiliar territory. Was democratic leadership more common in education, or was Winnetka unusual? Given the very undemocratic process we had just gone through, should we begin to move away from those democratic practices? Would we be fools not to scale back faculty and staff involvement in decision making? This was and remains one of the biggest questions our board has faced: What do we do when democratic processes fail? Do we retreat into a more hierarchical approach or do we just keep plowing ahead, hoping that people will be nicer next time? It took some time for me to come to what in the end is the obvious answer. I will leave you in suspense and circle back to this at the end.

Third, it was unclear how to best communicate with the public. The board's communication with the public had not been able to head off this controversy. How can the board answer public criticism about an ongoing process that is not public—especially when a reaction could derail the progress? This relates not only to negotiations, but also to other issues such as personnel. How can the board encourage the public to be patient with a process they necessarily know little about? How can the board convey complex ideas to an involved public that is sometimes swayed by emotion and slogans? I think our board was already comfortable with the idea that things can be messy, not simple, but the question was how to convey that to impatient constituents. I will admit right now that I have no greater idea how to manage this than I did my first day on the board. All we can do, I believe, is try hard, be sincere and honest, urge patience, and refer back to the district values.

Finally, and probably most to the point, what is the correct board–superintendent relationship? Here is where I had the most questions. I believed that the correct board–superintendent relationship was dependent on the board finding a balance somewhere between unthinking trust in the administration and micromanagement, but I had no real idea where that balance should be. Was the balance point different on different issues—on finances, curriculum, communications, district management style, political ramifications of decisions, or the district culture? What fiduciary responsibility does the board have to oversee the superintendent? Should a superintendent's qualifications as a professional educator mean that her decisions about curriculum need no review by the board? Does the fact that the board was elected mean that its decisions about political matters need no review by the superintendent? I believed that when you got those balances right you would have a board and superintendent working well together, with respect for each other's roles. I believe now that the solution to these essential questions lies not in the balance between trust and micromanagement, but in the messier practice of exercising shared leadership and 360-degree learning.

These were the questions that were on my mind, and they felt rather concrete to me, rather manageable. I thought maybe a good solid talk with a long-standing board member would set me straight, and I could get on with my new job. I wanted, to be perfectly candid, simple and workable answers to these questions. Instead, what I got from our board and from our superintendent was something altogether less concrete and less simple. What I got was a more amorphous conversation about values. I felt like someone who signed up for a bookkeeping class who was suddenly given readings on the history and art of mathematics. It was interesting but I was not sure how it was going to help me get my job done.

I was wrong. Only after listening to our superintendent talk about the culture and district values (and hearing the same message reflected from others in the district, at Summer Institutes, the annual new teachers retreat, and throughout the community) did I begin to appreciate that I was missing a piece. The board must participate in formulating those values to really know them. It must really know them in order to model them and articulate them to other members of the school community. It must model and articulate them to reinforce those values to everyone involved with the schools and to build respect and trust for the board. When all this is accomplished, the board–superintendent relationship will be very strong because it is rooted in a common vision and will set a tone for the entire district. So you see there was a lot I did not know that I did not know. This was the work in front of us, and I had no idea it was even there.

Learning on the Job: Three Lessons I Did Not Realize I Was Learning

Luckily for me, our superintendent has made learning on the job a great experience. The thing about having her teach you is that you do not realize you are being taught. You will sit there on the couch in her office, new on the job, saying some dumb thing, and she will sit there calmly, seemingly agreeing and mentioning a thing or two, until all of a sudden you find yourself telling her why that was a dumb idea in the first place, and that you really feel quite differently about the matter. It is similar to what she calls "leading from behind" (i.e., sitting in the figurative back of the room while helping the leaders in the front get to a good place). I have seen her do it. I know she's done it to me many times, although I have only caught her at it a time or two.

Here is a recent example. In an effort to maximize communication we decided to send a letter not only to every parent, but also to every household in the district. We thought this should be the first of a series of letters—something our superintendent seemed hesitant to undertake, although she did not really say so. Now, we are a lean district, and there are few staff members available to physically put together 5,000 letters. So, board members offered to help, which they did in over 2 days' time. Those 2 long days gave the board plenty of time to think it over and decide that we really did not need those other village-wide mailings after all, and I was able to spend the next week with a heating pad on my shoulder.

Because I was made vice president of the board in my first year and then president a year later, I spent a lot of time on our superintendent's couch. From that vantage point, I watched her spend a lot less time than I had expected reading memos, having meetings, or putting out "fires in the inbox," and a lot more time just being available to talk. I came to realize that was very productive time, as it helped her build community while also keeping her in touch with what people were thinking and saying. In fact, most of what she did those first years after the negotiations was very deliberately done to strengthen the district and the culture, and she did it in three important ways. She (1) brought people together; (2) spoke openly about values; and (3) worked hard to make sure leadership was shared in the district. This was fascinating for me to watch, and it gave me a model as I tried to learn how to be a good board president. But more importantly, by doing these three things, she created a culture that reinforced itself, allowing the board, staff, new teachers, administrators (including herself), and parents to learn from each other in a 360-degree way. It also happily brought the board into the fun part of leadership. I want to share with you what those efforts looked like on the ground.

Bringing People Together

The members of the board—particularly the new ones—were determined to get out there among the public and faculty, to give a personal face to the board. We came up with the idea of making a budget presentation to the teachers association, in which we could introduce ourselves and perhaps share some of the finer points of school board finance. In preparing, we began to realize how much mistrust there was, as we learned to address whispered suspicions regarding "hidden" funds, and so on. Happily, the presentation went fairly well and the fact that we could comfortably discuss the intricacies of such things as tax levies added somewhat to the board's credibility. We became encouraged. We then did a series of "meet the new school board members" meetings with the Parent-Teacher Association (PTA). I believed that having fresh faces, unassociated with the negotiations, was very important, and we worked hard not to be drawn into the prevailing "us versus them" mentality.

Still, there were wounds. When the superintendent brought one of our most outstanding teachers to the board for approval as our new curriculum coordinator, a veteran board member could not help but let those wounds show, asking the candidate if she would be capable of going from the teacher to the administrator ranks. It could not have been clearer; she was asking if the candidate was willing to leave her coworkers and go to the "other team." The candidate looked stricken.

I jumped in to assure her that we were all on the same team. Thankfully, she took on the job. This brings to mind how difficult and awkward it sometimes was to be a new board member working to change relationships and mindsets without seeming to suggest that you "know better" than experienced and dedicated sitting board members.

In bringing people together, the board president has to first and foremost bring the board members together. The way I handled this was to admit frequently and eagerly (and honestly) how little I knew about an issue, all the while insisting on talking it out with the board until I understood it thoroughly. That conversation, which my fellow board members will confirm can take some time, frequently leads to a better understanding of the issue, to better defined opinions by individual board members, and to everyone having a better understanding of and respect for others' opinions. It also leads to a more collegial feeling among board members and to a preponderance of decisions by consensus. It may go against conventional advice that we learn by listening and not by talking, but to fully understand something I need to talk it out, and I think most other people do as well.

Our superintendent had many more plans for the board to informally relate with the staff. Before I describe these to you, I need to say something about how we have been able to do this. It is undeniable that putting board members and staff together in informal situations risks inappropriate conversations, especially about personnel issues. For such efforts to work, there has to be a very real acknowledgement of the boundaries between appropriate and inappropriate conversations, and the board members in particular must be ready and able to quickly steer out-of-bounds conversations back in-bounds. All of this takes a lot of courage on the part of the superintendent, and it is not foolproof, but I believe the benefits have outweighed the risks in Winnetka.

Visiting the schools. One of the most interesting efforts is our superintendent's Friday tour of the school buildings with board members. Any available board member joins her to walk through a building, often with the principal, stopping in classrooms occasionally to see what is going on and to chat with the teacher. The board members are there as learners, not as overseers, and the teachers are eager to share what is going on in their classrooms. As a new board member, I saw these informal tours as purely benefiting me, as I was able to meet faculty and staff, get to know the buildings, take a look at some vintage boiler rooms, see classrooms in action, and witness firsthand some of the educational practices we heard so much about. (In fact, it is important to note that these tours are an excellent way for board members to learn more about the philosophy and practice of the schools from the experts—the teachers—without being explicitly told they are being taught anything.) Let us be honest, school board members really like schools and children. That is why we joined a school board rather than some other board, and that is why it is sometimes difficult to get us to remember that we are not the educators. Touring a building with rows of tiny sneakers in the hallways is something that delights and energizes us.

I did not appreciate how important these tours were to the staff, however, in building relationships and breaking down barriers, until I began to hear the teachers' reactions. Many of them told us how surprised and pleased they were that board members would "take the time" to tour the buildings. (I personally am waiting for someone to thank me for "taking the time" to comb through policy manuals, read budgets, and decipher the latest state legislation. That takes much more time and is much less fun.) If our tour bogged down and did not get to all the classes we intended to see, the teachers we did not visit would be disappointed. And new teachers who initially (and much to our surprise) were unnerved by having school board members touring their classrooms became more comfortable as they got to know us better and as they witnessed the relationship of mutual trust and respect between the board and the superintendent. Clearly, getting the board members into the buildings was important.

In the spring of my first year as board president, our superintendent asked me if I would join her for the annual tradition of walking through the buildings and giving tenure letters to newly tenured teachers. Again, it was a rewarding afternoon, requiring minimal effort and giving me maximum satisfaction, but I was struck by how much everyone in the buildings seemed to appreciate it. When I reflected on it, I realized that the budget presentation to the teachers association took about 100 hours of work. This walk-through was about two hours of sheer enjoyment. I could not be sure which effort created more good will and trust for the board.

I began to reflect on the seemingly casual practice of building bridges by informal contact, and I began to see something more intentional about it. Our superintendent's leadership style involves lots of conversations on her couch, as I mentioned, but it also involves lots of casual conversations while walking around. A leadership book I picked up at a school board conference[2] said Lincoln did much the same thing, and called it "management by wandering around [MBWA]," a phrase coined in the 1982 book *In Search of Excellence* (Peters & Waterman). Having come from a business model where work was done through structured meetings, this MBWA model initially seems sloppy, empty, aimless. Knowing that Lincoln was none of these things, and seeing how our informal gatherings created such powerful connections and stronger understandings, I realized that this is one of the leadership tools our superintendent uses to build community. Board members see firsthand the professional and thoughtful ways the staff brings educational philosophy into the school. This reinforces the value of staff opinions for board members, who become more responsive to learning from people who other more hierarchically-minded boards might only see as subordinates. The staff sees the board members as interested in what they are doing in their schools, and asking articulate and relevant questions. This helps the teachers feel less intimidated by the board members and more willing to ask real questions of people who would more likely be viewed as "bosses" in other more hierarchically-minded districts. It is another effective way to open us up to 360-degree learning.

Special gatherings. Our superintendent also created more formal opportunities for board members to relate to and learn from the faculty. To my mind, the most effective is the Summer Institute, a 3-day seminar held the week after school ends. This is a well-organized and thoughtful seminar run by staff and often facilitated by nationally known educational experts. Board members, administrators, faculty, associates, and other staff come together in large and small group settings to discuss the district's history, values, and goals. I am always grateful to be included. At first, board members are hesitant to offer their layperson opinions and teachers are hesitant to speak up in front of board members, but pretty soon, we are just speaking to each other as people. We learn to take risks with each other and we learn from each other. The same thing happens at the New Teacher Retreat, where board members join new teachers and their mentor teachers at a dinner, share stories, and then roast marshmallows around a campfire. Bridges are built, trust is created, and we learn from each other. It is another 360-degree learning experience.

Relations within the board. I do not want to fail to mention that board members must also make the effort of getting to know each other. We did not undertake that effort in any formal way, but we all worked hard to develop a friendly and supportive environment by making sure everyone's voice was heard at meetings, by acknowledging board members' efforts, by being genuinely interested in each other's lives, and by bringing snacks to meetings that promised to go late. As the board president, I felt a responsibility to be sure that the culture of our board was strong and healthy, and if it seemed that one or more board members were feeling out of the mainstream, I would try to check in with them to see how they were doing. I tried to make all board members feel welcome and valued, and used humor a lot. I particularly encouraged new members to share their ideas, as it gives the rest of the board the benefit of their thinking and it reduces the significant danger that someone not actively participating in a board decision will begin to feel marginalized and less committed to the group's decision. Still, bringing the board together is not a one-person effort, and I do not think that a one-person effort would work anyway.

At one point it became very important to bring board members together when someone who had been perceived as critical of the board later joined it. This new board member clearly wondered how he would be accepted, and it *was* a real issue for one or two long-standing board members. I made time to chat with the new member after meetings, and through my word and manner tried to demonstrate to him and to others that I welcomed him and felt confident he would be a great addition to the board—as he indeed was. I believe this new member was pleased and relieved to be accepted, and the positive climate we created helped buffer any negative expectations from other board members and from the public, who were able to see that we would not permit ourselves to be fractured.

Written communications can also help bring board members together. Although we are careful about the use of e-mail, I am a big proponent of periodically sending friendly e-mails to board members, reminding them of meetings or coordinating schedules, all the while being sure to rib one of our board members for his undying allegiance to the University of Illinois and his relentlessly orange sport shirts. (During baseball season, however, you cannot rib our new board president about the Boston Red Sox *at all*.)

These sorts of things may seem small, but I think they are incredibly important. In dealing informally with board members, the president must try to be efficient and on top of things, of course; but he or she should also be friendly and pleasant and occasionally bring some humor into the mix. Board members are volunteers, taking time out of their busy lives to try to serve the community, often at the expense of work and family. They should be respected for that commitment and we should do everything possible to make that service pleasant, rewarding, and to the extent possible, fun.

Both within the board and with the board's dealings with others, we worked to adopt the advice our attorney gave us during negotiations: "assume positive intent." That usually works—either because the other person actually did have positive intent, or because faced with our dogged good will, any negative intent thawed before it could do any harm. (This advice is a corollary to Mark Twain's saying "When in doubt, tell the truth. It will confound your enemies and astound your friends.") Anyway, as Pollyanna-ish as it sounds, it is both the right thing to do and wonderfully effective.

Speaking About Values

I mentioned that talking about organizational values—and building things out of pipe cleaners and feathers—was not something this big-firm lawyer was well prepared for. What were we doing talking about values? Is the role of the board fiduciary and oversight, or it is more strategic and visionary? I think many board members arrive with the belief that someone else (a Washburne or other educator, or the superintendent) has defined the district's values and goals, and the board's role is to make sure the administration stays on the straight and narrow. Talking about values is difficult and unfamiliar, and the topic is murky and undefined.

In the wake of the difficult negotiations of 2001, our superintendent talked a lot about the culture of the district and the values of the organization. She felt single-handedly responsible for maintaining the unique child-centered culture of the schools and brought enormous passion to the matter. At the time I wondered if this conversation about values and culture was truly necessary for the future direction of the district, or whether it was just necessary for our superintendent to make sense of what happened. How would the experience of these negotiations really affect the culture? Was the culture that important, or that fragile? Could we not just move on? I could not get a read on this from the board members who had gone through negotiations, as they were so upset about the whole thing, and I could not get a read from the new board members, like me, who had not gone through the experience.

It was undeniable, however, that our superintendent's statements about values—in her opening day statement, her remarks at the Summer Institute, and so on—strongly affected board members, faculty, and administrators. The willingness to share her very passionate thoughts on the matter was much appreciated by the faculty, and teachers made a point of coming up to me to express that appreciation. Intellectually, our superintendent's methods of sharing those values, through poetry and literature as well as through traditional educational writings, said a lot about how she thought. People seeking a simplistic, definitive game plan do not do so through poetry, which tends to invite messy and unique interpretations.

In the Summer Institute after negotiations, Bena Kallick, a nationally known educational consultant who has worked with the district for many years, led us in a wonderful conversation about messy dilemmas and how a district committed to progressive education is necessarily faced with competing truths. It was of course a topic very much on our superintendent's mind, and one she followed up with at the next fall's opening day speech. The speech was made to the faculty and staff, but board members attended too. As usual, while we may have thought we were there to lend support, there was plenty to learn. In her speech that day, the superintendent talked about how our willingness to accept messy dilemmas affects leadership of the district.

As I read, I realized a paradox about our district. We are on one hand strong because we choose to live, explore, and make sense of the tensions. We don't choose to turn our back on the complexities of life in schools. On the other hand it makes us so vulnerable. We don't have easy, comforting answers. Like living all of life, we are taking a risk.

To stay true to those complexities, to avoid either/or thinking, our superintendent recommended having a "true dialog with one another" in which we "suspend assumptions and enter into a genuine 'thinking together.' " This was good advice for the school board too.

Before I leave this topic of values, I want to describe a couple of events that helped me learn to be a little "messier" in my thinking, and that helped me remember that the best work is done in a collaborative fashion. Early on in my board service there was a lot of parent concern over our ability to challenge all the children in the classroom—to diversify education not only for those children who were struggling, but particularly for those children who were not, all within the context of an inclusive classroom. Parents called for an answer, and fast. It seemed reasonable to have the administration look at the issue and report back within a couple of months. That is what a law firm would do. As someone with no training in education, I did not realize that diverse learning styles were a big topic in progressive education, or that resolving the issues brought to us would (and should) take more than a couple of months.

As a new board member I kept my ideas to myself, long enough to listen to the other board members. They did not want the board to define what needed to be done. They did not want to create a rigid time frame. They were willing to put the matter in our superintendent's hands, despite some unhappy parents. Was that the right thing to do? Was the board too blindly trusting of the administration? In fact, the process our superintendent put in place allowed the faculty to carefully consider what it does for children, to put together a thoughtful Diverse Learners Study, to help all staff explore the concepts and how they relate to our philosophy, and ultimately to present to the parents a wonderful seminar showing the ways the teachers reach and challenge all the students in a classroom. The Diverse Learners Study was my first introduction to our superintendent's method of "leading from the back of the room." It was messy, it took time, but it was the only way to go.

Another example involved a program called Character Counts. A few years ago the parent community was deeply concerned about social and emotional learning, and particularly concerned with bullying. At the same time, the village police chief felt that the village, including the schools, should adopt Character Counts as a community-wide initiative. The chief called a meeting of various school and community representatives and presented the program. At first glance, Character Counts had some things going for it. It is absolutely ready to go, no additional work required; it had some nice looking handouts; and it was being strongly pushed by the chief. Rather than bowing to the simple and expedient solution, however, our superintendent created a committee to consider what type of social/emotional program would be best for the district. Teachers and administrators ended up creating a program just for Winnetka, custom-made for each of the various schools and age groups. A committee was formed at the middle school to expand the initiative into the curriculum, and I was invited to participate as liaison from the school board. The energy and passion that the teachers and administrators brought to the project allowed the resulting initiative to be enthusiastically adopted by the teachers in that building, resulting in a program that has become an important part of the school day. It is also a program that has earned some recognition and fostered new and creative thinking in some of the younger grades in the district. In contrast, Character Counts or any program picked off the shelf and planted into the curriculum would have had a much harder time being accepted.

As I became more impressed with the importance of talking about values in the district, I began to let the statements I made as board president to the staff and community reflect my understanding about the district's culture and philosophy. In short, I began to speak more freely from the heart. It was never the kind of learned statement that might come from an educator, but I think hearing the board president acknowledge and honor our educational goals and culture helps the faculty feel that the board members "get it" and appreciate their work. I particularly remember having a long-time faculty member tell me how much she appreciated my speeches. She told me she was surprised and pleased to have the board president speak about the school's goals and values in a way that showed a willingness to learn. I was pleased that those talks had such a strong effect on her; I was bemused that she had such low expectations of me to begin with; and I was relieved that an English teacher did not find significant fault with my sentence structures. Whether in speeches or in other settings with faculty and staff, having the board members learn about and discuss educational philosophy and the attendant messy dilemmas helps faculty feel more confident that the board will be less likely to interfere in the good work of education or succumb to demands for simple solutions. Having the board conversant in these ideas also increases the likelihood that those ideas will be absorbed and reflected back to the faculty, parents, and community.

So is joining in the conversation about the district's values really important? If it is (and I believe it is), why does it seem so foreign at first? Harvard professor Richard Chait and coauthors William Ryan and Barbara Taylor argue in *Governance as Leadership: Reframing the Work of Nonprofit Boards* (2005) that nonprofit board members tend to do just what I initially tend to do—focus too much on administrative matters rather than on the important "generative" leadership thinking in which the organization creates strategies, policies, and actions. According to Chait,

> When you think of a decision-making flow, all we are suggesting is that boards get at the headwaters. They need to get way upstream; they tend to wade in much too far downstream. Generative thinking is getting to the question before the question. It's actually the fun part of governance. It's not about narrow technical expertise. Generative work is almost always about questions of values, beliefs, assumptions, and organizational cultures. That's what makes it interesting, but also what makes it important is to have people in those conversations who understand the institution, but have some degree of distance. (Salls, 2005, pp. 15–16)

Without this fundamental conversation about values, culture, and who we are as a district, the board is limited to more managerial tasks—and then left to second-guess the values chosen by others. As a board member, I would hate to miss the conversation—it *is* the fun part. I believe the board, with its degree of distance and ability to reflect the community's thoughts, does add something to the analysis. But most importantly, I think having the board in on the conversation about values is part of the commitment to shared leadership. Unless the board is part of that essential conversation, it will not have ownership in the concepts, it will not be conversant, and it will not reflect those values to the staff, the administrators, the public, and even the superintendent. How important is that? I cannot quantify it for you, but I know the look of relief in the eyes of a teacher or administrator after hearing something that reassured them that the board really does "get it."

One final thought on why talking about values is important, and that is the most important reason—to keep everyone focused on the essential purpose of education—*to do what is best for the kids*. I have recently heard from a number of experts, involved with districts all over the country, that school boards are getting worse every year as board members focus more on adult issues like private ambitions, political agendas, and self-aggrandizement. Management of school boards has increasingly taken more of the superintendent's time, at the expense of education. This may seem obvious to superintendents, but as a board member it is surprising and depressing. To think that superintendents increasingly view school boards as an obstacle to doing a good job is heartbreaking for those of us who want to believe that board service helps, rather than hinders, the education of our nation's children. Perhaps talking about values will help us all remember why we are in these positions in the first place.

Continuing to Share Leadership

Winnetka has always prided itself on using the democratic model of decision making, but sharing leadership is really hard; it takes a certain amount of courage as well as faith in your educational partners. Can you trust that they will understand and protect the organization's values? What about turnover; will the new people take the time to learn before rushing into change? If you give the partners a new voice in decision making, will they go too far, trying to use force rather than logic to influence the decision? The faith it takes to continue to share leadership is severely tested in times of turmoil. What do you do if members of the staff or community choose not to engage in a real democratic conversation about an issue, but rather use power (a petition, strike, or other simplistic appeal to the media or the public) to impose their will? What do you do if the staff begins to go directly to individual board members to circumvent their principal and superintendent? What do you do if a vocal minority of the public tries to force the firing of a teacher through a strident letter-writing campaign that threatens to disrupt an ongoing remediation process? In short, what do you do if democratic processes do not seem to work? While our superintendent addresses it from her perspective in her chapter, these questions have certainly had to be addressed by the board as well.

After a particularly bad experience, it is natural to think about scaling back your commitment to shared leadership, not necessarily punitively (although there is that instinct too) but in self-protection. "Fool me once, shame on you; fool me twice, shame on me," whispers in one ear. After all, the board has been given the authority and the duty to make decisions on behalf of the community. If the only input the board gets is from people who want to throw vegetables[3] rather than study issues, maybe the board needs to simply exercise that authority on its own. Maybe the board needs to be more top-down.

In the other ear, however, you hear a voice urging you not to give up on democratic processes. If we know those processes make for a better organization, is it not the job of the board and administration to maintain their commitment to such principles, rather than take the easy way out? Remember, most of the public wants the board to stand up to the vocal minority when necessary, to engage in a thoughtful dialog with everyone involved, to be deliberative in its decision making, and ultimately to do what the board believes is the right thing for the entire community.

After listening to these voices for several years, I finally know where I stand. In retrospect, the answer is obvious: *There is no simple answer*. It is a classic paradox, and in this paradox two things are true:

First, the board must try to protect the district and its people from future damage. It would be naïve to ignore the abuse of the democratic process and hope it gets better, and it would be unfair to leave the organization and its people at risk. So what can the board do? It must learn what motivates the people who use power to force their hand. It must show the damage power plays cause to the organization and to individuals. It must reassure the majority that the district will not be hijacked by a vocal minority. It must look to the long-term good of the organization. It must remind everyone involved about the limitations of shared leadership; the board is open to 360-degree learning, but it must—not *can*, but *must*—ultimately make the decisions it is entrusted to make. This sounds like a battle cry, but it is not. It is exactly what our superintendent accomplished by (1) bringing people together; (2) speaking about values; and, yes, (3) continuing to share leadership.

That is the second and paradoxical piece. The board must continue to share leadership because in the long run, shared leadership is the best leadership. It is that simple, but it is not that easy. It is not easy because shared leadership is hard to manage, takes courage, and occasionally requires a lot of mopping up. It is also often not much fun to invite the very people who have been throwing vegetables at you into the discussion, especially when they come away from the experience thinking they have triumphed. Boards may be used to being yelled at by the occasional uninformed and strident member of the public, but it is lonely sitting up in that seat, quietly sticking with your principles while your reputation is being attacked. This is not the fun part of board service, and I guarantee no one wants to share *that* part of leadership.

But in the end, it is the right thing to do, and when the board continues to share leadership it makes a strong statement to the silent majority about the goals and values of the district. There will always be a small percentage of the community who will abuse shared leadership for whatever reason. All we can do is to try to make the rest of the community as strong as possible so that they will not succumb to the virus of that small percentage. On my wall is a calendar of quotations my Quaker grandmother (a former school board member herself) first started sending me 30 years ago. One of the quotations this month reads:

Some citizens are so good that nothing a leader can do will make them better. Others are so incorrigible that nothing can be done to improve them. But the great bulk of the people go with the moral tide of the moment. The leader must help create that tide.[4]

We must eventually ignore the incorrigible few, assume positive intent in the rest, and try to create the right tide.

One last thought on shared leadership. In Winnetka, even while there have been those bumps in the road, shared leadership has become part of the district culture and has spread to include a number of new constituents. Not only are teachers, administrators, staff, the board, parents, and students involved in decision making, but so are a number of community organizations including the Winnetka Caucus and the

Winnetka Public Schools Foundation. In addition, citizens seek to form advisory groups to consider and evaluate matters affecting the schools.

Our use of advisory groups brings up a lesson I learned about shared leadership and the time it can take. In the wake of a successful referendum in 2003 the village grew more aware of the complexity of public school finances, and began to ask for a more in-depth analysis of the types of financial information that would be most useful to the public. Residents called for a citizens' advisory committee on the topic. It sounded like a good idea, and it had some strong support on the board. I told our superintendent that I thought this would be a great way to increase public understanding of our financial picture (particularly of the complex state laws restricting the ability to increase tax levies) and to increase our understanding of what the citizens want to know. She agreed. Best of all, I continued, using citizen volunteers this way would really save her some time. Reiterating her support, she gently corrected me; it would not save her time, but cost it.

As much as citizens groups can be valuable, they must be well structured, and she would need to do that.

And that is what happened. The superintendent was closely involved in structuring the committee, welcoming the members, and setting the agendas. There were many thoughtful meetings over a period of months, and the citizens' group created a comprehensive list of the most frequently asked financial questions and their answers. The group suggested a written Financial Guide and an Annual Schools Report, and the superintendent ultimately wrote those two documents over a spring break.

This was a worthy project and a lot was accomplished, but I learned something—that sharing leadership is rarely a time-saver. For a district to maintain its culture of shared leadership the superintendent must serve as the keeper of the processes that allow for democratic decision making, and this responsibility is a complicated one.

Successes: The Power of a Strong Board–Superintendent Relationship

I have described the three types of leadership practices our superintendent has quietly and unobtrusively nurtured in the district: (1) bringing people together; (2) speaking about values; and (3) sharing leadership. Those practices were reflected and reinforced by a board that truly and deeply believes in the values and goals of our district. The board and superintendent had developed a very strong relationship rooted in these common values and based on a mutual respect. I believe that relationship made the district stronger, gave the district additional credibility in the public eye, and was a major factor in the successes of the next couple of years.

Can you go out to the public to make the case for an operating tax referendum without having a strong and mutually supportive board–superintendent relationship? Maybe so, but I would not want to do it. The intensive effort of 50 or more public presentations before every kind of audience was tough enough as it was. While the presentation was about finances, it was also fundamentally about the district's values and goals. What kind of school system does our community want? What are we willing to sacrifice for it? Long-time residents knew about the historical values of the school system and wanted to see the superintendent and board reflect those values. Younger families wanted to be sure no sudden change was underway that would undermine the education of their children. The strong board–superintendent relationship made our public appeal much stronger, and helped spread awareness of the values and goals of our educational system.

Recently we completed another round of negotiations and I am thrilled to say things turned out much differently this time. Our superintendent had put in an enormous amount of time preparing for these negotiations, almost from the day after that November board meeting in 2001. After 4 years of "getting to know you"—Friday school tours, Summer Institutes, board attendance at opening day gatherings, opening day assemblies and picnics and holiday parties—and concerted efforts to explore and enunciate our values, more of the faculty knew and trusted the board members. Our superintendent had used her opening day speech to honestly address her hopes and fears about the coming negotiations, and the board and faculty heard her. By the time we got into the negotiating room, the teachers' negotiating team and board were unified in wanting a negotiation process that honored the shared leadership values of the district. The process we created and used did just that; the end result was fair; and we finished early. I do not know what else you could ask for.

One of the most exciting successes is the way our 360-degree learning has become institutionalized in the district. We do not participate in 360-degree learning because we happen to be individually curious people; we do so because it is built into the fabric of the district. The Summer Institute welcomes and expects a process of self-reflection and examination. Our new teacher retreat and mentoring program creates a forum for new teachers to learn from senior teachers, and that creates a climate in which asking questions and learning from each other is expected. Our teachers participate in a Masters program that invites ongoing learning. The board tours the schools, learning about education from our wonderful teachers and, most importantly, the real experts—the kids. Our superintendent has very deliberately woven these learning experiences throughout the institutions of our district, and they are there to stay. At one new teacher retreat an experienced faculty member was giving the new teachers a history of the district. On the timeline, together with the tenure of Carleton Washburne and the construction of Crow Island School, was 2003—the year the board began attending the faculty holiday party. The institutions of the district are built on the principles we have worked on in the last few years, and I know they will outlast the tenures of all of us.

The Future

That is my story so far. I hope it has some insights for you. I do not claim to know how to replicate our strong board–superintendent relationship and I do not claim that a strong relationship will inoculate a district from turmoil (in fact I know that is not the case). But I do know that the work done by our superintendent and board in preserving the district's culture and fostering the superintendent–board relationship strengthened everything about our district. In particular, I have learned an enormous amount about leadership from my fellow board members and our superintendent and I will always value that knowledge.

The challenge for us now is to sustain the culture in the future, based not on individuals or personalities, but on the institutions into which we have woven the practice of shared leadership. The job of exploring and reflecting the district culture is never ending, as new board members, faculty, administrators, PTA officers, and parents come to the district. I hope each of those new people will be educated into the district culture and the philosophy of shared leadership as I was. Some of that education may come out of formal training, but most of it will come out of the shared leadership opportunities and the 360-degree learning that happens here. That is the type of education I value the most.

In my final address to the faculty as board president I described this sort of education. It was at an annual dinner where we honor long-term and retiring staff and sing "The Circle Game" and reflect on changing times. My twin sons were graduating from the district and within a year my youngest daughter would be as well, so the sense of changing times was definitely on my mind. I talked to the group about how as a new parent I had not fully understood the district philosophy, but chose to be patient with it and trust the teachers to make it all work out. In the following years I was able to watch the educational philosophy at work, both as a parent and as a board member, and I recited some of the opportunities given to me: the Summer Institute, working with educational experts, watching the thoughtful and persuasive Diverse Learners Study presentation, and talking to the teachers in the classrooms on Fridays. I concluded:

So things change, the circle turns, my kids go to high school. I am still an absolute amateur when it comes to understanding our educational philosophy, but I am now an unabashed fan. William Butler Yeats wrote: "Education is not the filling of a pail, but the lighting of a fire." You lay the groundwork and light a spark, and what happens is magic. Or as one of our fourth grade teachers said recently, "I only teach one subject: curiosity."

Thank you for everything you do every day in the schools and for the kids. Thank you for teaching to the child, for understanding them, for challenging them, for respecting them, for nurturing them in times of difficulty, for celebrating with them in times of joy. Thank you for educating me as you educated my children.

And so I remain, a board member whose education is a work in progress. But surrounded by wonderful board members, talented teachers, effective staff, and a very wise superintendent, I—like most people—have a chance of understanding and conveying the philosophy and culture of our district to the next generation. And that is the basis of a very strong district indeed.

Notes

1. The Winnetka Caucus is a group of approximately 70 residents serving 2-year terms, which seeks the names of promising board members, interviews them, and then "slates" or recommends a candidate for each open seat. Only in times of extreme controversy does anyone run opposed to the Caucus candidate. This has the happy effect of bringing people into board service who (1) have good business and board experience and necessary business skills such as accounting, marketing, communication, or law; (2) are selected to represent the various facets of the community; (3) have not been forced by the campaign process to take a firm public position on educational issues, but rather are able to join the board, learn the issues, and then form an informed opinion; and (4) did not join the board out of a desire to see their name on a campaign button.

2. Phillips, D.T. (1992). *Lincoln on leadership: Executive strategies for tough times* (pp. 14–15). New York: Warner Books.

3. This was the advice given by a graduating eighth grader last spring, and it has since become something of a mantra for our board. She told her classmates not to be like the

audience in the movie *Young Frankenstein*, who threw cabbages and tomatoes at the tap-dancing monster when he stumbled. At least he tried, she admonished. Instead, we should have the courage to try new things, to learn new things; "to take risks, be supportive of people who do and remember . . . do not throw vegetables."

4. Scattergood Calendar, September, 2005. Quotation attributed to a 19th-century Japanese philosopher.

References

Chait, R.P., Ryan, W.P., & Taylor, B.E. (2005). *Governance as leadership: Reframing the work of nonprofit boards*. Hoboken, NJ: John Wiley & Sons.

Peters, T., & Waterman, R. (1982). *In search of excellence*. New York: Harper & Row.

Salls, M. (2005, April 4). *Why nonprofits have a board problem*. Harvard Business School: Working Knowledge for Business Leaders. Retrieved September 3, 2005 from http://hbswk.hbs.edu/item.jhtml?id=4735&t=nonprofit

Walters, J.D. (1993). *Secrets of leadership*. Nevada City, CA: Crystal Clarity Publishers.

Most of us started our superintendency committed to keeping our eye on the higher purposes of education, vowing not to get bogged down in the managerial details. John Wiens shares his quest for an intellectual understanding of the role, a meaningful theory of leadership, and the creation of an environment that helped others pursue similar quests.

CHAPTER 9

Educational Leadership as Civic Humanism

JOHN R. WIENS

Mommy, how do we know that we're not just characters in a book and someone isn't just reading us?

Why do you ask?

Well, because we're always reading about other people, and I was just wondering.
—Anais, 2004 (age 4) and Her Mother[1]

To Anais's grandfather, this conversation frames the ethical-political condition of humankind, thereby capturing rather nicely the ironic situation in which one identifiable group of people, educational superintendents, live their lives. Anais is a thinker—she wonders about what she "knows." She is humble enough to say she wonders and courageous enough to say it out loud. Thoughtful superintendents also wonder, for example, about whether they are leading or being led. In rare moments of private contemplation they wonder about their rights and responsibilities to lead and be led. In moments of clarity they are able to see the potential to lead—to imagine the improbable—to initiate conversations that contribute, or have contributed, to making the world a better place. In moments of pensiveness they may, like I did, wonder whether their work has anything to do with what they studied in their educational administration programs at university. They may in their wonder realize that education, and, by extension, educational leadership, are everyone's birthright and potential—and that who they are, and what they do as people, often does and can have a positive effect on others and the world. And they may realize, like I did, that being a superintendent is a privilege afforded to few—a privilege that tests our very humanity at the same time as it grants us great opportunities to enhance humanity.

I like the way Hannah Arendt (1968), perhaps the greatest political thinker of the twentieth century, talks about education:

> What concerns us all and cannot be turned over to the special science of pedagogy is the relation between grown-ups and children in general or, putting it in even more general and exact terms, our attitude toward the fact of natality: the fact that we have all come into the world by being born and that this world is constantly renewed through birth. Education is the point at which we decide whether we love the world enough to assume responsibility for it and by the same token save it from that ruin, which, except for renewal, except for the coming of the new and the young, would be inevitable. And education, too, is where we decide whether we love our children enough not to expel them from our world and leave them to their own devices, nor to strike from their hands their changes of undertaking something new, something unforeseen by us, but to prepare them in advance for the task of renewing a common world. (p. 196)

These are hopeful—however lofty—and seemingly abstract sentiments. First, to superintendents, they suggest that we are not in this alone. While we may feel often that we are the only ones willing to accept these tough responsibilities, they do not and cannot fall on us alone. There is room for individual and personal decision and discretion, and Arendt suggests that what we decide, individually and collectively, has the potential to make a world-shattering difference. Finally, she suggests that our authority comes from our humanity, our being human, more so than from our positions, status, and training. To be a superintendent is, above all else, to be a human being concerned with advancement of the human condition. It is my view also that when we look first to our humanity, as opposed to our positions and qualifications for our authority and our responsibility, it changes the job as conventionally conceptualized and practiced. "To educate" means, as it always has, "to lead forth to a good life." And in a democracy, as Arendt suggests, to educate means preparing children to assume responsible citizen roles in the world for the sake of a better world. These are hard things to remember as a superintendent in a world preoccupied with managerial and systems accountability.

A Qualified Confession

I am a baby boomer—born in the late 1940s and schooled in the 1950s and 1960s. I have a love–hate relationship with organizations, institutions, and systems. Long before I understood the systems world–lifeworld dichotomy framed by Jürgen Habermas (1987), I worried, in my soul, that systems and their trappings dehumanized the world.

Roughly put, Habermas posited that systems are essential artifacts of our increasingly complex, multifaceted, globalized world but that systems' world characteristics—an emphasis on hierarchical positions, predetermined policies and procedures, guaranteed strategies and outcomes, and the like—tend to push aside human lifeworld considerations, making the world generally less hospitable. Systems frown on the individual initiative, changing priorities and purposes, and unpredictable consequences that mark our everyday lives—instead promising an end to human error and randomness. Thus, while systems are necessary to provide explicit focus, direction, and a measure of certainty among inevitably contentious and infinitely competing interests in the world, systems also deny or discredit real-life occurrences that fall outside their realm. In doing so, systems deny the legitimate, and perhaps preferable, possibilities that individuals and groups external to formal systems might present for enhancement of the human condition. In today's world, systems often trump people—we might say schooling systems lead superintendents, rather than the other way around.

I must confess that, in some ways, I am the ultimate systems or "organization man," having been a vice-principal, principal, coordinator, and superintendent in the school system and the president of two provincial and one national organizations as well as a director or board member of many more. I am now a dean in a university, one of the oldest, most entrenched institutions in the history of this Western world. Despite this traditional orientation, even before I became a superintendent, I believed that educational leadership did not have to be or be done the way it was.

Now, the not so humble qualifier: I have come to believe that, with the help of others, I have found a better—more human and educationally defensible—perspective on educational leadership. Those of us with responsibilities for maintaining, sustaining, and enhancing systems must, in order to mitigate their harmful possibilities, be skeptical of the very necessity or goodness of their existences. We must surely continuously examine not only a system's efficiency, effectiveness, and efficacy but also how systems might distract us from humanity—our capacity for moral imagination about how the world might be more free, just, and civil. A twist on a well-known phrase might be in order: "The unexamined school system is not worth superintending." And to that end, regular and systematic (but not to the point of paranoia) examination was exactly what I initiated, encouraged, and engaged in as a practicing superintendent.

My Superintendency

I was a superintendent in Seven Oaks School Division[2] for 18 years, the last 12 as superintendent and chief executive officer (CEO). In Manitoba, Canada, school "divisions" are just, for the most part, school districts with a different name. As in the United States, they are somewhat autonomous politically and geographically circumscribed entities. Significantly, in Canada, public education is an exclusively provincial prerogative—there is no explicit federal government presence in education. In addition, in Manitoba and Saskatchewan, school boards have the right to levy property taxes in support of their programs and communities—a condition that significantly enhances their ability to respond to local concerns and to operate autonomously. Thus, while school boards are generally sensitive to their communities' reactions to increased taxation, they do retain the discretion to introduce new programs or services and to fund them locally. In that sense, they are very much the type of local political systems that Thomas Jefferson envisioned as "councils"—local jurisdictions institutionalized and supported by governments to ensure that citizens had opportunities to participate in matters that affected their everyday lives, and to provide a necessary check on state and federal governments. I have often described this situation in Manitoba in Arendtian terms as "an island of freedom" (Arendt, 1965, p. 250) in an ocean of stricture and compliance. Manitoba is just a good place to be a superintendent for these and other reasons that will become evident.

The thorough and comprehensive examinations of teaching and learning that the board, the superintendents, and school administrators undertook while I was superintendent could be described as continual, occasional, and episodic, extending another terminology from Habermas (1987, p. 275). As superintendents, we *continually*, in private and public conversations, particularly with principals, asked questions like, "How does that (hiring, policy, procedure, activity) fit with our (agreed upon) notions of education and our educational responsibilities?" and "How might we change this discipline question into an educational one?" While we anticipated some resentment with this line of questioning, we generally found quite the opposite. Among ourselves, we superintendents chalked up this unexpected reaction to two factors: (1) principals were no longer forced to come up with the "right" answer—we were looking more for "good" answers than right or "true" ones; and, (2) the questions somehow removed the onus from the individual principal—we were now somehow in this together as educational colleagues. In other words, management questions tend to imply fault and blame; educational questions somehow imply shared responsibility.

By *occasionally* I mean regular occasions like board retreats and meetings, administrator's meetings, staff meetings, and meetings of external bodies. Here examination took a different form: "Why did we set things up this way?"; "Please remind us why we started this in the first place"; and "What would happen if we didn't have boards or superintendents?". While at first this seemed awkward and uncomfortable, a return to first conditions and first principles became welcome and reassuring. More than once, a trustee, superintendent, or principal remarked on how glad they were that we had had these connections, as it provided them with both the justification and the vocabulary to respond to public questioning. Last, by *episodic* I mean infrequent or "once in a lifetime" occurrences, such as a resident's challenging the idea of property taxation or the approval of a new program like peace education, or a policy like "safe and respectable schools and workplaces."

As superintendents, we began to look forward to these challenges as opportunities to "educate" the board, the principals, and the public. One of my favorite and, I believe, our most beneficial exercises was when the superintendents' team would try to imagine how the implementation of controversial decisions might affect each principal and each school community. We were always striving to keep the seemingly autocratic and arbitrary demands of the system in check by weighing them against educational needs and people's interests, and vice versa.

All of this, of course, begs the question of how we as a district got to this point, which means revisiting my own educational leadership journey.

Being Led or Leading?

Superintendents are very busy people. If superintendents are asked about their work they will regale you with stories of 18-hour days, 7-day weeks, hundreds of meetings, and being always "on call." If you ask them why they sought, took, and stay in the job they're less likely to say it's because of the money, status, and prestige than to say that they enjoy the continuous and often surprising challenges, they love the people they work with, and they think they might be making a difference. What all of them would agree on is that they are very busy, so busy that they do not have time to read . . . or think. In acknowledging this, they have reaffirmed the ancient dichotomy of "living the human life" and "living the human life *well*." In that dichotomy are two aspects to life and living—the *vita activa* and the *vita contempliva* (Arendt, 1958, pp. 12–17), or the life of action and the life of contemplation. When superintendents talk about their busyness, they in effect are saying that they have chosen, or been chosen, to emphasize the *vita activa* over the *vita contempliva*. Inadvertently they may even be saying that the life of continuous activity is preferred and privileged—in other words, better than the contemplative life.

I was one of those superintendents for whom, at the beginning of my career, there existed no dichotomy. I worked, mostly labored, 16 to 18 hours a day, 6 or 7 days a week. I thought that that was how to do the job and how it had to be done. And still, I was asked by board members, principals, teachers, and my family what I did with my time. My stock responses were that the work is never done (true), or that I was the superintendent and it was my job to see that everything got done and on time. What is remarkable and in retrospect terribly ironic was that I had quit two previous positions because I did not want to work for someone who was acting like I was. I had accepted all my administrative positions on the basis that things did not need to be done in the usual way. There was a "better way" and I could show people what it was. I did not realize that the only thing I was doing differently was working longer and harder than everyone else. In spite of my bold claims, I was allowing the job or, more accurately, my perceptions of the job and myself, to "lead" me. My previous brief foray into educational thought had been momentarily forgotten.

My career of being a teacher and teacher leader had taken some severe hits in the early 1980s. I was a 7-year principal and president of the Manitoba Teachers' Society, the provincial teachers' professional body and union. At the time the presidency was a one-year term and when, at the end of that term, I decided not to return to my former principal position, I had a most difficult time acquiring a job. I was trying to relocate to Winnipeg at a time of teacher surplus and the strong union protection of existing teachers—the very things I had fought for. I was turned down three times for positions in the Manitoba

Teachers' Society. I was not the only former president who saw working for the professional body as a desirable life choice. I was offered a teaching position only to have it withdrawn when it went to the board for approval, and it was only in the summer that I was granted a term position as a junior high teacher.

Having been hooked on leadership, administrative and political, and being denied the opportunities I wanted, I turned to reading, encouraged by my new principal, Dr. Otto Toews.[3] I became enthralled with developmental theory, particularly Lawrence Kohlberg's theory of moral development (Kohlberg & Mayer, 1972) as the aim of education. The emphasis on the "moral" resonated with me. It was largely because of this newfound intellectual stimulus that I decided not to pursue a political career at the national teacher's federation level. A year later I was hired as a deputy superintendent almost immediately after I had completed my master's in education, and 6 years later, in 1989, was named superintendent and CEO of Seven Oaks School Division No. 10 in Winnipeg, Manitoba. This was a position that I would hold for the next 12 years, and I began a time of great personal and professional transformation, culminating in a doctorate in education and a subsequent career as a dean of a faculty of education.

The Vita Activa: From Manager to Superintendent as Teacher

Although not then aware of the classic dichotomy between thought and action, I started my career in the superintendency as most others did, as a systems manager who had been a successful classroom manager (teacher) and school manager (principal). Although my work was greatly influenced by my time as a teacher politician, I saw my job mainly as ensuring that my part of the system, in this case curriculum implementation and professional development, operated smoothly. It was my job to uphold and promote the chief superintendent's work, to keep the principals and teachers happy, and to skillfully convince the board and the public of the necessity, value, and goodness of our division's activities. I became a manager of the corporate culture, reinforcing the existing hierarchies and the chain of command and communication, and safeguarding the reputation of the system, and within that, solving problems and resolving conflicts. It fit nicely with my academic study, in which organizational and scientific management theories were challenged only by my counseling courses. It was not easy to reconcile the two, but if push came to shove, the management imperative prevailed. Without much hesitation I became socialized, and contentedly I might add, to the role of superintendent as expert manager and supervisor.

The reading I did substantially upheld my previous education. *A Nation at Risk* (National Commission on Excellence in Education, 1983) came out, reinforcing the "Effective Schools"[4] literature with its behavioristic and positivistic sciences approach, which had been embraced by academics and practitioners alike. However, the reform movement made me increasingly uneasy. First, being a progressive in theory if not in action, it seemed to me that the propositions and recommendations of *A Nation at Risk*, its predecessors, and its offspring were simply a throwback to a more authoritarian time—an attempt to recapture a glorious, golden age in education that never was. As a union leader I had been exposed to what I believed were systemic inequities and discrimination and I wanted no part in promoting and legitimizing them again.

Thus, early in my superintendency, I was relieved when Larry Cuban's (1972) book, *The Management Imperative and the Practice of Leadership in Schools*, appeared, with its critical probing of the management priority in educational administration and the implication that instructional leadership was possible, given the appropriate understandings and predispositions. Based upon his juxtaposing of management, leadership, and politics, and fired up by my discontent and a barely disguised missional zeal, I ventured for the first time into the realm of public scholarship, writing a lengthy tome for the 1992 Canadian Society for the Study of Education conference entitled, "The Superintendent as Teacher: The Seven Oaks Commitment." Needless to say, while embraced heartily at home, it was received with a robust, incredulous skepticism at a Canadian Association of School Educational Administrators' session. I attributed this response to the fact that I, as a practitioner, was challenging academics' long-held theories in the field of educational administration and, in a sense, I was discrediting their work and challenging their imaginations. In retrospect, we were both right *and* wrong. I had neglected my scholarly responsibility to recognize the achievements of scholars in the field and they, for the most part, had become locked in a management paradigm. Ultimately, we have both been vindicated as the study of educational leadership has become more integrated into the study of educational administration.

Not to be deterred, I continued to make the case that the superintendency was like teaching, deriving its authority and entitlement primarily from the fact that we were teachers first and that teaching was central to the education enterprise. I did not realize that I was still in the old trap, conflating education and schooling and instrumental curriculum skill with educational expertise. It was about this time that my colleague David Coulter introduced me to the philosophy of education literature that he was studying in his doctoral program at Simon Fraser University in Vancouver. We were both particularly intrigued with the work of Kieran Egan, an educational theorist whose work not only resonated with us on several levels but whose approach to the study of education and schooling we found most appealing. Sharing our philosophical work with superintendent colleagues in Seven Oaks, the board, and the principals, we collectively embarked on a mission to make the culture of the division and the practice of the superintendency more educational and educative. Our premise and justification was provided by Egan (1990, p. 135): "At a professional level it means that, in order to educate, teachers must be in some significant sense scholars; teaching is properly a learned profession." Our activities, which became practice, were built upon what we deemed to be the promise of that premise and upon the "Cuban trichotomy," as I called it at the time, where the superintendent was instructional leader or teacher as well as manager and politician.

Superintendent as Teacher and Scholar

As part of our conscious shift from superintendents as managers, we adopted a new nomenclature for our superintendents' group. We became the superintendents' team, as opposed to the cabinet and the central administrative council. We declared our intention to be "teachers" first in everything we did, and proclaimed that our practice and actions would be governed by educational rather than management and political purposes. Following Egan, we would also be, "in some significant sense scholars."

In the interest of scholarship, we decided to emphasize the work of educational philosophers—people like Egan, Richard Peters, Robin Barrow, Maxine Greene, John Dewey, and John Goodlad, who built on ideas from Plato, Aristotle, Erasmus of Rotterdam, Jean Jacques Rousseau, and the like. Our meetings—board meetings, principals' meetings, superintendent's meetings—took on a scholarly manner and tone, using educational theory and philosophy and their languages as conceptual tools to create seminars in educational thought. Our topics ranged from the purposes of education to the purposes of high schools, from education reform to educational renewal, from democratic education to schooling as socialization, from teachers as professionals to teachers as laborers, from accelerated education (à la Henry Levin) to special education, from human rights to multiculturalism—just to name a few. Any board member or division employee could "introduce" topics and/or lead discussions on topics of their choice. We sent out articles for reading and set aside other times for discussion.

It was a heady time. We were the division's "teachers"—we accepted responsibility for the division's education, and I believe it helped us think more deeply about our own educational responsibilities. There was relatively little resistance to these "dialogical times," and only when there were urgent problems to be responded to did we preempt them. Matters such as teacher evaluation policies, pay equity provisions, bus routes, and the purchase of school bus tires were deferred if the discussions extended beyond preset times. We enjoyed great support from the board, our teachers' associations, and our employee unions, with whom we worked closely, inviting them to all board meetings except in closed sessions. The people with whom we worked most closely, the board and principals, felt that we were spending more time doing the right work and enjoying it more, and that we were better able to explain to the parents and the public why we were doing what we were doing and why we simply could not follow the prevailing education reform path. The payoff was not only greater understanding, but also greater acceptance.

There are several practices, and departures from practice, that I believe stand out—to this day. I wonder if they could not and should not become standard practice in school systems everywhere:

- Instead of annual or regular strategic planning exercises that emphasize strategic objectives, actions, and outcomes, we emphasized regular dialogue on educational purposes, conditions, activities, and likely and perceived consequences.
- As noted above, there was an attempt to set aside some time at most administration and board meetings for "educational" discussion or presentation, which may or may not have had any relevance to the "business" of the meeting, before governance and administrative matters.
- The superintendents' team initiated a distinguished lecture series, inviting renowned educational scholars[5] to share their work with the community.
- A contingent of board, superintendents, administrators, and teachers was invited to attend the American Educational Research Association (AERA) conference every year, with the expectation that they would become discussion leaders in the division.

- The division encouraged and sponsored board, administrator, and teacher presentations at various provincial, national, and international conferences.
- In conjunction with teachers and their local associations, the division developed a professional evaluation model that placed most of the emphasis for professional improvement on the teachers themselves. Principal supervision was deemed necessary only in infrequent or emergent situations. That this was accomplished during the height of the "school failure" and subsequent accountability movements was possible because the policy review had been initiated prior to that time and we had a supportive and trusting relationship with our teachers' association.[6]

Admittedly, there were also initiatives that fizzled for a variety of reasons, some having to do with the failure to involve teachers, parents, or students at the outset, and others because they were seen as an encroachment on teachers' private times or we underestimated the resources required to sustain them. These included the formation of teacher research teams, which I believe foundered because of insufficient methodological support and insufficient release time; the Teacher Team Leader project, an attempt to support educational dialogue groups for teachers, which ran aground because of scheduling problems; the community "Dialogue on Education" initiative, a public forum on education that could not muster enough public interest; and the Board-Student Liaison Committee, an attempt to give students a voice in school improvement efforts that unfortunately was misused by some trustees and students to push individual agendas.

Nevertheless, the "education" initiative, on the whole, had a huge impact on the Seven Oaks community and does to this day. The language largely remains. The emphasis on thoughtfulness and participation as part of the division's culture and reputation remain, and the focus on preparing all children for democratic participation is strong. However, somewhat sorrowfully, I admit that the move to broaden our efforts to *systemic* educational-political action was a much rockier journey.

Beyond Our Borders

Although not necessarily inevitable, it is readily understandable and explainable that many of us saw it as our responsibility to share our educational journey with others. Ours was a public enterprise for the public good, and had to meet the tests of transparency and general acceptance, not only for the sake of dialogue but also to share what we thought to be possible and desirable, even in a time of public disenchantment with schools. We told our stories unabashedly and forthrightly, by whatever means and in whatever settings available to us. In a real sense, they became vehicles for public engagement in educational policy discourse.

The superintendents' team encouraged and supported the public contributions and positions of the Seven Oaks Board of Trustees, the principals, the teachers, and other employees, as well as students and community members. Seven Oaks representatives participated in *any* organization with educational connections, particularly at the provincial level, including board, superintendent, teacher, principal, and union organizations. They were often supported by release time to carry out their responsibilities locally, provincially, and beyond. In addition, we prepared vigorously to present at every open legislative or regulative change hearing and always began with what became known as an "educational" preamble that stated the division's core values and beliefs regarding education. Our board of trustees, in opposition to its provincial parent group, supported the Manitoba Teachers' Society and the Seven Oaks Teachers' Association in support of teachers' rights in collective bargaining when they were challenged by the government of the day. Various groups from the division participated in all meetings regarding school reform (hearings, curriculum meetings, public consultations, and the like). The division had a presence and made an appearance in all matters educational in the province.

Suffice it to say that, on our terms—people taking on our stances and emulating our work—we experienced somewhat limited success. We wanted to show that local boards of trustees and their executive officers could act inclusively and democratically, could assume and uphold unpopular positions such as supporting teachers and unions, and could advocate for the resources to look after all children educationally. In other words, we upheld the ideals of local autonomy and the demands for public inclusiveness, responsiveness, and responsibility, and encouraged others to do the same thoughtfully. Our civility and eagerness, although sometimes embraced, were at other times mocked or simply ignored by government, other divisions, educational organizations, and the media. From our perspective, managerial concerns and current political ideologies continued to rule the day, and to tyrannize and neglect the educational agenda, particularly on the public policy front.

Thus, when we, as a division, refused to participate in a government-mandated grade 3 testing program, the superintendents' team instead quietly negotiated an alternative rather than force a public confrontation on the basis of educational conviction, even though by now, because of our principals' work with their school communities, the division enjoyed great parental support. As time went on, we more or less withdrew from the public policy front as much as possible, going about our business quietly so as not to attract too much attention in case some government office might attempt to inflict censure or sanction on us. We did not bother them, and they did not bother us. Without fanfare, the division simply refused or minimally agreed to participate in government "accountability" initiatives like planning schemes, testing regimes, predetermined parental involvement, and schools of choice, deciding whether to participate based upon our notions of education. Ultimately, we felt vindicated in these decisions because in virtually all cases, these "reforms" have proven to be either fleeting, unsuccessful, or simply deemed "wrong"—both educationally and/or ethically.

On the positive side, the students, teachers, parents, principals, superintendents, and board have always remained respected members of the broader community. A large percentage of the division's employees and graduates were involved in leadership positions throughout the city and the province. Seven Oaks children and young people regularly distinguish themselves not only in university and college, but also in music, the arts, and athletics. I believe these accomplishments reflect the solid ethical and political grounding they received from their schooling, but unfortunately, this is not the kind of human consequence that easily lends itself to the empiric evidence or causal claims so popular today. Ironically, it was in the last years of my superintendency that I discovered a set of conceptual resources to help me understand the human activity I was pursuing. I found them in the work of Hannah Arendt's explication of the human condition, particularly her perceptions of the *vita activa* and the *vita contempliva*.

Understanding the *Vita Activ*a

In her book *The Human Condition*, Arendt (1958) revisits the ancient differentiations of human activity—labor, work, and action. I find the classical distinctions she makes helpful in understanding the activities of the superintendency, and, as mentioned, see their connection to Cuban's (1972) trichotomy of management, instructional leadership, and politics. Her distinctions also have a family resemblance to the various aspects of education as theorized by Egan, a matter that I will allude to later. Finally, I will use the labor-work-action classifications to organize my thoughts on the successes, failures, accomplishments, and frustrations regarding our Seven Oaks activities. I recommend this framework to all educational leaders as a way to critically examine their work and make judgments about how to proceed. I know for certain that it resonates with graduate students of educational administration, particularly those who are already practicing administrators.[7]

Labor

Labor, for Arendt, is the human activity that sustains human life. It is primarily biological and material in nature—eating, sleeping, procreating, raising children—and it is repetitious and only ends with death. Labor is an almost automatic activity that requires constant motion but minimal thought because of its cyclical sameness. It also requires knowledge of the rules of the survival game, or at least tacit knowledge of what has "caused" survival in the past. Labor has a strong family resemblance to Cuban's management imperative. For example, if superintendents and/or CEO's do not prepare, administer, and balance budgets it is unlikely that they will be permitted to initiate other activities. Budgets are the lifeblood of systems. Like staffing, budgets have to be managed through the same processes every year—failing to do so seriously undermines the health and credibility of the system. While the process may be mind-numbing, it is essential. The very fact that labor is essential and familiar in its ubiquity means that many people *hold on to it as the essence of their activity*. All superintendents must be managers—and some never move beyond management.

Work

Work, on the other hand, differs from labor first and foremost because it leaves some permanent evidence of previous activity behind. This permanent evidence is like the work of an artist, adding an enriching but not necessarily essential artifact, and representing the worker to the world. While the results of work may not be apparent upon its completion, evidence of it remains in some form, whether the worker is present or not. Work, thus, is a reflection of the worker—like a building is a reflection of the architect; it says something about him or her, his/her beliefs, values, and mentality. Furthermore, work, in order to be recognized as such, must make a public appearance. Whereas labor always "labors" behind the scenes, work appears in the open, otherwise, it has no earthly value. In fact, it actually has less earthly value than labor because while labor itself may be largely invisible, the neglect of labor results in the most horrendous consequences. So work is not so much a necessity as an opportunity—more sociological and psychological than biologic.

In school systems, work is the activity that depends upon identifiable, recognizable individuals or groups of individuals. The initiatives of the superintendents' team and the division primarily fell under the category of work, as does Cuban's notion of instructional leadership, Egan's idea of romantic understanding, and my notion of the superintendent as teacher. It mattered who initiated these concepts and initiatives, who performed the associated activity, and who participated, because in education it's people's ideas, sentiments, and activities that both show up while they're around and remain after they're gone. Because of this, "work" is more rare than labor.

Action

Action, according to Arendt, is the highest and rarest form of human activity, and it comes most often in the form of speech and example. The classic site of action, for Arendt, was the Greek polis, where free and equal men gathered to debate what was good for the city-state. Participation was open only to men of means, whose privilege released them of the obligations of feeding, rearing, and providing for their families. Unencumbered by menial matters and necessity, they were free to debate, motivated only by their opportunity to shine—to impress, to express new ideas—and to enhance the status and situation of Athens and Greece. Of course, if we insisted today on those preconditions, there would be very little action in today's world.

Ideally, action would now transcend partisan politics and enduring chauvinism, sexism, racism, and discrimination, but retain certain aspects of the ancient concept. Action has never had the quality of permanence, the reliability of cause and effect, or the possibility of control or management. When we say something, our words become anyone's property to use as they wish—they can claim an idea for their own or pass the message on inadvertently or at will, and the words may have unintended consequences wholly disconnected from the intent of the person who uttered them. The same is true of one's public or overt behaviors, which can be interpreted and misinterpreted, with motives denied or attributed, and results either extremely consequential or inconsequential. In short, if one wishes to live a safe, unchallenged life, one avoids action if at all possible. Action holds an element of risk and entails a loss of control while the activity of action is momentary with consequences that may go on and on.

On the other hand, if one wishes to make their contributions count, they cannot avoid action, with all its pitfalls and pratfalls. Action is akin to Cuban's politics and Egan's philosophical and ironic understanding. The possibility for actions are, of course, enhanced under certain conditions—conditions that we strived to achieve as superintendents in Seven Oaks so as to promote the actions—mostly speech and initiations of dialogues—we believed in. Arendt and Habermas, among others, have outlined such conditions as nonhierarchical, noncoercive, nonexploitative, and nondiscriminatory instances and situations. They are the conditions we associate with the human gift we as people hold most dear—the right to exercise human freedom which, along with action, Arendt believes makes being human possible and bearable.

I understand now that what the superintendents' team was intuitively trying to do was provide, for everyone, the conditions for freedom and action to exist and flourish—for people to be human in the fullest sense—to be the initiators, or leaders, of education. My intent was to not only make the division as democratic as possible but also to have us achieve an appreciation for democracy as the closest avenue we humans have for actualizing freedom and action. Thus, repeatedly, the superintendents tried to initiate dialogue where people could come to the table as welcome equals. We believed dialogues on education provided those opportunities because we had come to realize that true democracies assume everybody's responsibility and right to participate in these dialogues.

In hindsight, calling ourselves "teachers" was somewhat disingenuous, in terms of equality, because teacher–learner relationships are inherently hierarchical and unequal. The superintendency is also necessarily hierarchical and somewhat tyrannical—systems do demand accountability and response. The trick was, of course, to make mutual dialogue more possible and more likely. This is where we had to rely on the *vita contempliva*, because the *vita activa* is incomplete without the *vita contempliva*. The *vita contempliva*, the life and world of the mind and thought and the imagination, can accommodate the ideals of equality, inclusion, and participation so critical to democratic dialogue, however impossible they are to achieve in real, everyday life.

Achieving a *vita contempliva*, while extraordinarily important, is virtually impossible in the superintendency because of the time demands and the culture of the position. The *vita contempliva* requires a kind of private quiet time for reflection and introspection. We achieved some of this through Monday superintendent's team meetings, but even these were often interrupted by perceived crises. On several occasions I announced to the board and the principals that the superintendents would be scheduling half or full days per week for reading and thinking—explaining that this was a necessary requirement of our jobs. Those announcements were tolerated—not embraced—and reactions ranged from "When will you get your work done?" to "I'll have to wait and see how this works out." In truth, private uninterrupted time never worked out, and was never institutionalized as part of the job. Principals forgot about it and called anyway, and superintendents somehow rarely got to their reading during "office hours." I still believe it should be part of the job description of superintendents, as such time is an expectation of all scholars.

The *Vita Contempliva*—Reading/Writing to Theory to Thought

As I indicated earlier, the prevailing literature on educational administration and educational leadership caused me considerable unease as a superintendent. Much of it seemed not only counterintuitive but also too prescriptive and too presumptive, generalizing to the point of meaninglessness for actual practice. My fears were not unfounded—administrators were able to make temporary intellectual connections but rarely were able to relate these to their daily tasks and challenges. Attempts to engage others in topics like organizational development, scientific management, structural functionalism, and the like caused eyes to glaze over and were most often met with a "So what?" Articles on the role of the principal, leadership traits, best practices, and the various familiar descriptors/models of leadership[8] (instructional, transformational, moral, participative, managerial, strategic, and contingent to name a few) made people feel guilty or alienated—that they had to label themselves, or find a match or latest niche, often with weak connections to educational purposes. The fact that the educational leadership literature basically matched or emulated the popular business management literature[9] (with its emphasis on excellence, change, effective "habits," total quality, and the like) did little to squelch my unease that these notions were developed without sufficient attention to the context of schools and classrooms.

Reading and Writing

As the reform movement marched inexorably over schools and school systems, a slow awakening occurred within the superintendents' team. First, it dawned on us that the language of reform was not primarily and centrally about education. Rather, it was about economic ideology, sometimes called "the business agenda"—full of phrases like economic advantage, competition, customer satisfaction, consumers, products, stakeholders, entrepreneurship, human resources, and the like. The words of education reform revealed its purposes, leaving us feeling betrayed. Second, any serious notions of education seemed absent from the debate—indeed, the discussion sounded to us like the promotion of a kind of economic patriotism (our country and its people will lose their "competitive advantage"). Finally, and relatedly, free enterprise seemed to be conflated with democratic citizenship and the enhancement of the democratic ideal. It was at this point that we decided that we needed to look outside the psychologically based (learning and teaching) and the sociologically framed (organizational change and design) literature for educational underpinnings. We found that critical theorists—feminists for example—had only begun to address prevailing notions of educational administration and that philosophers had generally ignored or avoided the topic (Leithwood & Duke, 1999).

In our view, the absence of philosophical underpinnings undermined contemporary perspectives on educational administration, including the superintendency. We felt we had to return to original questions about education: What is it about humans that they need and want education? What does it mean to be an educated person? What are the public purposes of education? What conception of educational leadership best fits with these understandings and the meanings we attribute to them? Our search was not in vain. When we began reading the work of educational philosophers—contemporary and historical—we found a treasure trove of resources with which to challenge the educational reform movement. We were no longer rebels with just a cause. We now had access to "weapons of mass instruction," to borrow a phrase from our teacher union.

We used these generous resources unsparingly—our written presentations to the board, the government, educational organizations, teachers, and parents were supported by quotations about equality, inclusion, participation—in other words, democracy as an aim of education—from the likes of Richard Peters, Gary Fenstermacher, Nel Noddings, Maxine Greene, Benjamin Barber, Jane Roland Martin, and Henry Levin. As our familiarity and confidence increased, we included the work of educational thinkers like Kieran Egan and John Goodlad and finally the work of political and critical philosophers like Jean Bethke Elshtain, Charles Taylor, Hannah Arendt, and Jürgen Habermas. What they all had in common was a deep sense of moral responsibility and a high regard for the potential of democratic ideals, and a significant level of anonymity, even among educators, which we tried to challenge.

Moving Toward a Theory of Education

As noted earlier, I had not found a theory of the superintendency or of educational leadership that appealed to me, and I set about conceptualizing a more satisfactory theory with my colleague David Coulter (Coulter & Wiens, 1999). Operating from the premise that educational leadership was significantly different from other kinds of leadership (business, military, partisan political, for example), and that what made it different was its foundation in concepts of education, we began our quest with a search for a comprehensive theory of education. My interest was in a theory clearly founded in supportable notions of what it meant to be human at its fullest and best—in both a concrete and an abstract sense—a theory that would allow and account for past human achievements, celebrate current conceptions of humanity at its best, and imagine the future achievement of a better understanding of the potential for good—no small order but a worthy one.

I have found satisfaction—for the moment—in combining the work of Hannah Arendt and Kieran Egan. Egan (1997) espouses a theory of education as cultural recapitulation, whereby individuals acquire and internalize enduring cognitive tools through education. He explicated the cognitive tools human cultures have employed from prerecorded history to the present, tools he claims have resulted in the achievement of various forms of understanding—somatic, mythical, romantic, philosophical, and ironic—and in doing so, identifies those people, from Plato and Aristotle to Dewey, who have shaped our notions of education and schooling. Arendt explores the grand educational dichotomies of the Western world—as already discussed, the life of action and the life of thought; the meanings of "public" and "private"; the human gifts of freedom and action (read as classical politics and moral philosophy); the concepts of childhood and adulthood and education and politics.

What they have in common is a belief that thought and action are inseparable and mutually interdependent; that the way people make sense of themselves and their world rests heavily on past experiences and how those experiences are understood, and that particular human understandings imply particular human possibilities which, in turn, imply particular human responsibilities and activities. For example, Egan's mythic understanding implies associative activity, like systems management; romantic understanding implies agonistic activity, like teaching; philosophical understanding implies affiliative activity, like education, and ironic understanding implies altruistic activity, like leadership. The ideally educated person has acquired the "mind tools" that result in corresponding thought and action, allowing him/her to draw on these understandings as necessary and appropriate. This framework provided a way for my understanding the understanding of others, and allowed me to examine my own understanding of the superintendent as an educated person; a person who had acquired these "mind tools" through experiences. Furthermore, it provided conceptual resources to explore limitations in my own or in others' thinking. These points cannot be fully dealt with in the scope of this work, but what is significant is that I found a theory of education on which to base a theory of educational leadership, a resonating compatibility between Egan's notions of educational thought and Arendt's notion of political action.

Thinking

What is educational leadership, then, based upon robust notions of education? For Arendt, education was about understanding the human condition and was the responsibility of all adults, for all children. For her, education was having children learn about what the world was like so that they could act upon it when they became adults to make it better. She made a sharp distinction between education and politics—what education is for children, politics is for adults: "Whoever wants to educate adults really wants to act as their guardian and prevent them from political activity" (1968, p. 177). Here Arendt identified something that we as superintendents had felt intuitively and uneasily. In describing ourselves as teachers, we were actually creating an incompatibility, a barrier to equality and political and educational participation. We began to see that we were engaged in an activity akin to ancient politics. Arendt's work seemed to coincide with my efforts to come to a meaningful and more egalitarian understanding of educational leadership.

By taking these very abstract notions of education and politics and by thinking carefully about them from a deep sense of purpose, Arendt concluded that the epitome of human action was classical politics—which shares little with contemporary politics except for some of the rhetoric. The Greek polis, its male chauvinism aside, exemplified classical politics—a place where all "free" people came together to put their best ideas forward for the good of the country. The ideas and ideals that animated and constituted the Greek polis, along with the Roman forum, informed and inspired Thomas Jefferson and the writers of the American Constitution (Arendt, 1965, pp. 232–255), and now were informing us. In theory, it was a place for all for the good of all—a place where people could demonstrate their authenticity (moral autonomy) in the name and for the cause of human solidarity. My colleagues and I decided that working toward this ideal as a model of educational leadership—where humanity, education, and democracy converged—was what we wished to do . . . a tough act to get right. All of this contributed to a homegrown theory of educational leadership, incorporating the essence of previous models of educational leadership and anchoring them on strong notions of education and democracy. The following became my private and public touchstones upon which I tried to build and by which I would judge our efforts as well as other theories of education leadership:

- Education is a normative and fundamentally moral concept and activity whose primary purpose is the preparation of all children for democratic participation.
- Education is the responsibility of all adults toward all children.
- The leadership relationship is an ethical–political relationship involving all adults and is open to all under the conditions of equality, mutuality, and reciprocity.
- Educational leadership, as a moral activity, is simply the initiation of dialogues on and about educational purposes, preconditions and conditions, activities, and potential consequences for individuals and society—in other words, educational leadership is more parasitic on notions of education than on notions of leadership.
- The aim of educational leadership activity is greater understanding about the human condition—what it means to be human, and what authority and responsibilities that implies.
- The educational attitude is one of a constant search for the common, public, or greater good for humankind—democracy, in abstract terms, is more a search for goodness than for truth and beauty.
- Human goodness is an intersubjectively determined and temporary state or condition that must always be renewed.
- The ultimate human interaction is public dialogue, which has its origins and sanctuary in the private human imagination.
- The purpose of schooling is to make education imaginable and democracy possible, even though neither can ever be guaranteed, as in "caused" or "assured."

These touchstones define or describe the bases upon which the activities described below rest.

Experimentation From a Deep Sense of Purpose

In retrospect, during my superintendency, I believe that we were engaged in a great human experiment with a deep sense of purpose—how to make ourselves better educational leaders and how to make the world better, as in more democratic and human. The experiment included not only the activities discussed earlier but also the following—all examples of educational leadership—initiated or supported by myself or my superintendents' team colleagues.

The Great Ongoing Education Dialogue

Beginning in the early 1990s, my superintendent colleagues and I have led and conducted, both inside and outside the school division, a series of public dialogues on "What does it mean to be an educated person?" Participants are asked to identify someone familiar to them who they believe to be educated and why they believe that. They may then be asked to think about how people become educated, what our school system does to "educate" children and young people, and what values are evident when we are at our best—or how our schools and school systems get in the way. Participants put their institutional roles and loyalties aside and usually chose someone close to them—a parent, grandparent, relative, or friend—and talked about values that we might consider to be the underpinnings of a democratic society. The words used most frequently to describe people included wise, caring, respectful, honest, moral, good listeners, and with a sense of humor. The words most used to describe the school and the division were responsive, responsible, democratic, empathetic, thoughtful, inclusive, and welcoming.

In political terms, this exercise provided a strong base from which to critique and evaluate the province's education reform initiatives. As an ethical exercise it greatly increased the number of people directly contributing to divisional policy development, administrative procedures, professional development, and curriculum projects—the governance and organizational aspects of educational renewal. It has spawned similar exercises in university classes and at educational retreats, and even prompted a dialogue at the national level on "What does it mean to be an educated Canadian?" (Wiens & Coulter, 2005). Such an effect reminds me that once an action is taken, no one can predict its reach and its scope.

Teaching Today for Tomorrow

Teaching Today for Tomorrow is a teacher-produced journal that was spawned by teacher involvement in local, national, and international professional development activities. Begun in 1993, it is an impressive example of teachers assuming professional responsibility for the further education of their colleagues, including administrators and professors, at the local, provincial, national, and international levels. It is an extraordinary example of educational leadership—a noncoercive, nonhierarchical dialogue on education—initiated by a group often referred to as a "trade union" by nonteachers.

Masters of Education Cohorts

Also initiated by teachers and administrators, the division's superintendents' team negotiated an agreement with the Faculty of Education at the University of Manitoba to offer a master's in education (Educational Administration, various curriculum studies, and/or Guidance and Counselling) via a cohort program mostly housed and conducted within the division. The board played its part by supporting the initiative via payroll deduction of tuition fees paid up front by the division, thereby signaling their support for ongoing scholarship and demonstrating their belief that ongoing professional education was a public as well as an individual benefit and had a public, and worthy, purpose. As a by-product of this initiative, the division has become known, and not pejoratively, as both the "Cerebral Division" and the "Intellectual Division."

The Experiment Continues: Advancing Community Schools

At the "trial and talking" stage prior to my departure in 2001, the division embarked upon a grand experiment to restore the local school as the center of community life. While there were parent centers in a few schools before, the current initiative involves community workers in every elementary school with collaborative projects, from "How to Help Your Children Learn to Read" to community celebratory dinners initiated, sponsored, and prepared by parents. This was a grassroots initiative par excellence—nobody knows for certain who started it and nobody seems to care. It is the type of educational leadership possible in a democratic culture.

To me these experiments are an example of, and a justification for, taking education and the transformative power of educational leadership seriously. They also provide a rationale for a more humanistic, less system-driven approach to the study and the practice of the superintendency and educational leadership in general. With these initiatives, the system stands ready in the service of the people, rather than the opposite. Such an approach is not only enjoyable and more civically responsible; it is truer to the very ideals upon which education and democracy were built.

How Does It All Fit and Where Does It All Lead?

As much as is possible under the circumstances, I have attempted to take the scholarly "observer-researcher" stance in assessing my time in the superintendency and the work that took place. At the same time, I have tried to contribute to the understanding of the potential historical contribution of educational philosophy to the development of concepts of educational leadership.

Aristotle used the term "citizen friendship" (cited in Morgan, 1992, p. 347) to define the ideal relationship between the state and the individual. The state is, of course, a collection of all its individuals bound by common purpose and acting in, and toward, "concord"(p. 357), a universally agreed upon ideal state of living together as a world. Education was the provision to children and young people of the cognitive means (outlined by Egan) and the corresponding ethical disposition for responsible civic action (outlined by Arendt). Together they constitute the ideal of "civic friendship"—a love for human authenticity, for human solidarity—for the human condition and for each person, which translates into a love for democracy and the common good. Arendt, following Aristotle, called for political judgment (1968, pp. 224–225) as the means and the ends of "civic friendship."

In my view, Arendt pointed the way for scholars and practitioners to think about the superintendency in particular, and educational leadership in general, with her introduction of the term "judgment" as central to the ethical-political realm of human thought and action. Judgment is what distinguishes the leader-actor from the manager-laborer and the professional-worker. It is judgment that causes and expresses unease with the valuation of education and educational leadership by scientific technical means and ends, by structural-functionalist arrangements, and by authoritarian–domination relationships. In other words, the depth and scope of our humanity, the consequences of educational activity, and the advantages and benefits of democracy cannot be measured by the economic criteria of return on investment, the social criteria of existing cultural arrangements, or the standard of living or competitive advantage measured by wealth. People and institutions cannot be measured with the same confidence and certainty (and presumed objectivity) we use to determine weight and size. In the judgment of the Seven Oaks parents, provincial testing positioned their children as political objects or economic resources and they wanted no part of it. Finally, it is judgment that determines what cognitive resources à la Arendt are appropriate to the educational and political tasks at hand and in what combination. Judgment is leadership capacity par excellence, and it deserves further study (Coulter & Wiens, 2002, p. 23).

The educational leader is not only aware of the public purposes of education but also has the skills, dispositions, and competence to make sound educational judgments. Many superintendents are able to be wise instinctively and intuitively, but it is better if they can also judge when and how they should act as the hero or the corporate CEO, and why, how, and when they should act privately or publicly. I found the conceptual resources and the explanations and justifications that correspond to educational leadership in the work of educational theorists and educational philosophers, as opposed to the scholarship on educational administration and leadership. And I found a name for the object of my study in the terms "civic humanism," or "classical republicanism" (Honderich, 1995, p. 375), a political outlook that considerably influenced the writers of the American Constitution.

Civic humanism, based on equality and inclusion, presumes a kind of embracing of our humanity, downplaying but not denying its frailty and foibles. I understand it to mean, ideally, that:

- If someone understands something deeply and better (for example, that education's primary purpose is education for a democracy), then they can imagine ingenious ways to pursue it, and they generally do not need to be managed or instructed.
- I content myself with the people who occupy the world the same time as I do—I believe they also must have purposes and responsibilities that somehow interact and coincide with our concurrent coexistence. I must be willing to engage (even invite) the most disagreeable into the dialogue of humanity, because this gives meaning to my life and my life's work.
- We were all given the gifts of freedom and action, and that it takes all of us to achieve peace and social justice—if anyone is left out of the story then we are either shortchanging ourselves or missing some miraculous possibility and we are all implicated in the failure or loss of humanity in our world.

From these standpoints, educational leadership as civic humanism, the superintendency at its best is simply initiating or extending the human conversation to our children and young people in the hope that future generations will have an enriched adventure in humanity and a better world to live in.

In any case, I was left, when I departed the superintendency, with a research and action agenda—to delve further into educational, moral, and political philosophy and to try to understand educational judgment and civic humanism better. The journey continues. It is my hope that my readers, including many who are not (formally) students or scholars, will be encouraged and inspired by the possibilities inherent in the relentless search—however sketchily presented—of one person to become a better person, with all that entails, and in so doing, imagine how they themselves can become better educational leaders (or even superintendents). And maybe Anais will someday read about her grandfather and his attempts to make the world a better place, and what she reads will help her become a better "leader" of and for the world—on her own terms, of course—which is what I hope for every "educated person."

Notes

1. Anais's mother is our daughter. Anais is our first granddaughter and one of the most intelligent, beautiful people in the world.

2. Seven Oaks School Division is a suburban-rural school district in the northwest corner of the city of Winnipeg, Manitoba, Canada. I was superintendent from 1983 to 2001 and the chief superintendent and chief executive officer from 1989 to 2001. By Manitoba standards, it was a large district with about 9,500 students when I left in 2001. The population was multiethnic and multicultural. In one survey, it was noted that 52 different languages were spoken in the district.

3. Dr. Otto Toews, principal of Munroe Junior High School in 1981, had just completed his doctoral thesis on principal decision making and regularly introduced me to new forms of scholarship.

4. The "Effective Schools" literature was a forerunner to *A Nation at Risk*, (National Commission on Excellence in Education, 1983) basically promoting the same prescriptions, albeit from a different agenda and different academic sources. The cures for the schools in both instances were strong leadership, clearly defined hierarchical structure, direct instruction, clear expectations, time on task, and the like.

5. The Seven Oaks Symposium Series became a feature of this division. Over time it included lectures and seminars with the likes of Henry Levin, Larry Cuban, Andy Hargreaves, Nel Noddings, Gloria Ladson-Billings, Gary Fenstermacher, Virginia Richardson, Thomas Sergiovanni, and others of that stature.

6. I had given the teachers' association in my earlier years in the superintendency a large measure of control and discretion in divisional professional development and the policy was initiated as a result of an extended discussion on teacher professionalism. Furthermore, the superintendents' team and the board regularly used the PDK Gallup Poll reports to emphasize local communities' satisfaction with their own schools' teachers.

7. I have taught many classes at the graduate level on educational administration and used the conceptual framework of *vita activa* to examine administrative work. I have yet to find any student who does not find it worthwhile to examine the practice of educational administration. The distinctions are not, of course, as sharp as I present them, nor the hierarchy as evident in reality and practice.

8. Scholars of educational administration are familiar with these descriptors. I now consider them to be "category mistakes"—they are chauvinistic and presumptuous, which, in fact, refer to activities rather than educational purposes, per se. For example, how can anyone claim to "transform" someone else or to make them more "moral"? Or is "managerial leadership" not an oxymoron? And, is not all leadership contingent? Finally, they remain mired in the hierarchical "management" paradigm.

9. The management literature, while strewn with terminology like excellence, change, quality, effective "habits," and the like, more often is sold as a "totalitarian" (e.g., TQM) solutions, prescription, or recipe for "business" success laid over an educational or schooling environment. This literature, in my view, tends to emphasize the inevitable, the predictable, and the simplistic. Who is against excellence and quality? Who determines change is inevitable or that some habits are better?

References

Arendt, H. (1958). *The human condition*. Chicago: The University of Chicago Press.
Arendt, H. (1965). *On revolution*. New York: Penguin Books.
Arendt, H. (1968). *Between past and future*. New York: Penguin Books.
Coulter, D., & Wiens, J.R. (1999). What is educational about educational leadership? *Education Canada, 39*(2), 4–7.
Coulter, D., & Wiens, J.R. (2002). Educational judgment: Linking the actor and the spectator. *Educational Researcher, 31*(4), 15–25.
Cuban, L. (1972). *The management imperative and the practice of leadership in schools*. Albany, NY: SUNY Press.
Egan, K. (1990). *Romantic understanding*. New York: Routledge.
Egan, K. (1997). *The educated mind*. Chicago: University of Chicago Press.
Habermas, J. (1987). *The theory of communicative action. Vol. 2: Lifeworld and system: A critique of functionalist reason* (T. McCarthy Sr., Trans.). Boston: Beacon.
Honderich, T. (Ed.). (1995). *The Oxford companion to philosophy*. New York: Oxford Press.
Kohlberg, L., & Mayer, R. (1972). Development as the aim of education. *Harvard Educational Review, 42*(4), 449–496.
Leithwood, K., & Duke, D. (1999). A century's quest to understand school leadership. In J. Murphy & K.S. Louis (Eds.), *Handbook of research on educational administration* (2nd ed., pp. 45–72). San Francisco: Jossey-Bass.
Morgan, M. L. (Ed.). (1992). *Classics of moral and political theory*. Indianapolis, IN: Hackett Publishing.
National Commission on Excellence in Education (1983). *A nation at risk: The imperative for educational reform*. Washington, DC: U.S. Government Printing Office.
Wiens, J.R., & Coulter, D. (2005). What is an educated Canadian? *Education Canada, 45*(1), 21–23.

COMMENTARIES

Constructivist Superintendents

BENA KALLICK

Being a superintendent is much like the new technology you purchase—the manual is difficult to read and understand, the help line is difficult to reach, and the consultation charge to learn from experts is costly. It is a job that requires enormous flexibility, attention to multiple perspectives, and an internal set of checks and balances to withstand the pressures of external demands from a public that has, in many ways, been distracted from the real purpose of a public education system. And, as in a democracy, the anchors for decision making are grounded in a deep knowledge of the Constitution and a belief that its mandate is to provide equal access and opportunity for all students to learn at the highest level possible.

The challenges to our public education system are many—as is evidenced by the stories told in this book. We have been catapulted into an age of information and communication made possible by technologies that allow us to know more than we ever imagined, with less certainty about what we know. We use business terms to describe the "business" of educating our children. We find ourselves accounting by numbers rather than by authentic demonstrations of student learning. Our legislation calls for No Child Left Behind—the most honorable goal of any superintendent. However, unlike our judicial system, educators are guilty until they prove themselves innocent. Systems are under scrutiny, often with insufficient measures for what really matters or what might serve as real evidence of student learning.

It is with that backdrop that this book took on its challenge—to tell the stories of how a superintendent faces his or her public as a learner as much as an administrator. Each story is laced with examples that demonstrate the strength and courage it takes to continue to dream, innovate, and imagine and, at the same time, to remain in concert with the community being served.

A superintendent has to spend time getting to know the educational community—the parents, the teachers, the administrators, the students—as well as the community who are not represented in the schools. Many superintendents are hired by a board of education that is looking for change. Yet change, in and of itself, does not necessarily make for a better school system. A superintendent must honor the culture he or she has entered and come to know what traditions to sustain, what transitions to promote, and how to be mindful of the possible transformation of the system so that the changes can be sustained long beyond his or her tenure.

The very best superintendents with whom I have worked all share some common characteristics (Costa & Kallick, 2000). They demonstrate habits of mind such as

- the ability to listen with understanding and empathy;
- the ability to be flexible in their thinking;
- the use of questioning and problem posing, rather than providing immediate reactions;
- clear and precise communication;
- a striving for accuracy with any material being used, presented, or depended on; and
- an openness to continuous learning.

They are persons who face their mistakes and learn enough to avoid repeating them. They are persons who do more listening than telling. They are persons who manage to represent authority without becoming too authoritative. They are persons who know when to make the decision and when to allow others to participate in decision making. They are persons who have managed to put students in the center of every decision that is made. In summary, they are persons who really believe in education as the center of our democratic system and they model democratic behaviors in all that they do. Perhaps we might call them *constructivist superintendents* because they are continually evaluating and reevaluating situations as they search for meaning. They know that there are no easy answers, so they try to ask significant questions.

As a consultant working with many superintendents across the country, I see a marked difference between the novice and expert superintendent. The expert has learned how to meet challenges with the courage and wisdom born of experience. He or she knows more about how to withstand the immediate pressures the board presents upon entry. For example, one superintendent I know described his learning curve to me. He tells the story of how, within the first 24 hours of his entering the district as a new superintendent, he had a meeting with the board in which he was told that they expected him to fire the high school principal before the opening of the next school year. He was told this in June. He did as he was asked—at the cost of a smooth entry plan that delayed real change for a long time. In his next job as superintendent, he was told by the board within three weeks of entry, "The honeymoon is over. Here are some things you must address." Although a highly successful superintendent in each district, he learned from his experience. He has just started in a new district, and he included a clause in his contract that would give him six months to get to know the district before being asked to address any key issues from the board.

When a superintendent has experience, it presents a challenge for the board and the community. In another district, the search firm hired to find a new superintendent has been meeting with the public and is hearing key issues that the public feels need to be addressed. The challenging question is—how can the new superintendent make certain that he or she hears the issues and has the support of the board and the community to gather his own perspective on a situation before taking action? Who identifies the issues to address, and how they should be addressed? Entering a new system is like entering a new culture—it takes time to learn the rituals, habits, and language. Even an experienced superintendent must learn to observe for a period of time—and must be given that time—before announcing actions.

Although a new superintendent knows the literature and the rationale of a thoughtful entry plan, the impatience of the community and the board may not allow for a thoughtful entry. The novice superintendent is caught between wanting to please the board and wanting to make a successful entry with the professional community. It takes considerable experience to know "how to go slow to go fast." The early investment in building thoughtful relationships and knowledge has enormous payoff later.

Another superintendent with whom I worked had to meet the challenge of the teachers' union before he could initiate any changes. Again, this superintendent was a very experienced and accomplished person. The union had geared up to resist his public stance on educational philosophy. He knew how to bide his time and work productively and carefully with the union, building relationships before moving in the direction of his vision. Much as Becky van der Bogert's story describes, he worked with the community, the board, and the teachers to develop a clear philosophy that would guide changes in practice. He made it a practice to meet with the head of the union and, at the same time, to encourage teacher participation in new decisions. The combination of keeping the union leaders well informed in addition to an emphasis on inclusiveness in decision making turned the situation around. On the other hand, a novice superintendent I am working with almost needs chains for restraint as she uncovers the lack of focus on curriculum in her new district. She has been networking with more experienced superintendents to learn how to reach a good balance between uncovering the issues and building the relationships that will allow for transformational change.

I want to note, as well, that habits of mind become as significant for the entire school community as they are for the superintendent. We cannot expect students to be any more thoughtful than the adult role models who surround them. The superintendent must walk the talk every day, if he or she expects to see lasting change in the school culture.

Although I have heard many say that this is a most difficult time to be a superintendent, I would guess that there has never been a "good" time. The system is set up so that there is always a tension between the superintendent and the board of education. It is part of the checks and balances of the system. However, the tension can either be constructive or destructive. Good superintendents are able to guide the board so that they become thoughtful, studious, and dedicated to all children. They are able to help the board learn about important issues and, at the same time, recognize the need the board members have to be representative of community voices.

This book contributes to the field. We know too little about how to celebrate the successes and learn from the mistakes of this job. Although we have many theories of leadership, we do not have enough of the stories that practitioners can tell, with honesty, about what really happens, and the legacy of good practices leave the field when people retire. Perhaps this book will serve as an invitation for superintendents to make explicit their own theories and experiences of leadership, so that their legacy endures and so that research better reflects their realities.

REFERENCE

Costa, A., & Kallick, B. (2000). *Exploring and discovering habits of mind*. Alexandria, VA: Association for Supervision and Curriculum Development.

COMMENTARIES

Making Our Own Minds[1] the Object of Our Learning: Three Reasons to Seek Self-Knowledge

BARRY JENTZ

In this book, school district leaders do an honest and credible job of describing their struggles with external forces and the surprises, disappointments, and puzzlements that naturally accompany those struggles. In some stories, we also see an internal focus, leaders stepping back to question "the entity"—the mind that engages the world—in an effort to gain a clearer picture of their own behavior, its consequences, and its antecedents. In other stories, however, leaders speak as if they share an unspoken assumption that the superintendent mind is an entity, stable and nonchanging, at once wise and considerate, if sometimes frustrated and perplexed. These superintendents reveal little of their own minds.

In recent years, the effort to make our own minds an object of inquiry (as opposed to its only being the subject of inquiry) has been called both "Reflective Theory and Practice" and "Transformational Learning." All the writers of this book may be perfectly capable of searching themselves to better understand the nature of their behavior along with its consequences and antecedents, and some have chosen not to "go there" if only because their savvy precluded it. Advocating transformational learning is one thing, showing oneself in the chaotic and painful process is quite another. Having spent 35 years in one-to-one consulting conversations with people in leadership positions, I know that the process of enlarging the capacities of one's own mind is indeed chaotic, painful, and often prolonged.

So, why take the risk of exploring the nature of our own behavior along with its consequences and antecedents? Why should we make our own minds the object of our learning?

We Need to Discover Discrepancies and Change Them[2]

We tend to be unaware of a set of discrepancies between how we think about ourselves and how we actually behave. As a result, our behavior generates mistrust and we lose credibility even as we intend to be trustworthy and credible. Trust and credibility are the bedrock of leadership, without which we cannot advance our agendas. So, we need to look inward to discover these discrepancies and change our mind-sets and skills to be consistent with our spoken values and principles.

Believing the Tape

"That's not my swing!" I cried as I watched the video. Admittedly, the person swinging the golf club looked like me, but *my* swing was balanced and smooth—not the spastic lurch I saw on the screen. "Okay, I'll put you on tape again," the golf pro replied. I was much younger then, and working with a group of colleagues to study golf as a way to gain insights into the learning process. Far from expert, I still could not believe that my technique could be so flawed. The pro played back the second video; again I opened my mouth to deny the evidence of my own eyes and then closed it as I finally faced the embarrassing truth that the image in my head was more real to me than the reality on screen. I might never have believed it without viewing the tape.

As an educator and consultant in the fields of communication and leadership, I have been using this same technique for 25 years—and always with the same powerful results. I ask leaders to go on videotape so they can confront the sharp discrepancies between how they see themselves (their self-images) and how they actually behave. Leaders who think of themselves as open and truthful see that, in reality, they often withhold information, communicate in opaque or veiled terms, and speak judgmentally without explanation or evidence; leaders who think they are good listeners discover that they seldom pay attention to what others are saying; leaders who think they promote an open culture of learning discover that they are closed and dismissive. And, even when confronted with the video evidence, their first reaction is usually denial: "That's not my swing."

As long as they remain blind to these discrepancies, leaders inadvertently foster mistrust—and lose the very credibility they are attempting to gain. Without trust and credibility they have no hope of advancing their agendas and forfeit the opportunity to create cultures of learning.

From denial to recognition. Imagine yourself as a leader faced with this scenario: Frank, an old friend, transfers into your organization. At your first staff meeting, he cracks two jokes and interrupts you three times. You do not comment during the meeting, but later you seek him out to talk. What do you say?

At first glance, this situation seems innocuous enough; hardly an acid test of leadership skills. I always begin my Harvard courses by presenting the scenario and saying to the students: "This is the only information you have. Prepare to: (1) give Frank the information in the scenario, and (2) listen actively when Frank responds." Then I send them to an adjacent room and, one by one, call them back in for a videotaped role-playing session in which I take the part of Frank.

After making individual tapes, we view and analyze them as a class. The students discover that though they advocate two-way interaction, their behavior is a one-way attempt to correct what they assume to be Frank's misbehavior. Though Frank may have important information for them about his behavior and the meeting, they brush it aside, saying literally or in effect, "That's not what we're here to talk about." Although the students understand that useful feedback is precise and descriptive, they watch themselves speak to Frank abstractly and judgmentally, as in "Keep behaving that way and you won't be in a second meeting." Students learn that, when they feel pressure to lead—when they are, in effect, "under fire"—they quickly lose their ability to take in and process unexpected information by listening actively to learn.

From recognition to practice. Taken together, these discoveries unsettle students. Determined to correct their mistakes in subsequent role-plays,[3] they often repeat their errors, and encounter the harsh reality of the intransigence of their own behavior. They are confused and even ashamed. I help them understand that their confusion is nothing to be ashamed of—that it is, in fact, a necessary starting point for a constructive process of deep reflection about the nature of their behavior, the thinking that gives rise to it, and the assumptions tacit in their thinking. Then, I put them back on tape to test—once again "under fire"—the products of this self-examination process.

Practice Makes Progress. Deeply held assumptions, along with the thinking and behavior that follow from them, can be difficult to acknowledge, let alone modify. Repeatedly "going on tape" is a useful exercise, but not a cure-all. Still, repeated exposures to their own powers of denial usually help students become more disciplined and reflective learners who, with the help of others, can take a hard look at their own practice and make needed adjustments. This discipline will be essential for administrators who are expected to serve as agents of change in organizations that labor under their own unacknowledged assumptions and deceptive self-images. To change such environments, administrators need to be able to practice what they preach.

Unfortunately, many of us can go an entire lifetime without experiencing the powerful jolt of a "That's not my swing!" moment. Carefully structured use of videotaped role-playing can bring that power to leadership education, and help students recognize the difference between the way they see themselves and the way they really behave. In so doing, this combination of role-playing, review, and practice can give students a set of insights and skills that will earn them trust and credibility, positioning them to create cultures of learning.

We Need to Discover Our Negative Relationship to Confusion and Change[4]

The significant problems we face have no easy, technical answers and are inherently confusing, rendering us (and members of our organizations) confused. Because we tend to be unaware of our confusion or ashamed of it, we hide it and bluff, deny, blame, or take charge, though we have no idea what is going on and why. So, we need to look inward and take on the task of discovering and changing our attitude toward confusion, and we must develop a mindset and skills that enable us to use confusion as a starting place for personal and organizational learning.

As a result of our consulting with superintendents and people in other leadership positions, my colleague, Jerry Murphy, and I have written about what we call the "lost leader syndrome." No matter how capable or well-prepared administrators are, they regularly find themselves confronting bewildering events, perplexing information, or baffling situations that steal their time and hijack their carefully planned agendas. Disoriented by developments that just do not make sense, and by challenges that do not yield to easy solutions, administrators become confused—sometimes even lost—and do not know what to do.

Inevitably, many administrators respond to these symptoms by simply denying that they are confused. Others hide their confusion—and their search for sense—because they see it as a liability (They tell themselves: "I'll lose authority if I acknowledge that I can't provide direction—I'm supposed to know the answers!"). Acting as if they are in charge, while not knowing what to do, they reflexively and unilaterally react by attempting to impose a quick fix to restore their equilibrium.

Sometimes, these responses of denial, hiding, or imposing a quick fix may even succeed in making the immediate symptoms go away, but they rarely address underlying causes. More often, they lead to bad decision making, undermine crucial communication with colleagues and subordinates, and make administrators seem distant and out of touch. In the long run, administrators who hide their confusion also damage their organizations' efforts to learn and grow from experience. Yet, despite these drawbacks, few administrators can resist hiding their confusion.

To counter these many harmful effects, we propose a five-step process for turning confusion into a powerful asset for personal and collective learning and, as a consequence, better decision making.

Step 1: Embrace Your Confusion

When confronted with disorienting problems, you need to do the one thing you least want to do—acknowledge to yourself that you are confused and that you see this condition as a weakness. You might take a deep breath and say to yourself, "I'm confused and that makes me feel weak." Paradoxically, fully embracing where you are will not lead you to wallow in your confusion, but rather free you to move beyond your inner conflict.

Step 2: Assert Your Need to Make Sense

Engage your colleagues with a statement like, "This new information just doesn't make sense to me. Help me understand what's going on and our options for dealing with it, before I make a decision." It is essential to assert your confusion. Unless you do so, with conviction and avoiding either bravado or apology, others will fulfill your worst expectations—concluding that you are weak—and they will be less willing to engage in a shared process of interpersonal learning.

Step 3: Provide a Structure

You must next provide a structure for the search for new bearings that both asserts your authority and creates the conditions for others to join you. A structure has as many as three parts: an explicit statement of purpose as joint inquiry to make new sense; a set of steps to guide the inquiry and a statement of how a decision will be made (if appropriate); and finally, a time period. Providing structure demonstrates that you can lead by putting "heads together" rather than pretending to have all of the answers yourself.

Step 4: Listen Reflectively and Learn

As your team begins to respond with input, including data, new ideas, and possibly disagreement, the leader needs to shift to a mode of reflective listening, which might sound like this

- "You seem to be saying that X caused Y. Do I have that right?"
- "You're torn between two explanations. On one hand, you think X accounts for Z; on the other hand, you think Y does?"
- "The more you think about it, you find yourself confused, too?"

Step 5: Openly Process Your Effort to Make Sense

Having listened reflectively to your team, it is critical to verbalize the new sense you are making aloud. This is far preferable to thinking through possibilities silently before making what appears to be a unilateral decision. Examples of open processing might sound like this

- "That's news to me. I haven't heard that before."
- "That really throws me. How did you get to that from what you were saying?"
- "That helps me a lot by pointing out X."

In the 21st century, as rapid change makes confusion a defining characteristic of management, the competence of administrators will be measured not only by what they know but increasingly by how they behave when they lose their sense of direction and become confused. Organizational cultures that cling to the ideal of an all-knowing, omni-competent executive will pay a high cost in time, resources, and progress, and will be sending the message to administrators that it is better to hide their confusion than to address it openly and constructively. Administrators can be confused yet still be able to exercise competent leadership by structuring a process of reflective inquiry and action.

As leaders, we must find the courage to look inside ourselves for insight into our negative attitudes toward confusion, and change those attitudes along with our behavior. Otherwise, we will continue to forfeit opportunities to build communities for learning and change on the ground of an ever-increasing body of shared confusion. At worst, we will continue to bluff, deny, blame, or take charge, though we have no idea what is going on and why.

We Need to Discover Our Blind Spots and Change[5]

For many of us, education is a calling, so when we choose to pursue a leadership position, we aspire to make significant improvements in a school or school system. Despite our honorable intentions and best efforts, we frequently fail because there lies in all of us, if not examined and consciously worked on, a predictable and repeated tendency to fall into either a Savior, Authoritarian stance ("I have the answers, follow me") or the opposite stance of Pal, Laissez Faire/Democrat ("You have the answers, and I am here to support you"). Saviors lose the people and Pals fail to produce results. Recognizing and then rejecting the extremes of Leader-Savior or Leader-Pal behaviors is a necessary first step. Developing into a person who can combine the best qualities of both stances to become an authoritative and collaborative leader takes many more steps, all of which presuppose receiving feedback and looking inward in search of self-knowledge.

Parents (of teenagers, in particular) know how difficult it is to find the authoritative–collaborative balance in parenting. In slang terms, it is the hard–soft or tough–tender balance: When do you set and hold the boundary conditions, and when do you make exceptions on the basis of extenuating circumstance? When do you put family culture, needs, and rules first versus putting an individual child's needs and requests first? Of course, few of us see ourselves at the leadership extremes of a Savior or a Pal. All of us tend to think that we have a reasonable balance. And we are almost always wrong. In a metaphorical shorthand, we tend to be blind to our lack of balance. We have a blind spot. Administrators will know what blind spots are by recalling their first conversations with a long-tenured, poor-performing teacher who sees his work as excellent. Every administrator's first experience with using reason and data to bring light to the darkness of another mind is unforgettable. It is the light that goes out, not the darkness. Seeing blindness in others, of course, is child's play compared with discovering our own blind spots, because by definition our blind spots do not exist in our own minds. Because they do not exist, when people tell us about them, we experience those people as clearly misguided or up to no good. So, we have a conundrum: Without discovering our blind spots, we cannot find balance. However, we cannot discover our blind spots because they do not exist.

With occasional exceptions, discovering our blind spots alone is arduous, prolonged, and costly for years to those around us, as well as to ourselves. By definition, there is little sense or hope in sending a blind man to look for sight. To start the process of discovery, we need feedback from others who are very skilled and very committed to us. Even then, the process of going from darkness to light is as arduous as it is necessary for becoming an effective change agent leader. Of course, there are conditions where an administrator's willingness to look inward, combined with feedback from colleagues, can produce discovery of blind spots. As a result, we can make significant changes in our minds and behavior, bringing better balance on the authoritative–collaborative dimension. Detailing those conditions would go beyond the scope of this piece.

The point here is that we do not know what we do not know, and a great deal of what we do not know is essential to our success. We can only discover what we do not know by being willing to look inside, making our minds the object of our inquiry, accompanied in the process by others who are willing to share their experience and guide us into territory where we have not ventured before. We must find the courage to venture within, to enlarge the capacity and capabilities of our own minds, because leadership for change requires pioneering steps into unknown territory in the external world. The quality of the footing we find there is finally determined, not by the nature of the external world, but by the nature and quality of our own minds, along with the quality of relationship we have with them.

Conclusion

We are all in a hurry. Understandably so, given the nature and quantity of the work we have embraced. There is so much hard, important work to be done that it is next to impossible to bring ourselves to a screeching halt and slow down in search of self-knowledge. So we try to glean someone else's self-knowledge, offered as shortcuts—lists, best practices, and steps—not unlike the steps offered here for how to make confusion a resource. Unfortunately, self-knowledge does not transfer well. The steps offered here are worse than useless to someone who has not changed his attitude toward himself when he is confused. That is slow, searching, uncertain, and difficult work.

The search for self-knowledge is not an end in itself for those of us committed to leadership in educational organizations. We want to improve our practice so we can make significant change. No doubt, danger accompanies turning inward, and that danger is popularly advertised in such terms as "navel gazing" and "wallowing in emotions" and "touchy-feely" and "psychological pablum" and "two-bit psychoanalysis" and "paralysis by analysis" and "spinning your wheels." No doubt, as well, danger accompanies not turning inward in a search for self-knowledge. The risk is that, unaware of discrepancies between our self-image and actual behavior, we cannot diagnose why we are mistrusted, so we cannot self-correct. Frightened by confusion, we hide it and bluff, deny, blame, and take charge—though we have no idea what is going on and why. Blind to the lack of balance in our leadership between authoritativeness and collaboration, we fail to make significant change in our organizations.

Notes

1. I am using the word *mind* to refer to the "package" of our behavior, the thinking or feeling that gives rise to it, and the assumptions embedded in our thinking that shape our thinking and consequent behavior.

2. The content of this section is taken from Jentz (in press).

3. As the course proceeds, the students face increasingly difficult interactions, as defined by the fact that they have no technical, easy answers. See Heifetz and Linsky (2002) for an extended discussion of this activity.

4. The content of this section is taken from Jentz and Murphy (2005) and Marshall (2005).

5. The content of this section is taken from Jentz (2006).

References

Heifetz, R.A., & Linsky, M. (2002). *Leadership on the line: Staying alive through the dangers of leading.* Cambridge, MA: Harvard Business School Press.

Jentz, B. (2006). *The entry plan handbook: How to begin a leadership position successfully.* Newton, MA: Leadership and Learning Inc.

Jentz, B. (in press). The power of videotape *in educating leaders. Phi Delta Kappan.*

Jentz, B.C., & Murphy, J.T. (2005). Embracing confusion: What leaders do when they don't know what to do. *Phi Delta Kappan, 86*(5), 358–366.

Marshall, K. (2005, February). Confessing error: Can a leader admit confusion and still lead? *Wharton Leadership Digest, 9*(5). Retrieved November 13, 2005, from http://leadership.wharton.upenn.edu/digest/02-05.shtml

PUBLICATIONS OF THE NATIONAL SOCIETY FOR THE STUDY OF EDUCATION

First Yearbook, 1902, Part I: Some *Principles in the Teaching of History*. Lucy M. Salmon.
First Yearbook, 1902, Part II: *The Progress of Geography in the Schools*. W.M. Davis and H.M. Wilson.
Second Yearbook, 1903, Part I: *The Course of Study in History in the Common School*, Isabel Lawrence, C.A. McMurry, Frank McMurry, E.C. Page, and E.J. Rice.
Second Yearbook, 1903, Part II: *The Relation of Theory to Practice in Education*. M.J. Holmes, J.A. Keith, and Levi Seeley.
Third Yearbook, 1904, Part I: *The Relation of Theory to Practice in the Education of Teachers*. John Dewey, Sarah C. Brooks, F.M. McMurry, et al.
Third Yearbook, 1904, Part II: *Nature Study*. W.S. Jackman.
Fourth Yearbook, 1905, Part I: *The Education and Training of Secondary Teachers*. E.C. Elliott, E.G. Dexter, M.J. Holmes, et al.
Fourth Yearbook, 1905, Part II: *The Place of Vocational Subjects in the High-School Curriculum*. J.S. Brown, G.B. Morrison, and Ellen Richards.
Fifth Yearbook, 1906, Part I: *On the Teaching of English in Elementary and High Schools*. G.P. Brown and Emerson Davis.
Fifth Yearbook, 1906, Part II: *The Certification of Teachers*. E.P. Cubberley.
Sixth Yearbook, 1907, Part I: *Vocational Studies for College Entrance*. C.A. Herrick, H.W. Holmes, T. deLaguna, Virgil Prettyman, and W.J.S. Bryan.
Sixth Yearbook, 1907, Part II: *The Kindergarten and Its Relation to Elementary Education*. Ada Van Stone Harris, E.A. Kirkpatrick, Marie Kraus-Boeltk, Patty S. Hill, Harriette M. Mills, and Nina Vandewalker.
Seventh Yearbook, 1908, Part I: *The Relation of Superintendents and Principals to the Training and Professional Improvement of Their Teachers*. Charles D. Lowry.
Seventh Yearbook, 1908, Part II: *The Co-ordination of the Kindergarten and the Elementary School*. B.C. Gregory, Jennie B. Merrill, Bertha Payne, and Margaret Giddings.
Eighth Yearbook, 1909, Part I: *Education with Reference to Sex: Pathological, Economic, and Social Aspects*. C.R. Henderson.
Eighth Yearbook, 1909, Part II: *Education with Reference to Sex: Agencies and Methods*. C.R. Henderson and Helen C. Putnam.
Ninth Yearbook, 1910, Part I: *Health and Education*. T.D. Wood.
Ninth Yearbook, 1910, Part II: *The Nurses in Education*. T.D. Wood, et al.
Tenth Yearbook, 1911, Part I: *The City School as a Community Center*. H.C. Leipziger, Sarah E. Hyre, R.D. Warden, C. Ward Crompton, E.W. Stitt, E.J. Ward, Mrs. E.C. Grice, and C.A. Perry.
Tenth Yearbook, 1911, Part II: *The Rural School as a Community Center*. B.H. Crocheron, Jessie Field, F.W. Howe, E.C. Bishop, A.B. Graham, O.J. Kern, M.T. Scudder, and B.M. Davis.
Eleventh Yearbook, 1912, Part I: *Industrial Education: Typical Experiments Described and Interpreted*. J.F. Barker, M. Bloomfield, B.W. Johnson, P.

Johnston, L.M. Leavitt, G.A. Mirick, M.W. Murray, C.F. Perry, A.L. Safford, and H.B. Wilson.

Eleventh Yearbook, 1912, Part II: *Agricultural Education in Secondary Schools.* A.C. Monahan, R.W. Stimson, D.J. Crosby, W.H. French, H.F. Button, F.R. Crane, W.R. Hart, and G.F. Warren.

Twelfth Yearbook, 1913, Part I: *The Supervision of City Schools.* Franklin Bobbitt, J.W. Hall, and J.D. Wolcott.

Twelfth Yearbook, 1913, Part II: *The Supervision of Rural Schools.* A.C. Monahan, L.J. Hanifan, J.E. Warren, Wallace Lund, U.J. Hoffman, A.S. Cook, E.M. Rapp, Jackson Davis, J.D. Wolcott.

Thirteenth Yearbook, 1914, Part I: *Some Aspects of High-School Instruction and Administration.* H.C. Morrison, E.R. Breslich, W.A. Jessup, and L.D. Coffman.

Thirteenth Yearbook, 1914, Part II: *Plans for Organizing School Surveys, with a Summary of Typical School Surveys.* Charles H. Judd and Henry L. Smith.

Fourteenth Yearbook, 1915, Part I: *Minimum Essentials in Elementary School Subjects—Standards and Current Practices.* H.B. Wilson, H.W. Holmes, F.E. Thompson, R.G. Jones, S.A. Courtis, W.S. Gray, F.N. Freeman, H.C. Pryor, J.F. Hosic, W.A. Jessup, and William C. Bagley.

Fourteenth Yearbook, 1915, Part II: *Methods for Measuring Teachers' Efficiency.* Arthur C. Boyce.

Fifteenth Yearbook, 1916, Part I: *Standards and Tests for the Measurement of the Efficiency of Schools and School Systems.* G.D. Strayer, Bird T. Baldwin, B.R. Buckingham, Frank W. Ballou, D.C. Bliss, H.G. Childs, S.A. Courtin, E.P. Cubberley, Charles H. Judd, George Melcher, E.E. Oberholtzer, J.B. Sears, Daniel Starch, M.R. Trabue, and Guy M. Whipple.

Fifteenth Yearbook, 1916, Part II: *The Relationship Between Persistence in School and Rome Conditions.* Charles E. Holley.

Fifteenth Yearbook, 1916, Part III: *The Junior High School.* Aubrey A. Douglass.

Sixteenth Yearbook, 1917, Part I: *Second Report of the Committee on Minimum Essentials in Elementary-School Subjects.* William C. Bagley, W.W. Charters, F.N. Freeman, William S. Gray, Ernest Horn, J.H. Hoskinson, W.S. Monroe, C.F. Munson, H.C. Pryor, L.W. Rapeer, G.M. Wilson, and H.B. Wilson.

Sixteenth Yearbook, 1917, Part II: *The Efficiency of College Students as Conditioned by Age at Entrance and Size of High School.* B.F. Pittenger.

Seventeenth Yearbook, 1918, Part I: *Third Report of the Committee on Economy of Time in Education.* William C. Bagley, B.B. Bassett, M.E. Branom, Alice Canister, J.E. Dealey, C.A. Ellwood, E.B. Greene, A.B. Hart, J.F. Hosic, E.T. Housh, W.H. Mace, L.R. Marston, H.C. McKown, A.E. Mitchell, W.C. Reavis, D. Snedden, and H.B. Wilson.

Seventeenth Yearbook, 1918, Part II: *The Measurement of Educational Products.* E.J. Ashbaugh, W.A. Averill, L.P. Ayers, Frank W. Ballou, Edna Bryner, B.R. Buckingham, S.A. Courtin, M.E. Haggerty, Charles H. Judd, George Melcher, W.S. Monroe, E.A. Nifenecker, and E.L. Thorndike.

Eighteenth Yearbook, 1919, Part I: *The Professional Preparation of High-School Teachers.* G.N. Cade, S.S. Colvin, Charles Fordyce, H.H. Foster, T.S. Gosling, William S. Gray, Leonard V. Koos, A.R. Mead, H.L. Miller, F.C. Whitcomb, and Clifford Woody.

Eighteenth Yearbook, 1919, Part II: *Fourth Report of Committee on Economy of Time in Education.* F.C. Ayer, F.N. Freeman, William S. Gray, Ernest Horn, W.S. Monroe, and C.E. Seashore.

Nineteenth Yearbook, 1920, Part I: *New Materials of Instruction*. Prepared by the Society's Committee on Materials of Instruction.

Nineteenth Yearbook, 1920, Part II: *Classroom Problems in the Education of Gifted Children*. T.S. Henry.

Twentieth Yearbook, 1921, Part I: *New Materials of Instruction*. Second Report by the Society's Committee.

Twentieth Yearbook, 1921, Part II: *Report of the Society's Committee on Silent Reading*. M.A. Burgess, S.A. Courtin, C.E. Germane, William S. Gray, H.A. Greene, Regina R. Heller, J.H. Hoover, J.A. O'Brien, J.L. Packer, Daniel Starch, W.W. Theisen, G.A. Yoakum, and representatives of other school systems.

Twenty-first Yearbook, 1922, Parts I: *Intelligence Tests and Their Use: The Nature, History, and General Principles of Intelligence Testing*. E.L. Thorndike, S.S. Colvin, Harold Rugg, Guy M. Whipple.

Twenty-first Yearbook, 1922, Parts II: *Intelligence Tests and Their Use: The Administrative Use of Intelligence Tests*. H.W. Holmes, W.K. Layton, Helen Davis, Agnes L. Rogers, Rudolf Pintner, M.R. Trabue, W.S. Miller, Bessie L. Gainbrill, and others.

Twenty-second Yearbook, 1923, Part I: *English Composition: Its Aims, Methods and Measurements*. Earl Hudelson.

Twenty-second Yearbook, 1923, Part II: *The Social Studies in the Elementary and Secondary School*. A.S. Barr, J.J. Coss, Henry Harap, R.W. Hatch, H.C. Hill, Ernest Horn, Charles H. Judd, L.C. Marshall, F.M. McMurry, Earle Rugg, H.O. Rugg, Emma Schweppe, Mabel Snedaker, and Carleton W. Washburne.

Twenty-third Yearbook, 1924, Part I: *The Education of Gifted Children*. Report of the Society's Committee, Guy M. Whipple, Chairman.

Twenty-third Yearbook, 1924, Part II: *Vocational Guidance and Vocational Education for Industries*. A.H. Edgerton and others.

Twenty-fourth Yearbook, 1925, Part I: *Report of the National Committee on Reading*. William S. Gray, Chairman, F.W. Ballou, Rose L. Hardy, Ernest Horn, Francis Jenkins, S.A. Leonard, Estaline Wilson, and Laura Zirbes.

Twenty-fourth Yearbook, 1925, Part II: *Adapting the Schools to Individual Differences*. Report of the Society's Committee, Carleton W. Washburne, Chairman.

Twenty-fifth Yearbook, 1926, Part I: *The Present Status of Safety Education*. Report of the Society's Committee. Guy M. Whipple, Chairman.

Twenty-fifth Yearbook, 1926, Part II: *Extra-Curricular Activities*. Report of the Society's Committee. Leonard V. Koos, Chairman.

Twenty-sixth Yearbook, 1927, Part I: *Curriculum-making. Past and Present*. Report of the Society's Committee. Harold O. Rugg, Chairman.

Twenty-sixth Yearbook, 1927, Part II: *The Foundations of Curriculum-making*. Prepared by individual members of the Society's Committee. Harold O. Rugg, Chairman.

Twenty-seventh Yearbook, 1928, Part I: *Nature and Nurture: Their Influence upon Intelligence*. Prepared by the Society's Committee. Lewis M. Terman, Chairman.

Twenty-seventh Yearbook, 1928, Part II: *Nature and Nurture: Their Influence upon Achievement*. Prepared by the Society's Committee. Lewis M. Terman, Chairman.

Twenty-eighth Yearbook, 1929, Part I: *Preschool and Parental Education: Organization and Development.* Prepared by the Society's Committee. Lois H. Meek, Chairman.

Twenty-eighth Yearbook, 1929, Part II: *Preschool and Parental Education: Research and Method.* Prepared by the Society's Committee. Lois H. Meek, Chairman.

Twenty-ninth Yearbook, 1930, Part I: *Report of the Society's Committee on Arithmetic: Some Aspects of Modern Thought on Arithmetic.* Prepared by the Society's Committee. F.B. Knight, Chairman.

Twenty-ninth Yearbook, 1930, Part II: *Report of the Society's Committee on Arithmetic: Research in Arithmetic.* Prepared by the Society's Committee. F.B. Knight, Chairman.

Thirtieth Yearbook, 1931, Part I: *The Status of Rural Education.* First Report of the Society's Committee on Rural Education. Orville G. Brim, Chairman.

Thirtieth Yearbook, 1931, Part II: *The Textbook in American Education.* Report of the Society's Committee on the Textbook. J.B. Edmonson, Chairman.

Thirty-first Yearbook, 1932, Part I: *A Program for Teaching Science.* Prepared by the Society's Committee on the Teaching of Science. S. Ralph Powers, Chairman.

Thirty-first Yearbook, 1932, Part II: *Changes and Experiments in Liberal-Arts Education.* Prepared by Kathryn McHale, with numerous collaborators.

Thirty-second Yearbook, 1933, *The Teaching of Geography.* Prepared by the Society's Committee on the Teaching of Geography. A.E. Perkins, Chairman.

Thirty-third Yearbook, 1934, Part I: *The Planning and Construction of School Buildings.* Prepared by the Society's Committee on School Buildings. N.L. Engelhardt, Chairman.

Thirty-third Yearbook, 1934, Part II: *The Activity Movement.* Prepared by the Society's Committee on the Activity Movement, Lois Coffey Mossman, Chairman.

Thirty-fourth Yearbook, 1935, *Educational Diagnosis.* Prepared by the Society's Committee on Educational Diagnosis. L.J. Brueckner, Chairman.

Thirty-fifth Yearbook, 1936, Part I: *The Grouping of Pupils.* Prepared by the Society's Committee. W.W. Coxe, Chairman.

Thirty-fifth Yearbook, 1936, Part II: *Music Education.* Prepared by the Society's Committee. W.L. Uhl, Chairman.

Thirty-sixth Yearbook, 1937, Part I: *The Teaching of Reading.* Prepared by the Society's Committee. William S. Gray, Chairman.

Thirty-sixth Yearbook, 1937, Part II: *International Understanding Through the Public School Curriculum.* Prepared by the Society's Committee. L.L. Kendal, Chairman.

Thirty-seventh Yearbook, 1938, Part I: *Guidance in Educational Institutions.* Prepared by the Society's Committee. G.N. Kefauver, Chairman.

Thirty-seventh Yearbook, 1938, Part II: *The Scientific Movement in Education.* Prepared by the Society's Committee. Frank N. Freeman, Chairman.

Thirty-eighth Yearbook, 1939, Part I: *Child Development and the Curriculum.* Prepared by the Society's Committee. Carleton W. Washburne, Chairman.

Thirty-eighth Yearbook, 1939, Part II: *General Education in the American College.* Prepared by the Society's Committee. Alvin Eurich, Chairman.

Thirty-ninth Yearbook, 1940, Part I: *Intelligence: Its Nature and Nurture. Comparative and Critical Exposition*. Prepared by the Society's Committee. G.D. Stoddard, Chairman.
Thirty-ninth Yearbook, 1940, Part II: *Intelligence: Its Nature and Nurture. Original Studies and Experiments*. Prepared by the Society's Committee. G.D. Stoddard, Chairman.
Fortieth Yearbook, 1941, *Art in American Life and Education*. Prepared by the Society's Committee. Thomas Munro, Chairman.
Forty-first Yearbook, 1942, Part I: *Philosophies of Education*. Prepared by the Society's Committee. John S. Brubacher, Chairman.
Forty-first Yearbook, 1942, Part II: *The Psychology of Learning*. Prepared by the Society's Committee. T.R. McConnell, Chairman.
Forty-second Yearbook, 1943, Part I: *Vocational Education*. Prepared by the Society's Committee. F.J. Keller, Chairman.
Forty-second Yearbook, 1943, Part II: *The Library in General Education*. Prepared by the Society's Committee. L.R. Wilson, Chairman.
Forty-third Yearbook, 1944, Part I: *Adolescence*. Prepared by the Society's Committee. Harold E. Jones, Chairman.
Forty-third Yearbook, 1944, Part I: *Teaching Language in the Elementary School*. Prepared by the Society's Committee. M.R. Trabue, Chairman.
Forty-fourth Yearbook, 1945, Part I: *American Education in the Postwar Period. Curriculum Reconstruction*. Prepared by the Society's Committee. Ralph W. Tyler, Chairman.
Forty-fourth Yearbook, 1945, Part II: *American Education in the Postwar Period. Structural Reorganization*. Prepared by the Society's Committee. Base Goodykoontz, Chairman.
Forty-fifth Yearbook, 1946, Part I: *The Measurement of Understanding*. Prepared by the Society's Committee. William A. Brownell, Chairman.
Forty-fifth Yearbook, 1946, Part II: *Changing Conceptions in Educational Administration*. Prepared by the Society's Committee. Alonzo G. Grace, Chairman.
Forty-sixth Yearbook, 1947, Part I: *Science Education in American Schools*. Prepared by the Society's Committee. Victor H. Noll, Chairman.
Forty-sixth Yearbook, 1947, Part II: *Early Childhood Education*. Prepared by the Society's Committee. N. Searle Light, Chairman.
Forty-seventh Yearbook, 1948, Part I: *Juvenile Delinquency and the Schools*. Prepared by the Society's Committee. Ruth Strang, Chairman.
Forty-seventh Yearbook, 1948, Part II: *Reading in the High School and College*. Prepared by the Society's Committee. William S. Gray, Chairman.
Forty-eighth Yearbook, 1949, Part I: *Audio-visual Materials of Instruction*. Prepared by the Society's Committee. Stephen M. Corey, Chairman.
Forty-eighth Yearbook, 1949, Part II: *Reading in the Elementary School*. Prepared by the Society's Committee. Arthur I. Gates, Chairman.
Forty-ninth Yearbook, 1950, Part I: *Learning and Instruction*. Prepared by the Society's Committee. G. Lester Anderson, Chairman.
Forty-ninth Yearbook, 1960, Part II: *The Education of Exceptional Children*. Prepared by the Society's Committee. Samuel A. Kirk, Chairman.
Fiftieth Yearbook, 1951, Part I: *Graduate Study in Education*. Prepared by the Society's Board of Directors. Ralph W. Tyler, Chairman.

Fiftieth Yearbook, 1951, Part II: *The Teaching of Arithmetic*. Prepared by the Society's Committee. G.T. Buswell, Chairman.
Fifty-first Yearbook, 1952, Part I: *General Education*. Prepared by the Society's Committee. T.R. McConnell, Chairman.
Fifty-first Yearbook, 1952, Part II: *Education in Rural Communities*. Prepared by the Society's Committee. Ruth Strang, Chairman.
Fifty-second Yearbook, 1953, Part I: *Adapting the Secondary-School Program to the Needs of Youth*. Prepared by the Society's Committee: William G. Brink, Chairman.
Fifty-second Yearbook, 1953, Part II: *The Community School*. Prepared by the Society's Committee. Maurice F. Seay, Chairman.
Fifty-third Yearbook, 1954, Part I: *Citizen Cooperation for Better Public Schools*. Prepared by the Society's Committee. Edgar L. Morphet, Chairman.
Fifty-third Yearbook, 1964, Part II: *Mass Media and Education*. Prepared by the Society's Committee. Edgar Dale, Chairman.
Fifty-fourth Yearbook, 1955, Part I: *Modern Philosophies and Education*. Prepared by the Society's Committee. John S. Brubacher, Chairman.
Fifty-fourth Yearbook, 1955, Part II: *Mental Health in Modern Education*. Prepared by the Society's Committee. Paul A. Witty, Chairman.
Fifty-fifth Yearbook, 1956, Part I: *The Public Junior College*. Prepared by the Society's Committee. B. Lamar Johnson, Chairman.
Fifty-fifth Yearbook, 1956, Part II: *Adult Reading*. Prepared by the Society's Committee. David H. Clift, Chairman.
Fifty-sixth Yearbook, 1957, Part I: *In-service Education of Teachers, Supervisors, and Administrators*. Prepared by the Society's Committee. Stephen M. Corey, Chairman.
Fifty-sixth Yearbook, 1957, Part II: *Social Studies in the Elementary School*. Prepared by the Society's Committee. Ralph C. Preston, Chairman.
Fifty-seventh Yearbook, 1958, Part I: *Basic Concepts in Music Education*. Prepared by the Society's Committee. Thurber H. Madison, Chairman.
Fifty-seventh Yearbook, 1958, Part II: *Education for the Gifted*. Prepared by the Society's Committee. Robert J. Havighurst, Chairman.
Fifty-seventh Yearbook, 1958, Part III: *The Integration of Educational Experiences*. Prepared by the Society's Committee. Paul L. Dressel, Chairman.
Fifty-eighth Yearbook, 1959, Part I: *Community Education: Principles and Practices from World-wide Experience*. Prepared by the Society's Committee. C.O. Arndt, Chairman.
Fifty-eighth Yearbook, 1959, Part II: *Personnel Services in Education*. Prepared by the Society's Committee. Melvene D. Hardee, Chairman.
Fifty-ninth Yearbook, 1960, Part I: *Rethinking Science Education*. Prepared by the Society's Committee. J. Darrell Barnard, Chairman.
Fifty-ninth Yearbook, 1960, Part II: *The Dynamics of Instructional Groups*. Prepared by the Society's Committee. Gale E. Jensen, Chairman.
Sixtieth Yearbook, 1961, Part I: *Development in and Through Reading*. Prepared by the Society's Committee. Paul A. Witty, Chairman.
Sixtieth Yearbook, 1961, Part II: *Social Forces Influencing American Education*. Prepared by the Society's Committee. Ralph W. Tyler, Chairman.
Sixty-first Yearbook, 1962, Part I: *Individualizing Instruction*. Prepared by the Society's Committee. Fred T. Tyler, Chairman.

Sixty-first Yearbook, 1962, Part II: *Education for the Professions*. Prepared by the Society's Committee. G. Lester Anderson, Chairman.
Sixty-second Yearbook, 1963, Part I: *Child Psychology*. Prepared by the Society's Committee. Harold W. Stevenson, Editor.
Sixty-second Yearbook, 1963, Part II: *The Impact and Improvement of School Testing Programs*. Prepared by the Society's Committee. Warren G. Findley, Editor.
Sixty-third Yearbook, 1964, Part I: *Theories of Learning and Instruction*. Prepared by the Society's Committee. Ernest R. Hilgard, Editor.
Sixty-third Yearbook, 1964, Part II: *Behavioral Science and Educational Administration*. Prepared by the Society's Committee. Daniel E. Griffiths, Editor.
Sixty-fourth Yearbook, 1965, Part I: *Vocational Education*. Prepared by the Society's Committee. Melvin L. Barlow, Editor.
Sixty-fourth Yearbook, 1965, Part II: *Art Education*. Prepared by the Society's Committee. W. Reid Hastie, Editor.
Sixty-fifth Yearbook, 1966, Part I: *Social Deviancy Among Youth*. Prepared by the Society's Committee. William W. Wattenberg, Editor.
Sixty-fifth Yearbook, 1966, Part II: *The Changing American School*. Prepared by the Society's Committee. John I. Goodlad, Editor.
Sixty-sixth Yearbook, 1967, Part I: *The Educationally Retarded and Disadvantaged*. Prepared by the Society's Committee. Paul A. Witty, Editor.
Sixty-sixth Yearbook, 1967, Part II: *Programmed Instruction*. Prepared by the Society's Committee. Phil C. Lange, Editor.
Sixty-seventh Yearbook, 1968, Part I: *Metropolitanism: Its Challenge to Education*. Prepared by the Society's Committee. Robert J. Havighurst, Editor.
Sixty-seventh Yearbook, 1968, Part II: *Innovation and Change in Reading Instruction*. Prepared by the Society's Committee. Helen M. Robinson, Editor.
Sixty-eighth Yearbook, 1969, Part I: *The United States and International Education*. Prepared by the Society's Committee. Harold G. Shane, Editor.
Sixty-eighth Yearbook, 1969, Part II: *Educational Evaluation: New Roles, New Means*. Prepared by the Society's Committee. Ralph W. Tyler, Editor.
Sixty-ninth Yearbook, 1970, Part I: *Mathematics Education*. Prepared by the Society's Committee. Edward G. Begle, Editor.
Sixty-ninth Yearbook, 1970, Part II: *Linguistics in School Programs*. Prepared by the Society's Committee. Albert H. Marckwardt, Editor.
Seventieth Yearbook, 1971, Part I: *The Curriculum: Retrospect and Prospect*. Prepared by the Society's Committee. Robert M. McClure, Editor.
Seventieth Yearbook, 1971, Part II: *Leaders in American Education*. Prepared by the Society's Committee. Robert J. Havighurst, Editor.
Seventy-first Yearbook, 1972, Part I: *Philosophical Redirection of Educational Research*. Prepared by the Society's Committee. Lawrence G. Thomas, Editor.
Seventy-first Yearbook, 1972, Part II: *Early Childhood Education*. Prepared by the Society's Committee. Ira J. Gordon, Editor.
Seventy-second Yearbook, 1973, Part I: *Behavior Modification in Education*. Prepared by the Society's Committee. Carl E. Thoresen, Editor.

Seventy-second Yearbook, 1973, Part II: *The Elementary School in the United States*. Prepared by the Society's Committee. John I. Goodlad and Harold G. Shane, Editors.

Seventy-third Yearbook, 1974, Part I: *Media and Symbols: The Forms of Expression, Communication and Education*. Prepared by the Society's Committee. David R. Olson, Editor.

Seventy-third Yearbook, 1974, Part II: *Uses of the Sociology of Education*. Prepared by the Society's Committee. C. Wayne Gordon, Editor.

Seventy-fourth Yearbook, 1975, Part I: *Youth*. Prepared by the Society's Committee. Robert J. Havighurst and Phillip H. Dreyer, Editors.

Seventy-fourth Yearbook, 1975, Part II: *Teacher Education*. Prepared by the Society's Committee. Kevin Ryan, Editor.

Seventy-fifth Yearbook, 1976, Part I: *Psychology of Teaching Methods*. Prepared by the Society's Committee. N.L. Gage, Editor.

Seventy-fifth Yearbook, 1976, Part II: *Issues in Secondary Education*. Prepared by the Society's Committee. William Van Til, Editor.

Seventy-sixth Yearbook, 1977, Part I: *The Teaching of English*. Prepared by the Society's Committee. James R. Squire, Editor.

Seventy-sixth Yearbook, 1977, Part II: *The Politics of Education*. Prepared by the Society's Committee. Jay D. Scribner, Editor.

Seventy-seventh Yearbook, 1978, Part I: *The Courts and Education*. Clifford P. Hooker, Editor.

Seventy-seventh Yearbook, 1978, Part II: *Education and the Brain*. Jeanne Chall and Allan F. Mirsky, Editors.

Seventy-eighth Yearbook, 1979, Part I: *The Gifted and the Talented: Their Education and Development*. A. Harry Passow, Editor.

Seventy-eighth Yearbook, 1979, Part II: *Classroom Management*. Daniel L. Duke, Editor.

Seventy-ninth Yearbook, 1980, Part I: *Toward Adolescence: The Middle School Years*. Mauritz Johnson, Editor.

Seventy-ninth Yearbook, 1980, Part II: *Learning a Second Language*. Frank M. Grittner, Editor.

Eightieth Yearbook, 1981, Part I: *Philosophy and Education*. Jonas F. Soltis, Editor.

Eightieth Yearbook, 1981, Part II: *The Social Studies*. Howard D. Mehlinger and O.L. Davis, Jr., Editors.

Eighty-first Yearbook, 1982, Part I: *Policy Making in Education*. Ann Lieberman and Milbrey W. McLaughlin, Editors.

Eighty-first Yearbook, 1982, Part II: *Education and Work*. Harry F. Silberman, Editor.

Eighty-second Yearbook, 1983, Part I: *Individual Differences and the Common Curriculum*. Gary D. Fenstermacher and John I. Goodlad, Editors.

Eighty-second Yearbook, 1983, Part II: *Staff Development*. Gary Griffin, Editor.

Eighty-third Yearbook, 1984, Part I: *Becoming Readers in a Complex Society*. Alan C. Purves and Olive S. Niles, Editors.

Eighty-third Yearbook, 1984, Part II: *The Humanities in Precollegiate Education*. Benjamin Ladner, Editor.

Eighty-fourth Yearbook, 1985, Part I: *Education in School and Nonschool Settings*. Mario D. Fantini and Robert L. Sinclair, Editors.

Eighty-fourth Yearbook, 1985, Part II: *Learning and Teaching the Ways of Knowing*. Elliot Eisner, Editor.
Eighty-fifth Yearbook, 1986, Part I: *Microcomputers and Education*. Jack A. Culbertson and Luvern L. Cunningham, Editors.
Eighty-fifth Yearbook, 1986, Part II: *The Teaching of Writing*. Anthony R. Petrosky and David Bartholomae, Editors.
Eighty-sixth Yearbook, 1987, Part I: *The Ecology of School Renewal*. John I. Goodlad, Editor.
Eighty-sixth Yearbook, 1987, Part II: *Society as Educator in an Age of Transition*. Steven E. Tozer and Kenneth D. Benne, Editors.
Eighty-seventh Yearbook, 1987, Part I: *Critical Issues in Curriculum*. Kenneth J. Rehage and Laurel N. Tanner, Editors.
Eighty-seventh Yearbook, 1988, Part II: *Cultural Literacy and the Idea of General Education*. Ian Westbury and Alan C. Purves, Editors.
Eighty-eighth Yearbook, 1989, Part I: *From Socrates to Software: The Teacher as Text and the Text as Teacher*. Philip W. Jackson and Sophie Haroutunian-Gordon, Editors.
Eighty-eighth Yearbook, 1989, Part II: *Schooling and Disability*. Douglas Biklen, Dianne L. Ferguson, and Alison Ford, Editors.
Eighty-ninth Yearbook, 1990, Part I: *Textbooks and Schooling in the United States*. David L. Elliott and Arthur Woodward, Editors.
Eighty-ninth Yearbook, 1990, Part II: *Educational Leadership and Changing Contexts of Families, Communities, and Schools*. Brad Mitchell and Luvern L. Cunningham, Editors.
Ninetieth Yearbook, 1991, Part I: *The Care and Education of America's Young Children: Obstacles and Opportunities*. Sharon Lynn Kagan, Editor.
Ninetieth Yearbook, 1991, Part II: *Evaluation and Education: At Quarter Century*. Milbrey W. McLaughlin and Denis (D.C.) Phillips, Editors.
Ninety-first Yearbook, 1992, Part I: *The Changing Contexts of Teaching*. Ann Lieberman, Editor.
Ninety-first Yearbook, 1992, Part II: *The Arts, Education, and Aesthetic Knowing*. Bennett Reimer and Ralph A. Smith, Editors.
Ninety-second Yearbook, 1993, Part I: *Gender and Education*. Sari Knopp Biklen and Diane Pollard, Editors.
Ninety-second Yearbook, 1993, Part II: *Bilingual Education: Politics, Practice, and Research*. M. Beatriz Arias and Ursula Casanova, Editors.
Ninety-third Yearbook, 1994, Part I: *Teacher Research and Educational Reform*. Sandra Hollingsworth and Hugh Sockett, Editors.
Ninety-third Yearbook, 1994, Part II: *Bloom's Taxonomy: A Forty-Year Retrospective*. Lauren A. Sosniak and Lorin W. Anderson, Editors.
Ninety-fourth Yearbook, 1995, Part I: *Creating New Educational Communities*. Jeannie Oakes and Karen Hunter Quartz, Editors.
Ninety-fourth Yearbook, 1995, Part II: *Changing Populations/Changing Schools*. Erwin Flaxman and A. Harry Passow, Editors.
Ninety-fifth Yearbook, 1996, Part I: *Performance-Based Student Assessment: Challenges and Possibilities*. Joan Boykoff Baron and Dennie Palmer Wolf, Editors.
Ninety-fifth Yearbook, 1996, Part II: *Technology and the Future of Schooling*. Stephen T. Kerr, Editor.
Ninety-sixth Yearbook, 1997, Part I: *Service Learning*. Joan Schine, Editor.

Ninety-sixth Yearbook, 1997, Part II: *The Construction of Children's Character*. Alex Molnar, Editor.

Ninety-seventh Yearbook, 1998, Part I: *The Adolescent Years: Social Influences and Educational Challenges*. Kathryn Borman and Barbara Schneider, Editors.

Ninety-seventh Yearbook, 1998, Part II: *The Reading-Writing Connection*. Nancy Nelson and Robert C. Calfee, Editors.

Ninety-eighth Yearbook, 1999, Part I: *The Education of Teachers*. Gary A. Griffin, Editor.

Ninety-eighth Yearbook, 1999, Part II: *Issues in Curriculum: A Selection of Chapters From Past NSSE Yearbooks*. Margaret Early and Kenneth J. Rehage, Editors.

Ninety-ninth Yearbook, 2000, Part I: *Constructivism in Education*. Denis (D.C.) Phillips, Editor.

Ninety-ninth Yearbook, 2000, Part II: *American Education: Yesterday, Today, Tomorrow*. Thomas L. Good, Editor.

One-hundredth Yearbook, 2001, Part I: *Education Across a Century: The Centennial Volume*. Lyn Corno, Editor.

One-hundredth Yearbook, 2001, Part II: *From the Capital to the Classroom: Standards-Based Reform in the States*. Susan H. Fuhrman, Editor.

One hundred and first Yearbook, Part I: *The Educational Leadership Challenge: Redefining Leadership for the 21st Century*. Joseph Murphy, Editor.

One hundred and first Yearbook, Part II: *Educating At-Risk Students*. Sam Stringfield and Deborah Land, Editors.

One hundred and second Yearbook, Part I: *American Educational Governance on Trial: Change and Challenges*. William Lowe Boyd and Debra Miretzky, Editors.

One hundred and second Yearbook, Part II: *Meeting at the Hyphen: Schools-Universities-Communities-Professions in Collaboration for Student Achievement and Well Being*. Mary M. Brabeck, Mary E. Walsh, and Rachel E. Latta, Editors.

One hundred and third Yearbook, Part I: *Developing the Teacher Workforce*. Mark A. Smylie and Debra Miretzky, Editors.

One hundred and third Yearbook, Part II: *Towards Coherence Between Classroom Assessment and Accountability*. Mark Wilson, Editor.

One hundred and fourth Yearbook, Part I: *Media Literacy: Transforming Curriculum and Teaching*. Gretchen Schwarz and Pamela U. Brown, Editors.

One hundred and fourth Yearbook, Part II: *Uses and Misuses of Data for Educational Accountability and Improvement*. Joan Herman and Edward Haertel, Editors.

About the Contributors

Allan Alson
Allan Alson has been the superintendent of Evanston Township High School in Illinois since 1992. He began his teaching career in Philadelphia and served as a teacher and administrator in several communities in Massachusetts. He was also the assistant director of the Boston Public Schools/Boston University Desegregation Collaborative. In Evanston, Allan has been involved in creating a wide array of community partnerships, including an award-winning school-based health center. In 1999 he founded the Minority Student Achievement Network, a national consortium of 25 urban-suburban districts devoted to improving the academic achievement of students of color. Currently he serves on the steering committee of the Chicago Public School's High School Transformation Project and on the advisory board of the Chicago-based Fry Foundation High School Initiative.

Beverly Hall
In 2005, Dr. Beverly Hall completed her 6th year as the superintendent of the Atlanta Public Schools. Prior to her Atlanta appointment, Dr. Hall served as superintendent of the Newark, New Jersey. Public Schools; Deputy Chancellor for Instruction, New York City Public Schools; and superintendent, Community School District 27 in Far Rockaway, Queens, New York. She was also a principal and teacher in the New York City schools. Born in Jamaica, West Indies, Dr. Hall immigrated to the United States after completing high school. She received both her bachelor's and master's degrees from Brooklyn College and her doctorate from Fordham University. In addition to serving as superintendent in Atlanta, Dr. Hall is chair of the Advisory Board of the Harvard Urban Superintendents Program. She is also a member of the Commission on Teaching.

Linda Hanson
Linda Hanson, Ed. D., began her teaching career in the kindergarten and third grade classrooms. She taught high school art and college design classes for a combined 9 years. She pursued an administrative path and served as an elementary principal, a dean of students, a high

school principal, and an assistant superintendent of elementary curriculum. She was superintendent of two high school districts in Illinois for 13 years: Mundelein High School District 120 and Township High School District 113 in Highland Park. She is now the president of School-Exec Connect, a search firm that specializes in finding educational leaders for school districts.

Paul D. Houston

Dr. Paul D. Houston has served as executive director of the American Association of School Administrators since 1994. He has established himself as one of the leading spokespersons for American education through his extensive speaking engagements, published articles, and his regular appearances on national radio and television. Dr. Houston served previously as a teacher and building administrator in North Carolina and New Jersey. He has also served as assistant superintendent in Birmingham, Alabama, and as superintendent of schools in Princeton, New Jersey, Tucson, Arizona, and Riverside, California. He has served as a consultant and speaker throughout the United States and overseas, and he has published more than 100 articles in professional journals.

Becky Bair Hurley

A graduate of Colgate University and Northwestern University School of Law, Becky Bair Hurley has practiced in commercial real estate for the last 20 years. She now devotes most of her time to organizations such as the Winnetka Plan Commission, the Winnetka Historical Society, and the District 36 School Board.

Barry Jentz

A founder and partner in Leadership and Learning Inc., Barry Jentz has consulted extensively with public and private school systems and school administrators for 35 years. He is a lecturer on education at the Harvard Graduate School of Education and has taught courses on leadership, communication, and supervision in their Urban Superintendents' Program and the Field Experience Program. He is also the co-author of a number of books and articles on educational leadership, including *Leadership and Learning: Personal Change in a Professional Setting* and *Entry: The Hiring, Start-Up, and Supervision of Administrators*.

Bena Kallick

Bena Kallick is a private consultant providing services to school districts, state departments of education, professional organizations, and public agencies throughout the United States and abroad. She received her doctorate in educational evaluation at Union Graduate School. Her areas of focus include group dynamics, creative and critical thinking, and alternative assessment strategies for the classroom. Her written work includes *Literature to Think About, Changing Schools Into Communities for Thinking, Assessment in the Learning Organization, and Habits of Mind* (a four-book series published by ASCD), coauthored with Arthur Costa. She is cofounder of Technology Pathways, a company dedicated to providing easy to use software that helps integrate and make sense out of data from curriculum, instruction, and assessment.

Paul Kelleher

Dr. Paul Kelleher serves as the Norine R. Murchison Distinguished Professor and chair of the Department of Education at Trinity University. Prior to joining the Trinity faculty, Kelleher served for 20 years as a superintendent of schools in Bedford and Lawrence, New York, and in Westport, Connecticut. He has also been a high school principal and teacher and a middle school principal. His research interests include the development and implementation of educational policy, the organization and administration of schools, and teacher recruitment, preparation, and retention. He graduated from Harvard College with a B.A. in English, received an M.A.T. degree from the Harvard Graduate School of Education, and an Ed.D. in educational administration from Teachers' College, Columbia University.

Larry Leverett

In March 2003, Larry Leverett began his tenure as the first African-American superintendent in Greenwich, Connecticut. Larry grew up in and attended public schools in Passaic, New Jersey. He graduated from Virginia State College and received his M.A. and Ed.D. degrees from Teachers' College, Columbia University. Larry began his career as a third grade teacher in Passaic, where he also served on the board of education. Prior to Greenwich, Larry was superintendent in Plainfield as well as in Englewood, New Jersey. He also served as assistant commissioner and director of urban education in the New Jersey Department of Education. Currently, in addition to being superintendent in Greenwich, Larry serves as a member of the Advisory Committees of the Urban Superintendents Program at Harvard University and of the Laura Bush Foundation.

Rebecca van der Bogert
Before joining the Winnetka Public Schools as superintendent in 1994, Dr. Rebecca van der Bogert served as superintendent in Lincoln, Massachusetts, and assistant superintendent for curriculum in Groton, Massachusetts, and as a principal, special education teacher, classroom teacher, and guidance counselor. She received her doctorate from Harvard University. She currently serves on the board of directors of the Center for Courage and Renewal; the advisory board of the Illinois Collaborative for Academic Social and Emotional Learning; the advisory board of Erika's Lighthouse; and the board of the Northern Suburban Special Education District. She has published books and numerous articles on the topics of leadership, democracy, and learning communities, including *Making Sense of School Leadership: Persisting Questions, Creative Opportunities*.

John R. Wiens
John R. Wiens is currently dean of faculty education at the University of Manitoba in Winnipeg, Manitoba, Canada. He was a superintendent in the Seven Oaks School Division from 1989 to 2001. As a school and district administrator for 31 years, his first loves are teaching, philosophizing, and being a grandfather.